# THE FIRST ROCK SONG

## Contributions of Divine Metaphors to the Theology of the Song of Moses

ISMAEL DORA

Volume 2

# THE FIRST ROCK SONG

## Contributions of Divine Metaphors to the Theology of the Song of Moses

ISMAEL DORA

ACADEMIC THEOLOGICAL STUDIES

**The First Rock Song**
Contributions of Divine Metaphors to the Theology of the Song of Moses
Copyright © 2022 by Ismael Dora

Published by Northeastern Baptist Press
        Post Office Box 4600
        Bennington, VT 05201

All rights reserved. No part of this book may be reproduced in any form without prior permission from Northeastern Baptist Press, except as provided for by USA copyright law.

All Scripture translations are the author's unless otherwise noted.

Cover design by Leason Stiles & Jared August

Hardcover ISBN: 978-1-953331-18-2

To my beautiful wife Emmania אֵשֶׁת־חַיִל who loves me dearly,
Who has sacrificed her life to allow me to study the Bible,
Who has been a source of encouragement for me,
This project is dedicated to you, honey.

# Contents

| | |
|---|---|
| Series Introduction | i |
| Foreword | iii |
| Preface | viii |
| **Chapter One** <br> Introduction | 1 |
| **Chapter Two** <br> The Song of Moses in Context | 31 |
| **Chapter Three** <br> Metaphor: God Is a Rock | 51 |
| **Chapter Four** <br> Metaphor: God Is a Father | 87 |
| **Chapter Five** <br> Metaphor: God Is an Avenging Warrior | 117 |
| **Chapter Six** <br> Conclusion and Recommendations for Further Study | 147 |
| Bibliography | 153 |

# Series Introduction

Northeastern Baptist Press publishes Christian books that inform, inspire, and encourage people to follow Jesus Christ. Realizing the need for an academic series that is tethered to the Baptist Faith and Message 2000, NEBP has developed the Academic Theological Studies (ATS) series.

The ATS series is comprised of doctoral dissertations as well as academic monographs that are carefully selected based on solid recommendations and rigorous peer review. Each study makes a unique and distinct contribution to the broader field of theology. Although all books in this series are specialized, they are not written for specialists. The ATS series provides the church at large with quality resources that have significant implications for practical issues. Toward this end, we publish within the fields of biblical studies, systematic and historical theology, Christian counseling, education, and pastoral ministry.

We foresee the ATS series growing into a significant collection of academic studies that provide the church with an accessible, yet academically rigorous avenue for theological inquiry.

Jared M. August<br>
Ralph H. Slater<br>
Series Editors

# Foreword
## By David C. Deuel

In this study, the author undertakes a biblical theological examination of three divine metaphors in the Song of Moses: God is a rock, God is a father, and God is a warrior. To conduct his investigation, he first develops a methodology for treating metaphor that honors the biblical text as a coherent message. Having carefully selected his view of metaphor and supporting method, he treats the biblical text of the Song of Moses exegetically with careful attention to the broader context of which it is a part. Finally, he draws theological conclusions based on his exegesis regarding what God is like as a rock, a Father, and a warrior, particularly in relationship to his people, Israel. This model study could be used in investigations of other early biblical poetry.

David C. Deuel
Academic Dean Emeritus
The Master's Academy International

# Preface

The topic of metaphor has stimulated production of scholarly works since the 1970s when several philosophers began to formulate various theories regarding this difficult subject. In the field of biblical studies, some scholars and exegetes have investigated metaphors in the Hebrew Bible, but much remains to be done since the majority of these works only focus on the poetic books, especially the book of Psalms.

This dissertation examines three divine metaphors in the Song of Moses: God is a rock, God is a father, and God is an avenging warrior. This study's approach looks at the literal meaning of the vehicle to see how it was used in ancient Israel and/or in the ancient Near Eastern neighboring nations. This paves the way for the literary and theological examination of the metaphor, which is conducted in three steps: a) identification and interpretation of the metaphor; (b) function of the metaphor; and c) theological observations regarding the use of the metaphor.

This project utilizes a linguistic approach to figurative language, meaning that the metaphors in the Song of Moses are studied and examined through the biblical text. This method helps the exegete to understand the metaphorical statements and the rhetorical effects they produced. It also helps to understand the intention of the original author of the Song as he communicated this message to his audience.

I thank my God for allowing me to study his Word and to produce this dissertation. I offer my thanks to my advisor, Dr. Mark McGinniss. He has been patient, encouraging, and helpful throughout the production of this work. I thank my two readers, Dr. Kenneth Gardoski and Dr. Wayne Slusser, who read my dissertation with great care and provided insightful comments during my oral examination. I also want to thank my friend, Dr. Jared August, for reading the entire dissertation and for providing constructive feedback.

A special thanks to my pastor, Dr. John McNeal Jr., for his impact on my life and for his support. His wife, Earlene, has always been a source of encouragement for me. I will not forget the faithful friends who have helped along the way: Mr. and Mrs. Louis Cureau, Ms. Janice Brooks, and Mrs. Retta Johnson. Special thanks to my mom, Mrs. Rosemarie Dora, who has devoted her life to helping my wife with the kids so that I can have enough time to study.

Finally, I want to thank my beautiful wife, Emmania, for all her hard work. She has been more supportive than I thought she would. She has shown love and offered herself wholly to help me in every way. Words would not be enough to describe how much I am grateful to her.

*Chapter One*

# Introduction

The Song of Moses is a masterpiece of poetic diction. A large part of its artistic power is due to the density of its metaphors. In his Song, Moses uses the power of imagery to communicate an important message about God and his relationship with Israel. As Ryken correctly observes, the poet uses various metaphors to portray God "as the Rock (Deut 32:4, 15, 18, 30, 31); as an eagle caring for its young (Deut 32:11); as a father disciplining and nurturing his children (Deut 32:6, 10, 13–14); as a mother who gave birth to Israel (Deut 32:18); as a divine warrior… (Deut 32:35–36, 40–42)."[1] Thus, to properly interpret and appreciate the message of this Song, the reader has to grasp the meaning of its metaphors. Unfortunately, current biblical scholarship has largely neglected this important task.[2] To date, only Christiane Wüste's monograph deals with the metaphors in this Song. However, this project is different from her work in at least two ways: (1) Wüste researched the metaphors "rock," "vulture," "and parent-child" employing a diachronic and synchronic approach. This project will primarily use a linguistic methodology and supplement it with the cognitive approach to examine these metaphors. (2) While Wüste's purpose was to offer a differentiated consideration of the

---

1. Leland Ryken, James C. Wilhoit, and Tremper Longman III, eds., *Dictionary of Biblical Imagery: An Encyclopedic Exploration of the Images, Symbols, Motifs, Metaphors, Figures of Speech and Literary Patterns of the Bible* (Downers Grove: InterVarsity Press, 1998), 206.

2. See Christiane Wüste, *Fels – Geier – Eltern: Untersuchungen zum Gottesbild des Moseliedes (Dtn 32)* (Göttingen: V&R Unipress GmbH, 2018).

# THE FIRST ROCK SONG:
## Contributions of Divine Metaphors to the Theology of the Song of Moses

complexities and tensions of the various images used for God, the purpose of this dissertation is to examine divine metaphors to see how they contribute to the theology of the Song.

Many articles have been written on the Song but none of them fully addresses its imagery.[3] Commentators often catalog the rhetorical devices in the Song without explaining their full meaning within the poetic unit or providing theological reflection.[4] As a result, their exegesis of the text often lacks completeness. Moreover, books have been published on the Song, but they, too, fail to examine its metaphors to see how they contribute to the theology of the Song.[5]

---

3. See, for instance, G. Ernest Wright, "The Lawsuit of God: A Form-Critical Study of Deuteronomy 32," in *Israel's Prophetic Heritage: Essays in Honor of James Muilenburg*, ed. Bernhard W. Anderson and Walter Harrelson (New York: Harper & Brothers, 1962); James A. Boston, "The Wisdom Influence Upon the Song of Moses," *JBL* 87, no. 2 (1968); Matthew Thiessen, "The Form and Function of the Song of Moses (Deuteronomy 32:1–43)," *JBL* 123, no. 3 (2004); Brian Britt, "Deuteronomy 31–32 as a Textual Memorial," *BibInt* 8, no. 4 (2000): 358–74; Patrick William Skehan, "Structure of the Song of Moses in Deuteronomy (Deut 32:1–43)," *CBQ* 13, no. 2 (April 1951): 153–63; Mark Leuchter, "Why is the Song of Moses in the Book of Deuteronomy?" *VT* 57, no. 3 (2007): 295–317; Thomas A Keiser, "The Song of Moses: A Basis for Isaiah's Prophecy," *VT* 55, no. 4 (October 2005): 486–500.

4. See for example, Telford Work, *Deuteronomy*, Brazos Theological Commentary on the Bible (Grand Rapids: Eerdmans, 2009). See also John D. Currid, *A Study Commentary on Deuteronomy* (Darlington: Evangelical Press, 2006); Richard D. Nelson, *Deuteronomy: A Commentary*, Old Testament Library (Louisville: Westminster John Knox Press, 2004); Edward J. Woods, *Deuteronomy*, TOTC 5 (Downers Grove: InterVarsity Press, 2011).

5. For instance, George Knight has written a commentary on the poem in order to "offer a theological interpretation of the Hebrew text." George A. F. Knight, *The Song of Moses: Theological Quarry* (Grand Rapids: Wm. B. Eerdmans, 1995), vii. Paul Sanders focuses solely on the provenance of the Song, looking at its language, date of composition, literary context, and intertextual links with other literature. Sanders argues that the vocabulary of the poem and the reference to other gods as well as its intertextual connections (for instance, with Hosea and Psalm 81) suggest that it is pre-exilic and is of northern origin. Paul Sanders, *The Provenance of Deuteronomy 32* (Leiden: Brill, 1996). More recently, Keith Stone has refined his dissertation and produced a good work on the poem, but his research is on a performance critical

Nevertheless, such an investigation on metaphors is needed because the Song communicates its message through metaphors. Thus, while scholars have studied the Song, this project will investigate its divine metaphors to appreciate their poetic power and to unlock their contribution to the theological message of the Song. For, according to Ronald Bergey, "En tout âge, ce chant a présenté à Israël un reflet de sa condition actuelle et de son avenir."[6] It is in light of this assessment that this dissertation analyzes the divine metaphors of the Song to see how they function to contribute to its theology.

However, before such an inquiry can be made, the project will survey some of the major theoretical perspectives on metaphor to select a methodology for this study. In doing so, several questions will be answered: What is a metaphor? How is a metaphor identified within a poetic unit? How does a metaphor interact with the poetic text to generate different cognitive meanings? The answer to these questions will also serve to delineate the methodology of the research.

# Definition of Metaphor

Although scholars have long recognized the use of metaphors in literature to stimulate the reader's imagination, they have not reached a consensus regarding a definition. This is due largely to the various theories they propose.[7] This study surveys some of the most common theoretical perspectives on meta-

---

analysis. He thoroughly analyzes the dynamics of the Song's performance within the traditional settings of Deuteronomy; in doing so, he provides a close reading of the Song. Keith A. Stone, *Singing Moses's Song: A Performance-Critical Analysis of Deuteronomy's Song of Moses* (Boston: Ilex Foundation, 2016). See also Tina Dykesteen Nilsen, *The Origins of Deuteronomy 32: Intertextuality, Memory, Identity* (New York: Peter Lang, 2018).

6. Ronald Bergey, "Le Cantique de Moïse — Son Reflet dans le Prisme du Canon des Ecritures," *RRef* 223, no. 3 (2003): 2. This quotation is translated by this writer as follows: "At any age, this Song has presented to Israel a reflection of its present condition as well as its future."

7. For a list of other theories, see Janet Soskice, *Metaphor and Religious Language* (Oxford: Oxford University Press, 1985), 1.

phor, particularly the works of Aristotle, I. A. Richards, Max Black, Lakoff and Johnson, and Janet Soskice, before providing a working definition for this study. These scholars were chosen not only because they provide a definition of metaphor but also because they are among those who have had the most influence on scholars who research metaphor in the Hebrew Bible.

## Aristotle

One of the earliest attempts to propose a scholarly treatment of metaphor can be traced back to Aristotle. In his *Poetics*, Aristotle declares, "Metaphor is the application of a strange term either transferred from the genus and applied to the species or from the species and applied to the genus, or from one species to another or else by analogy."[8]

By *analogy*, Aristotle understood metaphor to be a mere substitution, an exchange of a literal word for a metaphorical one. In this case, the metaphor does not have any rhetorical function. He notes, "When B is to A as D is to C, then instead of B the poet will say D and B instead of D. And sometimes they add that to which the term supplanted by the metaphor is relative."[9] For Aristotle, it is important to discover the literal meaning to which the metaphor alludes.[10] In short, the basic thrust of his model is to regard and treat metaphor as a device of embellishment added for ornamental effect.[11] This view has remained current until the beginning of the twentieth century especially with the work of I. A. Richards.[12]

---

8. Aristotle, *Poetics*, vol. 23 in *Aristotle in 23 Volumes*, trans. W. H. Fyfe (Medford, MA: Harvard University Press, 1932), 1457b.

9. Ibid.

10. For a thorough critical assessment on Aristotle, see Paul Ricoeur, *The Rule of Metaphor: Multi-disciplinary Studies of the Creation of Meaning in Language*, trans. Robert Czerny, Kathleen McLaughlin, and John Costello (Toronto: University of Toronto Press, 1977), 9–43.

11. In her work, Kittay credits Aristotle with an appreciation of the cognitive function of metaphor and claims that it was Aristotle's followers who had merely treated the figure as decoration or comparison. Eva Feder Kittay, *Metaphor: Its Cognitive Force and Linguistic Structure* (Oxford: Clarendon Press, 1991), 4.

12. For a list of scholars who followed Aristotle, see Maren R. Niehoff, *Jewish*

## I. A. Richards

In 1936, I. A. Richards established some principles for the theory of language and metaphor, which continue to impact metaphor studies today. In his work *The Philosophy of Rhetoric* he defines metaphor as a "shift, a carrying over of a word from its normal use to a new use."[13] He writes, "In the simplest formulation, when we use a metaphor we have two thoughts of different things active together and supported by a single word, or phrase, whose meaning is a resultant of their interaction."[14] For Richards, the two thoughts are (1) the *tenor* which denotes the underlying idea, and (2) the *vehicle*, that is, the means by which the underlying idea is expressed.[15] Richards rightly observes that the vehicle is not added to the tenor for ornamental or aesthetic effect, as the Aristotelian school advocates. Rather, it works in tandem with the tenor to "give a meaning of more varied powers than can be ascribed to either."[16] Because words are "interinanimated," Richards insists, complete utterances should determine the meaning of metaphors within specific literary contexts, not isolated words.[17] His analogy illustrates this well:

> A note in a musical phrase takes its character from, and makes its contribution only with, the other notes about it; a seen color is only what it is with respect to the other colors co-present with it in the visual field; the seen size or distance of an object is interpreted only with regard to the other things seen with it. Everywhere in perception we shall see this interinanimation (or interpenetration as Bergson used to call it). So

---

*Exegesis and Homeric Scholarship in Alexandria* (Cambridge: Cambridge University Press, 2011), 38–39. For a summary of the various views of metaphor from Aristotle to the twentieth century, see Mark Johnson, "Metaphor in the Philosophical Tradition," in *Philosophical Perspectives on Metaphor*, ed. Mark Johnson (Minneapolis: University of Minnesota Press, 1981), 5–7.

13. I. A. Richards, *The Philosophy of Rhetoric* (Oxford: Oxford University Press, 1936), 93.
14. Ibid., 96–97.
15. Ibid., 96–97.
16. Ibid., 100.
17. Ibid., 47–65.

with words, too, but much more; the meaning we find for a word comes to it only with respect to the other meanings of the other words we take with it.[18]

One of the strengths of Richards's model is the recognition that words cannot determine meaning apart from the whole context. Lexicons and dictionaries, for example, are inadequate to determine the meaning of a metaphor because they do not consider the interaction between the tenor and the vehicle.[19] In this way, he considers the meaning of a metaphor as contextual and dialectical. Because of his focus on "interaction" between the elements of metaphor, his model later was labeled the "Interaction Theory of Metaphor" and was followed by many scholars, notably Max Black.

## Max Black

In 1962, Black further developed the interaction view of I. A. Richards. Essentially, Black argues that metaphor is "a loose word, at best, and we must beware of attributing to it stricter rules of usage than are actually found in practice."[20] For Black, the detection of the "characteristic transforming function involved in metaphor," which is *analogy* or *similarity*, must determine the original meaning of a metaphor.[21] This analogy includes two subjects: (1) the principal subject, that is, the literal word; and (2) the subsidiary subject, the metaphorical word describing the principal subject.[22] Moreover, instead of seeing the subsidiary subject as one component, Black deviated from his predecessor in arguing that it is a "system of associated commonplaces," a list of

---

18. Richards, *The Philosophy of Rhetoric*, 69–70.
19. The terms "tenor" and "vehicle" will be used consistently in this project to refer to the two subjects of the metaphor.
20. Max Black, *Models and Metaphors: Studies in Language and Philosophy* (Ithaca: Cornell University Press, 1962), 28–29.
21. Ibid., 27.
22. Ibid.

traits that belong to a particular society.[23] As such, when the principal and the subsidiary meet, they create new meaning in a metaphor.[24]

> Black further insists that the subsidiary subject always illuminates the principal. It does so by suppressing some details to emphasize others that are more important. Hence, it organizes thoughts about human beings in a new manner. For instance, in the statement, "man is a wolf," the wolf-system of related commonplaces is in view. However, according to Black, only human traits which "can without undue strain be talked about in 'wolf-language' will be rendered prominent."[25] The context of the metaphor will determine which human traits fit and which ones should be pushed into the background.[26] Such an activity, Black said, provides a sort of "filtering" or "screening" for the reader.[27]

## George Lakoff and Mark Johnson

Lakoff and Johnson in 1980 developed and expanded the study of metaphor in their seminal work *Metaphors We Live By*.[28] These scholars argue that metaphor is a property of concepts used effortlessly by ordinary people in their everyday lives. They define metaphor as "understanding and experiencing one kind of thing in terms of another."[29] They contend that the biblical poets purposefully used metaphors to "illuminate our experience, explore the consequences of our beliefs, challenge the way we think, and criticize our ideologies."[30]

---

23. Black, *Models and Metaphors*, 40.
24. Ibid., 38–39.
25. Ibid., 41.
26. Ibid.
27. Ibid., 42.
28. George Lakoff and Mark Johnson, *Metaphors We Live By*, 2nd ed. (London: University of Chicago Press, 2003).
29. Ibid., 193.
30. See also George Lakoff and Mark Turner, *More than Cool Reason: A Field Guide to Poetic Metaphor* (Chicago: University of Chicago Press, 1989), xi.

# THE FIRST ROCK SONG:
## Contributions of Divine Metaphors to the Theology of the Song of Moses

The main idea of this theory is that the conceptual system in terms of which a human being thinks and acts is essentially "metaphorical in nature."[31] Such concepts are structural and reside primarily in thoughts and only derivatively in language. These metaphoric structures then serve as a filter for all human experience. Lakoff and Johnson's illustration on the metaphorical concept "argument is war" captures well the essence of this theory:

ARGUMENT IS WAR

Your claims are *indefensible*.
He *attacked every weak point* in my argument. His criticisms were *right on* target.
I *demolished* his argument.
I've never *won* an argument with him.
You disagree? Okay, *shoot!*
If *you* use that *strategy*, he'll *wipe you out*. He *shot down* all *of my* arguments.[32]

According to Lakoff and Johnson, the concept "argument is war" structures the way people think and speak about argument. Since metaphor is "not just a matter of language, but primarily a matter of human thought," when talking about argument in terms of war, many other concepts related to verbal battle are implied.[33] That is why the metaphor *argument is war* defines and "structures the actions we perform in arguing."[34] This approach, known as "Cognitive Theory of Metaphor," has had an impact on biblical studies ever since its inception.[35]

---

31. Lakoff and Johnson, *Metaphors We Live By*, 3.
32. Ibid, 5.
33. Ibid., 6.
34. For more information, see Zoltán Kövecses, *Metaphor: A Practical Introduction*, 2nd ed. (Oxford: Oxford University Press, 2010), ix–x.
35. Many biblical scholars follow a cognitive approach to study metaphor in the Hebrew Bible. See for instance, Stienstra who develops the conceptual metaphor "YHWH is the Husband of His People" in her work on Hosea, Ezekiel, Isaiah, and Jeremiah. Nelly Stienstra, *YHWH is the Husband of His People: Analysis of a Biblical*

*Introduction*

## Janet Soskice

Soskice has integrated the approaches of both Richards and Black into her own theory of metaphor. She defines metaphor as "that figure of speech whereby we speak about one thing in terms which are seen to be suggestive of another."[36] She writes, "It should not be thought that metaphor is primarily a process or a mental act, and only secondarily its manifestation in language. Metaphor is by definition a figure of speech and not an 'act', 'fusion', or 'perception'. Were this not the case we should not know where to look for metaphor at all."[37]

Although metaphor is a figure of speech, explains Soskice, exegetes should think of it as a sum of the meaning of a complete utterance in context instead of isolated words because sometimes "it may take more than one sentence to establish a metaphor."[38] But the reader can establish a metaphor as soon as he can detect that "one thing is being spoken of in terms suggestive of another."[39]

Additionally, in establishing her theory of metaphor, Soskice borrows the term "interinanimation" from Richards because she thinks that Richards' theory "has come nearest to providing a satisfactory account" of metaphor.[40] Her interinanimative theory neither regards metaphor as a mere replacement for literal speech nor as strictly emotive. She states, "Metaphor should be treated as fully cognitive and capable of saying that which may be said in no

---

*Metaphor with Special Reference to Translation* (Leuven: Peeters Publishers, 1993), 1; Brian Doyle, *The Apocalypse of Isaiah Metaphorically Speaking: A Study of the Use, Function, and Significance of Metaphors in Isaiah 24–27* (Leuven: Peeters Publishers, 2000), 1; see also Marc Zvi Brettler, *God Is King: Understanding an Israelite Metaphor*, JSOTSup 76 (Sheffield, UK: JSOT Press, 1989); and Job Y. Jindo, *Biblical Metaphor Reconsidered: A Cognitive Approach to Poetic Prophecy in Jeremiah 1–24*, HSM 64 (Winona Lake, IN: Eisenbrauns, 2010), 1.

36. Soskice, *Metaphor and Religious Language*, 15.
37. Ibid., 16.
38. Ibid., 21.
39. Ibid., 22.
40. Ibid., 44.

other way. It should explain how metaphor gives us 'two ideas for one,' yet do so without lapsing into a comparison theory."[41]

## Evaluation

Aristotle's definition is a good starting point but has its weaknesses because it treats metaphors as simply artistical or ornamental devices.[42] As Soskice correctly declares, this Aristotelian view "reduces metaphor to the status of a riddle or a word game and the appreciation of metaphor to the unravelling of that riddle."[43]

The "interaction theory" as advocated by Richards and later Black is helpful for its focus on sentences rather than on words. Black, for instance, proposes to look at metaphors as having two subjects (the frame and the focus) called "associated commonplaces" because these two always interact with each other.[44] The problem with Black's idea, as Soskice mentions, is his insistence that each metaphor must have two distinct subjects.[45] This idea can only work in a comparative type of sentence, namely A is B. Mac Cormac correctly explains that Black's interaction view "allows for a reversal of his own terms—the focus may become the frame and the frame the focus."[46]

The cognitive theory of metaphor is also striking because it rightly understands the cognitive function of metaphor. However, its weaknesses lie in the fact that it minimizes the linguistic aspect of metaphor. Lakoff and Johnson (and later Turner) refuse to call metaphor a figure of speech. Weiss correctly points out that this cognitive model "treats metaphor primarily as a figure of thought, as opposed to a figure of speech, and it examines the mental processes involved in the creation and interpretation of metaphor."[47] This use

---

41. Soskice, *Metaphor and Religious Language*, 44.

42. Mark Johnson, *The Body in the Mind: The Bodily Basis of Meaning, Imagination, and Reason* (Chicago: University of Chicago Press, 1987), 67.

43. Soskice, *Metaphor and Religious Language*, 25.

44. Black, *Models and Metaphors*, 69.

45. Soskice, *Metaphor and Religious Language*, 43–46.

46. Earl R. Mac Cormac, *A Cognitive Theory of Metaphor* (Cambridge, MA: MIT Press, 1985), 25.

47. Andrea L. Weiss, *Figurative Language in Biblical Prose Narrative: Metaphor*

of metaphor is so broad that it sometimes leaves room for speculation.[48] As Jackendoff and Aaron assess, this model needs to add a criterion of incongruity and a more restricted scope for the term metaphor.[49]

The definition for this study will bear much similarity to Soskice's theory for several reasons. First, Soskice sees metaphor as a figure of speech and consequently a linguistic phenomenon.[50] This is important for this study which begins with the biblical text to understand how the divine metaphors contribute to the theology of the Song. Such a focus on language does not deny the cognitive aspects of metaphor. For, as Soskice further explains, although metaphor is primarily a linguistic phenomenon, it should be treated "as fully cognitive and capable of saying that which may be said in no other way."[51] Kittay agrees with Soskice when she writes, "The linguistic utterance of metaphor exists in relation to a language whose organization reflects and helps shape a conceptual system."[52] In other words, the canonical text is what gives rise to the cognitive function of the metaphor, not vice-versa. Therefore, the emphasis is primarily on the text rather than the ideas that sit behind the text.[53] Hence, the conceptual aspect of metaphor will be used to supplement the linguistic aspect, not to replace it. Second, in her definition, Soskice explains the phrase "seen to be suggestive of another" to signify "seen so by a competent speaker," that is, someone who knows the phonology, morphology, syntax, and semantic as well as the culture of the language.[54] This is to say that a competent speaker will use linguistic labels that are associated with both the tenor

---

*in the Book of Samuel*, VTSup 107 (Leiden: Brill, 2006), 16.

48. The focus on language allows the reader or the exegete to discover the original intent of the author of the song. Thus, speculation is kept to a minimum.

49. Ray Jackendoff and David Aaron, review of *More than Cool Reason: A Field Guide to Poetic Metaphor*, by George Lakoff and Mark Turner, *Language* 67, no. 2 (1991): 320–38.

50. Soskice, *Metaphor and Religious Language*, 15.

51. Ibid., 44.

52. Kittay, *Metaphor*, 15.

53. In her work, Kittay says that she aims to "understand the cognitive force of metaphor through the elucidation of metaphoric meaning." Kittay, *Metaphor*, 15. This is what this study seeks to accomplish also.

54. Soskice, *Metaphor and Religious Language*, 15.

and the vehicle. As Soskice notes, "A metaphor is only a metaphor because someone, speaker or hearer and ideally both, regards it as such; the intentional component is essential. It is thus the speaker's meaning, what he was thinking in uttering the speech act, that is determinative in whether he was speaking non-metaphorically, metaphorically or even nonsensically."[55] Third, contrary to Lakoff and Johnson, Soskice rightly understands the criterion of incongruity or deviance in metaphor. This is essential because each metaphor always breaks the semantic rules, that is, the tenor and the vehicle belong to different semantic domains. A right understanding of the criterion of incongruity leads to a better appreciation and handling of the poetic device.

Overall, Soskice provides the most succinct and accurate definition of a metaphor because she deals with the written text and how to read it in context. Her view is accepted as the basis for this study, given one minor adjustment. Contrary to Soskice, the definition of metaphor in this study already includes its basic function, that is, to generate different cognitive meanings. This distinction is important because, as this study already pointed out, metaphor as primarily a linguistic phenomenon has cognitive force. As such, the metaphor is best defined as that figure of speech which transfers a meaning from one realm to another to generate different cognitive understandings of reality. This definition is the backbone for this study.

## Identification of Metaphor

Having established a definition of metaphor, this study must still explain how a metaphor can be identified in a poetic unit. For, as Ina Loewenberg correctly asserts, "Any satisfactory formulation of the principle of metaphor requires the identifiability of metaphors since they cannot be understood or produced unless recognized as such."[56] Hence, after examining various theories that identify metaphors, Loewenberg demonstrates that semantic theory is the

---

55. Soskice, *Metaphor and Religious Language*, 136.
56. Ina Loewenberg, "Identifying Metaphors," in *Philosophical Perspectives on Metaphor*, ed. Mark Johnson (Minneapolis: University of Minnesota Press, 1981), 155.

right source of that formula since all metaphors involve semantic change.[57] Kittay agrees with Loewenberg when she states that a metaphor always involves some sort of incongruity, especially when the utterance is interpreted.[58] Therefore, to interpret the metaphorical utterance, Kittay has developed a model called "componential semantics."[59] Her model will be used throughout this study to identify metaphors in the Song of Moses.

## Componential Semantics

Kittay provides a clear method to identify the presence of metaphor. She proposes that one must first recognize literal and conventional meaning and then locate the deviant language. This is important because a term can be used both literally and figuratively in the Bible. For example, in Ps 105:37–45, the psalmist recounts various instances of God's provisions for Israel during the wilderness wandering. Yhwh provided quail for Israel and satisfied them with manna.[60] Furthermore, the psalmist said that Yhwh opened the צור (*tsur*; "rock") and water flowed out. In this context, the term צור (*tsur*; "rock") is used to refer to a mass of stone (i.e., an inanimate and solid material). According to Kittay, this meaning "consists of a content, represented as a set of concepts, a set of conditions which relate to the permissible semantic combination of

---

57. Loewenberg, "Identifying Metaphors," 155.

58. Kittay, *Metaphor*, 65. See also Ryken who argues that "a metaphor is always a fiction or a 'lie'. It asserts something that we know is not literally true." Leland Ryken, *Sweeter than Honey, Richer than Gold: A Guided Study of Biblical Poetry* (Bellingham, WA: Lexham Press, 2015), 50.

59. Componential semantics is the method that analyzes the meaning of a word by breaking the sense of a lexeme into its component parts. For instance, the word "man" can be represented as encompassing *human, male, adult*, in contrast to "girl": *human, female, non-adult*. As Weiss notes, this model allows its users to identify the "necessary and sufficient" elements that distinguish the meaning of a word from others. See Weiss, *Figurative Language in Biblical Prose Narrative*, 40–47.

60. This project uses the transliteration "Yhwh" when referring to the tetragrammaton יהוה, the covenant name of God (Ex 3:14).

# THE FIRST ROCK SONG:
## Contributions of Divine Metaphors to the Theology of the Song of Moses

the term."[61] This phenomenon is called "first-order meaning."[62] However, the same term "rock" is used in the Song of Moses to refer to a deity.[63] In this case, the language is incongruent. This incongruity is called "second-order meaning" because God is not a stone or something solid.[64] As Ryken correctly admits, "At a literal or grammatical level, a metaphor is always a fiction or 'lie.' It asserts something that we know is not literally true."[65] Thus, the first step is to recognize that the language is figurative in order to locate the incongruity.

To locate the incongruity, Kittay proposes that one identify the "unit of discourse which constitutes a metaphor."[66] This entails paying attention to *context* (historical, literary, cultural, etc.) as the key determining factor of a metaphor (or any literal sentences), not the grammatical unit. Kittay's observation about paying attention to the context is important. For, as Dille writes, "Metaphors do not function in isolation."[67] Thus, to ignore the world (context) of the metaphor is tantamount to calling everything a metaphor. That is why Kittay puts forth the following conditions to decide on which utterance contains a metaphor. (1) There must be a competent speaker of the language to ensure the utterance is not an error; (2) the context should persuade the reader that the utterance is not substantially different from his own expectations, as in the case where there is an alteration; (3) the utterance should display a certain degree of oddity (deviance) and that the incongruent element, when read within the context, belongs to at least two distinct semantic fields; and (4) there is a violation of the selection restrictions in the utterance.[68] Kittay's method of identifying metaphors can be illustrated with an example from the Song of Moses.

In Deut 32:6c Moses asks, "Is not he your father who has acquired you?" On the surface this question contains no incongruity since it may allude to

---

61. Kittay, *Metaphor*, 65.
62. Ibid.
63. See, for instance, Deut 32:4.
64. See Kittay, *Metaphor*, 70.
65. Ryken, *Sweeter than Honey, Richer than Gold*, 50.
66. Ibid., 41.
67. Sarah J. Dille, *Mixing Metaphors: God as Mother and Father in Deutero-Isaiah* (London: T&T Clark International, 2004), 1.
68. Kittay, *Metaphor*, 49–50.

a biological father.⁶⁹ In other words, the statement could describe a human relationship. However, the surrounding context suggests that it is God who is the father of Israel (32:6a). Since the term 'God' has the selection-restriction of *deity, spirit*, and the pronoun 'you' (=Israel) has the selection-restriction of *human*, the utterance is incongruent when read within its context. Thus, the statement is metaphorical.

## Distinction between Metaphor and Other Figures of Speech

Kittay emphasizes *semantic incongruity* or *deviance* as a primary means to identify metaphor in a poetic unit. Nevertheless, semantic incongruity is not a phenomenon peculiar to metaphor only. For instance, Deut 32:36 reads,

| | |
|---|---|
| For Yhwh will judge his people, | A |
| And to his servants He will show compassion; | B |
| When he sees that the hand is gone, | A |
| And there is nothing, bound or free. | B |

The context of this verse shows that the word יָד translated as "hand" is not used in its literal sense. Rather, it signifies strength.⁷⁰ It is a metonymy and as such, it stands for man's ability to do something, usually with hands.⁷¹ Therefore, the utterance is incongruent as it stands. But does this incongruity suggest that the metonymy be also called "metaphor"? Kittay answers this question by saying that such figures of speech do not violate their semantic fields. In essence, literary terms like metonymy, irony, hyperbole, and synecdoche may present some incongruities, but they always stay within their

---

69. All translations are the student's unless otherwise noted.

70. Charlie Trimm, *"YHWH Fights for Them!": The Divine Warrior in the Exodus Narrative* (Piscataway, NJ: Gorgias Press, 2014), 15–16.

71. Ethelbert William Bullinger, *Figures of Speech Used in the Bible, Explained and Illustrated* (Grand Rapids: Baker Book House, 1968), 547.

# THE FIRST ROCK SONG:
## Contributions of Divine Metaphors to the Theology of the Song of Moses

semantic domain.[72] Gibbs agrees with Kittay in his distinction between metaphor and metonymy when he states:

> There are key differences between metaphor and metonymy, despite the fact that both express mappings between things. In metaphor, there are two conceptual domains, and one is understood in terms of another, usually very different, knowledge domain. Metonymy involves only one conceptual domain, in that the mapping or connection between two things is within the same domain.[73]

Now a word must be said about simile since the literature is often divided on the issue of whether simile and metaphor are interchangeable[74] or altogether distinct in their rhetorical effects.[75] The peculiarity of a simile is that it can either be used literally or metaphorically. For instance, the statement in 2 Kgs 21:20, "He [Amon] did evil in the eyes of Yhwh, as his father Manasseh had done," is a literal statement. It does not have any incongruity because both Amon and Manasseh have the selection-restriction of human. However, in Deut 32:11, the language is figurative and involves the mapping of a source domain onto a target domain.[76] The verse reads,

---

72. Soskice, *Metaphor and Religious Language*, 8.

73. R. W. Gibbs, *Researching Metaphor in Researching and Applying Metaphor*, The Cambridge Applied Linguistics Series (Cambridge: Cambridge University Press, 1999), 36. See also Zacharias Kotzé, "A Cognitive Linguistic Methodology for the Study of Metaphor in the Hebrew Bible," *JNSL* 31, no. 1 (2005): 113.

74. For instance, Fogelin argues that the difference between simile and metaphor is in only a "trivial grammatical way: metaphors are similes with the terms of comparison suppressed." Robert J. Fogelin, *Figuratively Speaking* (New Haven: Yale University Press, 1988), 357. See also George A. Miller, "Images and Models, Similes, and Metaphors," in *Metaphor and Thought*, ed. A. Ortony (Cambridge: Cambridge University Press, 1993), 228–29.

75. For this view, Black argues that metaphor and simile are completely different. He declares, "In discursively comparing one subject *with* another, we sacrifice distinctive power and effectiveness of a good metaphor." See Black, *Models and Metaphors*, 31.

76. Soskice explains that the difference between simile and metaphor is only one of grammar. For her, true similes can accomplish the same effect as metaphor. See Soskice, *Metaphor and Religious Language*, 58.

| | |
|---|---|
| Like an eagle rouses its nest, | A |
| Over its young it hovers; | B |
| | |
| He spread out his wings, sheltered him | A |
| Lifted him on his feather. | B |

In this verse, the poet uses the imagery of נֶשֶׁר (an eagle) caring for its young to explain the protective care that Yhwh provides for his people "through the hostile wilderness."[77] Using componential semantics, it is clear that the eagle may be represented as *birds of prey, carnivore, winged bird*, while Yhwh can be represented as *deity, spirit*.[78] Here, the body parts of the eagle are thus applied figuratively to Yhwh by means of the simile, and as such, the utterance deviates to another domain. Contrary to the other figures of speech that contain an incongruity within their semantic field, similes may possess a criterion of incongruity that violates the semantic domain. That explains why Soskice states, "Metaphor and simile, while textually different, are functionally the same."[79] Nevertheless, while similes can function much like metaphors, they are not the same.[80] The textual difference between the two is sufficient to show that they are two different rhetorical devices: simile is simile, and metaphor is metaphor. Therefore, the analysis of simile will not be included in this analysis of divine metaphors of the Song.

## Metaphor at Work in Biblical Studies

During the last four decades or so, much has been written about metaphor in biblical studies. Scholars who research biblical metaphors do so from a

---

77. William P. Brown, *Seeing the Psalms: A Theology of Metaphor* (Louisville: John Knox Press, 2002), 22.
78. See Ryken, Wilhoit, and Longman, *Dictionary of Biblical Imagery*, 223.
79. Soskice, *Metaphor and Religious Language*, 59.
80. For more information regarding literary terms used throughout this thesis, please consult Richard A. Lanham, *A Handlist of Rhetorical Terms*, 2nd ed. (Berkeley, CA: University of California Press, 1991); Michael S. Mills, *Concise Handbook of Literary and Rhetorical Terms* (USA: Estep-Nichols Publishing, 2010).

variety of perspectives. Some works are concerned with theories of metaphor and how metaphor works in the biblical text; other works focus on specific metaphors or trace one metaphor throughout a passage or a book. Van Hecke and Labahn offer a useful overview of a range of methods scholars utilize to study metaphor to see how it creates meaning in a biblical text.[81] In this section, a review of some recent perspectives on metaphor will be presented in order to understand the proper place of this dissertation in Old Testament scholarship.

## Theoretical and Methodological Works on Biblical Metaphor

Several works deal with the theoretical aspect of metaphor but only three are selected because they share at least two features that are in line with this project: They understand metaphor as primarily a phenomenon of language, as opposed to thought; and they focus on authorial intent. The first theoretical work worth noting is Peter Macky's *The Centrality of Metaphors in Biblical Thought*. Macky provides a method for interpreting metaphors in the Bible. He evaluates various theories of metaphor before providing his own definition.[82] He argues that words can have various meanings and that it is through "speech act" that a speaker can narrow potential meanings down in order to find the meaning intended by the author. Therefore, quoting multiple passages from both the Hebrew Bible and the New Testament, Macky focuses on authorial intent to understand what the biblical writers were thinking when they wrote metaphorical expressions.[83] Macky's insistence on authorial intent

---

81. Pierre Van Hecke and Antje Labahn, eds., *Metaphor in the Psalms*, BETL 231 (Leuven: Uitgeverij Peeters, 2010).

82. Macky defines metaphor as a "figurative way of speaking (and meaning) in which one reality, the Subject, is depicted in terms that are more commonly associated with a different reality, the Symbol, which is related to it by Analogy." Peter Macky, *The Centrality of Metaphors to Biblical Thought: A Method for Interpreting the Bible* (Lewiston, NY: E. Mellen, 1990), 49.

83. Macky, *The Centrality of Metaphors to Biblical Thought*, 9. Vanhoozer correctly points out that every text must possess a single meaning and that meaning should reside in the original author's intention. For him, the author has authority

is valid because, as E. D. Hirsch explains, a text means exactly what its author meant by it. Thus, meaning is static and objective.[84] Such a focus on authorial intent rejects any reader-response based theory which argues that the meaning of a text resides in the reader's mind (i.e., the way the reader understands and interprets the text).[85] Although Macky provides many biblical examples in his theoretical model of metaphor, his treatment of the topic is insufficient because he does not provide any practical exegetical insights for the reader.

Another theoretical work frequently cited in biblical studies is David Aaron's *Biblical Ambiguities*.[86] Aaron endeavors to construct "a model for gradient judgments — that is, a method for judging statements and placing them on a non-binary continuum of meaning."[87] Arguing that the Hebrew Bible, like the other ancient texts, contains a kind of logical ambiguity or nonequivalence, Aaron encourages readers to seek meanings that are different from the literal sense and find out the one meaning that best describes the metaphor in

---

upon the text, not the reader. So, "the author is the ground of the 'being' of meaning." See Kevin J. Vanhoozer, *Is there a Meaning in this Text* (Grand Rapids: Zondervan, 1998), 47.

84. E. D. Hirsch Jr., *Validity in Interpretation* (New Haven: Yale University Press, 1967), 44. See also Kaiser who states that only one verbal is to be connected with any passage of Scripture unless the writer of the text gives literary and contextual clues that he has several aims in view for this exceptional passage. Walter Kaiser, Jr., "The Single Intent of Scripture," in *Evangelical Roots: A Tribute to Wilbur Smith*, ed. K. S. Kantzer (Nashville: Thomas Nelson, 1978), 138.

85. See for instance Antje Labahn who claims that metaphorical meaning is not created by the author and therefore is not located in the text; rather, the meaning is created when someone reads or hears the metaphor. Therefore, metaphors are literary devices that bear multiple senses and suggest various meanings to the readers or hearers according to their own presuppositions. For her, when an author applies the notion of intertextuality to metaphor, one brings over from the intertexts all the various interpretations the metaphor had in those contexts, not just the simple meaning of the metaphor. Antje Labahn, "Metaphor and Intertextuality: 'Daughter of Zion' as a Test Case. Response to Kirsten Nielsen 'From Oracles to Canon' — and the Role of Metaphor," *SJOT* 17 (2003): 49-67.

86. David H. Aaron, *Biblical Ambiguities: Metaphor, Semantics and Divine Imagery*, Brill Reference Library of Ancient Judaism 4 (Leiden and Boston: Brill, 2001).

87. Ibid., 7.

view.[88] To help understand statements that fall in between "literal" and "metaphorical," he introduces a third category called "conceptual ascriptions," which he illustrates as follows:

> Father-son language in the Hebrew Bible is fundamentally *ascriptival*, in both functional and structural ways, and for most of these expressions, metaphor is not involved. In this case, the functional ascription regards how one comes into the world (God as creator) and the structural ascription regards the attribution of authority to whomever it is that occupies the hierarchical station of "father" within a clan. Both are meant quite literally in the manner that ascription is closer to literal than it is to any figurative mode of expression. When we fail to recognize this, we guarantee a distortion of the biblical concept.[89]

Aaron's model is important for biblical studies because it allows "for more accurate assessments of ancient utterances."[90] In fact, Aaron recognizes that the Bible contains both literal and figurative statements. Therefore, a focus on the intention of the original author is needed to properly interpret figurative expressions. Moreover, Aaron rejects the notion that all thought is metaphorical in nature, as advocated by Lakoff and Johnson.[91] This correct reading of the Bible explains his skepticism regarding Brettler's idea that the statement "God is king" is metaphorical. For Aaron, "any notion of God as king of all celestial beings was understood as a literal charge of leadership."[92] Nevertheless, despite Aaron's success in providing a mechanism for identifying metaphorical expressions in biblical studies, his work is incomplete because it focuses solely on theory.

In a similar vein, Janet Soskice's *Metaphor and Religious Language* is helpful not only for its emphasis on the linguistic aspect of metaphor and its focus on authorial intent, but also for its clear method of identifying metaphor

---

88. Aaron, *Biblical Ambiguities*, 28–29.
89. Ibid., 63.
90. Ibid., 69.
91. Ibid., 101–24.
92. Ibid., 41.

in the biblical text. As noted earlier, Soskice explores the nature of metaphor and explains how it should be distinguished from other figurative tropes such as metonymy and synecdoche. She recognizes that metaphors are primarily a phenomenon of language but are cognitive and indispensable. In sum, Soskice sets out four conditions that any model of metaphor must satisfy: (1) It should not treat metaphors as either mere substitutions or merely emotive. (2) It must recognize the cognitive function of metaphors. (3) It must explain how one gets two ideas for one in a metaphorical sentence. (4) It must show that there is a competent speaker who utters the speech, and that the utterance is not made in error. Soskice concludes her work with three chapters dealing with how to speak about God and His works through metaphor.[93] However, like Macky and Aaron, Soskice does not bridge the gap between theory and practice because she does not offer any exegetical benefits for the reader beside a description of the theory.

While the above scholars seek to simply construct a theory or a model by which biblical metaphors can be examined, others are concerned with the actual study of metaphors to see how they function within a biblical text. Nevertheless, regardless of the theory of metaphor a scholar chooses to follow, the metaphor is treated either as a phenomenon of thought, that is, a system of human origin that resides inside one or more cognitive spaces of given human beings, or as a characteristic of language (linguistic theory of metaphor).[94] This is another way of saying that there are two models of metaphor: cognitive and linguistic. Everything else is simply a variation of one or the other (or both). For this reason, the next section will survey three representative works for each camp to examine their strengths and weaknesses before deciding on a methodology for this study.

---

93. Soskice, *Metaphor and Religious Language*, 97–161. See also Soskice's recent monograph *The Kindness of God: Metaphor, Gender, and Religious Language* (Oxford: Oxford University Press, 2008).

94. Cognitive theory of metaphor is the approach advocated by Lakoff and Johnson (including Mark Turner). Linguistic theories of metaphor are text-based approaches advocated by Aristotle, I. A. Richards, Max Black, Janet Soskice, Eva F. Kittay, and others.

# THE FIRST ROCK SONG:
## Contributions of Divine Metaphors to the Theology of the Song of Moses

## The Cognitive Theory of Metaphor in Biblical Studies

One of the most frequent theories used by biblical scholars in studying metaphors is the cognitive theory of metaphor developed by George Lakoff and Mark Johnson.[95] One such scholar is Sarah Dille, who examines five sets of mixed metaphors for God in five different biblical passages within their cultural and literary contexts. Dille deals with the woman-in-labor and warrior (Isa 42:8–17), the redeemer and father (Isa 43:1–7), the artisan and parent (Isa 45:9–13), the mother and husband (Isa 49:13–21), and the husband and father (Isa 50:1–3).[96] She focuses on metaphor coherence to understand the meaning of kinship metaphors where they interact with non-kinship metaphors that appear in the same texts. Her conclusion is that there is no consistent view of God as father or mother in Deutero-Isaiah.[97] Rather, these metaphors are independent of each other, and it is only within the larger context of Deutero-Isaiah that the individual metaphors can highlight some divine aspects such as God as a creator, redeemer of human beings, and protector. Perhaps one of the greatest weaknesses of this work is due to the fact that Dille begins with the conceptual cognitive approach to examine these metaphors. Consequently, she sometimes draws arbitrary and subjective conclusions. In Isa 43, for instance, Dille provides an analysis of the metaphors "God is a father" and "God is a redeemer" but fails to explain how these two metaphors cohere to underline the aspect of the love of God.[98]

Marc Zvi Brettler analyzes the kingship metaphor of God and what it means to Israel.[99] Brettler contends that in order to understand the metaphor "God is king," a comparison of how Israel described earthly and divine kings is required. For him, the biblical writers were cautious to use elaborate language when talking about divine kingship in order to avoid terms associated with hu-

---

95. Lakoff and Johnson, *Metaphors We Live By*, 1980.
96. Dille, *Mixing Metaphors*.
97. Dille, *Mixing Metaphors*.
98. Ibid., 74–101.
99. Brettler, *God Is King*. See also Marc Zvi Brettler, "Incompatible Metaphors for YHWH in Isaiah 40–66," *JSOT* 78 (1998):97–120.

man kingship that can potentially conflict with Israel's view of the character and sovereignty of God. Like Dille, Brettler discusses some arbitrary notions which he associates with the kingship metaphor. For example, in his analysis of Prov 21:30 and Job 42:3, he contends that these texts speak of God's kingship, yet the language of these wisdom texts does not contain any royal terminology.[100] Thus, Brettler at times seems to force the data to fit his kingship umbrella and this again is due to the way he uses the cognitive approach.

Another scholar who has used this approach in his study of metaphor is Alec Basson.[101] Using concepts from cognitive anthropology and conceptual metaphor theory, Basson analyzes divine metaphors in eight Psalms of lament (Pss 7, 17, 31, 35, 44, 59, 74, and 80). For each psalm, he describes the literary type (genre), the poetic features, as well as the contextual examination of the divine metaphors. Basson relies heavily upon the conceptual world underlying the divine metaphors to explore in detail the cognitive relationship between the way Yhwh is portrayed and the psalmist's own experiences. However, because Basson starts with the cognitive approach, some of his conclusions seem subjective. Moreover, he fails to draw theological conclusions from his study of these Psalms of lament and thus leaves the reader without any sort of theological insights.

In sum, scholars who follow the cognitive conceptual model of Lakoff and Johnson begin with the ideas that sit behind the text rather than the text. Simply stated, these authors seek to understand the cognitive or abstract factors giving rise to the divine metaphors in the text. Such an approach risks finding metaphors where there are none. It can potentially construct false biblical metaphors that were not in the mind of the biblical authors.

## The Linguistic Theory of Metaphor in Biblical Studies

Contrary to the cognitive approach, which begins with a concept or a thought to explore the metaphors in the biblical text, the linguistic approach

---

100. Brettler, *God Is King*, 54–55.

101. Alec Basson, *Divine Metaphors in Selected Hebrew Psalms of Lamentation* (Tübingen: Mohr Siebeck, 2006).

# THE FIRST ROCK SONG:
## Contributions of Divine Metaphors to the Theology of the Song of Moses

begins with the text proper. In doing so, it provides a safer ground for analyzing this rhetorical device because it is through the written text that one can discern the intention of the original author.[102] Many scholars utilize this approach to research metaphors in the Hebrew Bible. For instance, Brent Strawn analyzes the uses of leonine imagery in the ancient Near East using both biblical and extra-biblical materials.[103] He examines the archaeological remains of Israel and the ancient Near East in order to understand the lion metaphor during the Late Bronze Age through the Persian period. According to Strawn, the lion metaphor is used as a "trope of threat and power."[104] In the Hebrew Bible, it is applied to the self, the monarch, the adversary, and Yhwh. He concludes that such uses of the metaphor lion are consistent with ancient Near Eastern cultures except for its biblical use for the monarch. That is, the ancient Near Eastern cultures used leonine imagery positively with kings or rulers to depict power and threat. However, the Bible uses the leonine imagery with the king in a negative way. According to Strawn, such a distinction "reflects something different or distinct about Israel's theology of kingship."[105]

Another scholar who uses the linguistic theory of metaphor is Kirsten Nielsen, who analyzes specific texts within Isa 1–39 to understand the tree imagery.[106] Nielsen commends scholars and exegetes to pay close attention to the literary history and the various interpretative possibilities that may exist for a biblical text. Thus, the exegete must seek to understand the cultural context in which the image works as well as the history of the image, "giving as far as is possible an account of the use made of the image before and after its placing in the existing literary context."[107] Nielsen concludes that the goal of

---

102. It can be said that, before the cognitive theory of metaphor, everyone was using a linguistic theory of metaphor of some sort.

103. Brent A. Strawn, *What Is Stronger than a Lion? Leonine Image and Metaphor in the Hebrew Bible and the Ancient Near East*, OBO 212 (Freiburg: Herder, 2005).

104. Ibid., 65.

105. Strawn, *What Is Stronger than a Lion*, 247.

106. Kirsten Nielsen, *There Is Hope for a Tree: The Tree as Metaphor in Isaiah*, transl. Christine Crowley and Frederick Crowley, JSOTSup 65 (Sheffield, UK: Sheffield Academic, 1989).

107. Ibid., 66.

the tree metaphors in the book of Isaiah is to alter the audience's perspective to match Isaiah's theological interpretation of the current political circumstances of Israel.[108]

More recently, Benjamin Foreman examines the animal metaphors in the book of Jeremiah.[109] He looks at how the book of Jeremiah utilizes animal imagery to describe the people of Israel. Foreman tackles three types of metaphors: pastoral metaphors, mammal metaphors, and bird metaphors. He concludes that animal metaphors contribute to the theology of the book of Jeremiah in many ways: by explaining how Israel has rejected Yhwh and is unable to return to Him without God's restoration, by describing the exile as a consequence of individual and collective sins, and by spelling out specific sins the nation of Israel has committed. In so doing, Foreman demonstrates that animal metaphors are "able to translate the prophet's abstract, or seemingly distant or unlikely, message into a tangible reality."[110]

In short, scholars who utilize the linguistic approach of metaphor rightly focus on the text to analyze metaphor. They rightly understand metaphor as a phenomenon of language. Therefore, their emphasis is primarily on the biblical text. Nevertheless, any study that intends to fully understand a metaphor should not ignore its cognitive value because metaphor functions to create a mental picture for the reader. As Kittay asserts, "Metaphor provides the linguistic realization for the cognitive activity by which a language speaker makes use of one linguistically articulated domain in order to gain an understanding of another experiential or conceptual domain."[111] That is why the cognitive view of metaphor by Lakoff and Johnson is necessary to supplement the linguistic view.

---

108. Nielsen, *There Is Hope for a Tree*, 167.

109. Benjamin A. Foreman, *Animal Metaphors and the People of Israel in the Book of Jeremiah* (Göttingen: Vandenhoeck & Ruprecht, 2011).

110. Foreman, *Animal Metaphors*, 257.

111. Kittay, *Metaphor*, 14.

THE FIRST ROCK SONG:
Contributions of Divine Metaphors to the Theology of the Song of Moses

# Methodology for Study

This study primarily focuses on metaphor as a phenomenon of language to gain a right understanding of the author's intention. As such, it uses the linguistic approach to analyze metaphors in the Song of Moses. The cognitive conceptual approach is used to supplement the linguistic approach in understanding the mental picture created by the metaphor. These two approaches are not mutually exclusive but are complementary. As the definition for this inquiry explains, metaphor is that figure of speech which transfers a meaning from one realm to another realm to generate different cognitive understandings of reality. Thus, it is important to begin with the written text to identify and analyze the divine metaphors and then to try to understand the world from which the metaphors originate in order to see how they generate different cognitive meanings.

Such an inquiry will not tackle issues related to the poem's date of composition or its provenance.[112] As stated earlier, much has been written on

---

112. Although this dissertation does not deal with the date of composition and provenance of the poem, this writer's position is that the poem was written by Moses, just before his death around 1405 BC. The judgment on the Mosaic authorship is based on three factors: (1) the internal evidence of the book itself (Deut 31:9, 24); (2) the multiple references containing the name of Moses in Deuteronomy (Deut 1:5; 4:44; 29:1; 31:1, 9; 32:45; 33:1); and (3) the multiple references connecting the name of Moses with the Torah within the Hebrew Bible (Josh 8:31–32; 23:6; 2 Kgs 14:6; Neh 8:1; Neh 13:1; 2 Chr 25:4; 2 Chr 34:14; 2 Chr 35:6). This paper also assumes an "early date theory," which places the Exodus exactly around 1445–1446 BC, in the third year of Amenhotep II (1447–1421) based on 1 Kgs 6:1 and Judg 11:26. Proponents of this theory cite 1 Kgs 6:1 as the primary evidence and argue that the verse dates the beginning of the construction of the temple. It reads, "Now it came about in the four hundred and eightieth year after the Israelites came out of the land of Egypt, in the fourth year of Solomon's reign over Israel, in the month of Ziv which is the second month, that he began to build the house of Yahweh." According to this theory, since the fourth year of the reign of Solomon was in 966 BC, the 480 years preceding the fourth year of Solomon would place the Exodus at 1445 BC. Therefore, since Moses gave the speech to Israel forty years after the Exodus, the book must have been written around 1405 BC. See Charles H. Dyer, "The Date of the Exodus Reexamined," *BSac* 140, no. 559 (1983): 235. See also Gleason L. Archer, *A Survey of Old Testament*

these issues. This inquiry will look at the MT as it is laid out in the *BHS*.[113] This investigation bears similarities to the work of Alison Ruth Gray who focuses on one psalm to analyze its metaphors.[114] Gray promotes a "metaphor-focused exegesis" as a complementary approach to the Psalms. She offers an investigation of the "word pictures" of Ps 18 to show how they interrelate throughout the poem, and how they help to understand its unity and purpose.[115] Gray attempts to consider each word in this poem as "a potential source of verbal or pictorial interaction, with the ability to engage or activate certain conceptual associations."[116] In so doing, she uses the lexical, semantic, pragmatic, and conceptual approaches to explain the content and function of the metaphors in the text. The author explains the importance of considering metaphors in the study of poetry in the Psalter because they create "scenes in the mind of the reader," and can provide information concerning the structure, purpose, and theology of a psalm.[117] She concludes that the metaphors in Psalm 18 help to develop a vast and rich picture of the synergy between Yhwh and the king of Israel in their victorious routing and subjugation of their common enemies.

This investigation also bears much similarity to William Brown's *Seeing the Psalms*. Brown examines the Psalms through the hermeneutical lens of metaphor, paying close attention to the ancient Near Eastern literature and iconography. Brown defines metaphor as a "manifestation of a language" which serves as "grids or filters through which reality is viewed and reconfigured."[118] The goal is to enable the reader to "perceive something differently."[119] Brown's work on metaphors demonstrates the necessity to understand a poem in its context since a term can mean different things. Because of that

---

*Introduction*, rev. and exp. ed. (Chicago: Moody Press, 1994), 239.

113. A. Alt et al., eds. *Biblia Hebraica Stuttgartensia*. Editio quarta emendata (Stuttgart: Deutsche Bibelgesellschaft, 1990).

114. Alison Ruth Gray, *Psalm 18 in Words and Pictures: A Reading through Metaphor* (Leiden: Brill, 2014).

115. Ibid., 5.

116. Gray, *Psalm 18 in Words and Pictures*, 207.

117. Gray, *Psalm 18 in Words and Pictures*, 1.

118. Brown, *Seeing the Psalms*, 6.

119. Ibid.

flexibility, readers should remove any preconceived notions about a metaphor until they have analyzed it in its context.

The method of analysis will be completed in three steps. The first involves identifying the divine metaphor within its poetic unit. This requires examining the structure of the verse (or verses) to see how the poetic lines correspond to each other. Then, the imagery of the vehicle is clarified and interpreted in order to understand how it informs the reader about the unit's tenor. The second step discusses the function of the metaphor from a rhetorical standpoint. In other words, it looks at the relationship between the speaker/author, speech/text, and audience/reader as the means of achieving certain persuasive effects. The third step draws some biblical and theological conclusions of the metaphor to understand the theological contribution of the metaphor to the Song.

## Identification and Interpretation of the Divine Metaphor

The first step in the analysis of the Song of Moses is to identify and interpret the divine metaphor. Part of the first step involves identifying the metaphor using the method of Kittay, who proposes to look at the entire poetic unit to locate the incongruity.[120] This is fundamental because sometimes the tenor and the vehicle may not be explicitly stated in the text, as is the case in a comparative type of statement where A is equal to B. For instance, in Deut 32:39–42, the epithet "warrior" is not used for God. However, the language of the poetic unit is that of a divine warrior (Yhwh) using his flashing sword and arrows to fight his foes. Since Yhwh is depicted as a human warrior who uses his martial weapons to combat his enemies, the incongruent language domain is recognizing as producing a metaphor, since the tenor is "God" and the vehicle is "warrior." The metaphor can thus be rendered as "God is a warrior." Once the device is successfully identified, discussion on the structure of the poetic unit will be presented to provide a visual representation of the various components and their interrelationship. Then the metaphor is interpreted. This interpretation includes a lexical and syntactical analysis of the

---

120. See Kittay, *Metaphor*, 70.

poetic unit as well as an understanding of the ancient Near Eastern world from which the metaphor originates.

## Function of the Divine Metaphor

The second step in the analysis of the Song of Moses will discuss the rhetorical function of the metaphor. Patrick and Scult define rhetoric as "the means by which a text establishes and manages its relationship to its audience in order to achieve a particular effect."[121] Thus, this step seeks to understand how that relationship is carried out. This is important because, as the product of an author, the Song of Moses was meant to persuade the original audience in a certain way. For this reason, an exegesis of the metaphor is not complete without a discussion of its rhetorical function. The rhetorical function of the literary device also enhances its theological contribution.

## Theological Contributions of the Divine Metaphor

This last step involves examining the theological contributions of the metaphor in the Song of Moses. It will be necessary to understand what theological message the poet wanted to communicate to his audience through these metaphors. For, as Lim declares, "Biblical texts were shaped purposefully and purposely in order to function as a permanent theological witness."[122] This is true for the Song of Moses which, according to Ryken, "is a catechetical capsule of God's history and relationship with Israel."[123] Therefore, such a biblical theological enterprise is required.

---

121. Dale Patrick and Allen Scult, *Rhetoric and Biblical Interpretation* (Sheffield, UK: Almond Press, 1990), 12.

122. Johnson T. K. Lim, "Toward a Final Form Approach to Biblical Interpretation," *STJ* 7, no. 1 & 2 (1999): 1–11.

123. Ryken, Wilhoit, and Longman, *Dictionary of Biblical Imagery*, 206.

THE FIRST ROCK SONG:
CONTRIBUTIONS OF DIVINE METAPHORS TO THE THEOLOGY OF THE SONG OF MOSES

## Overview of the Dissertation

Chapter 1 explains the methodology taken in this systematic inquiry. A survey of the major theories of metaphor is presented and Janet Soskice's definition is selected as the basis for this research. According to this theory, metaphor is primarily a linguistic phenomenon, as opposed to a cognitive or mental idea. Furthermore, to make a successful identification of each metaphor and provide an enhanced discussion of each, Kittay's componential semantics is followed. This method proposes first to understand literal and conventional meaning and then to locate the incongruity. Such a method avoids the mistake of talking about metaphor when, in fact, there is none.

Chapter 2 discusses some preliminary issues such as setting the Song of Moses in its historical context and providing a structure that fits the analysis of the divine metaphors of the Song. Chapters 3, 4, and 5, constitute the heart of the dissertation. Chapter 3 discusses the metaphor "God is a rock" because it is a predominant metaphor in the poem, occurring no less than six times.[124] (More specifically, the term צוּר meaning "rock" is used as a divine metaphor in Deut 32:4, 15, 18, 30–31, and 37.) Chapter 4 examines the metaphor "God is a father" (vv. 6–14). Chapter 5 tackles the metaphor "God is an avenging warrior" (vv. 22–25; 39–42; v. 43). As such, it explains the deeds of Yhwh, especially how he fights against the Israelites when they disobey his covenantal laws and how he fights his foes who misunderstand his judgment on Israel. Chapter 6 draws the results of the investigation to an end and outlines a conclusion pertaining to other study on interpreting biblical metaphor.

---

124. George V. Wigram, *The Englishman's Hebrew Concordance of the Old Testament* (Peabody, MA: Hendrickson Publishers, 2013), 1069–70.

*Chapter Two*

# The Song of Moses in Context

Before embarking on the journey of analyzing the divine metaphors of the Song, it is essential to set it in its proper context. For, as Futato argues, "Context is essential for interpretation."[1] Osborne goes further to say, "Unless we can grasp the whole before attempting to dissect the parts, interpretation is doomed from the start. Statements simply have no meaning apart from their context."[2] Futato and Osborne have made a good observation regarding setting a text in its proper context because a word can have multiple meanings.[3] Moreover, the meaning of a word may change over time.[4] Thus, it is unwise to assume that the meaning of a word in a context can equally apply to every other text. Simply put, the divine metaphors of the Song cannot be properly interpreted and understood apart from their contexts: historical, literary, cultural, and geographical. For this reason, this chapter will cover the

---

1. Mark D. Futato, *Interpreting the Psalms: An Exegetical Handbook* (Grand Rapids: Kregel Publications, 2007), 144.

2. Grant R. Osborne, *The Hermeneutical Spiral: A Comprehensive Introduction to Biblical Interpretation* (Downers Grove: InterVarsity Press, 2006), 37.

3. See Gordon D. Fee and Mark L. Strauss, *How to Choose a Translation for All Its Worth: A Guide to Understanding and Using Bible Versions* (Grand Rapids: Zondervan, 2007), 47.

4. See Moisés Silva, *Biblical Words and Their Meaning: An Introduction to Lexical Semantics* (Grand Rapids: Zondervan, 1994), 138–69. See also Stephen Ullmann, *Semantics: An Introduction to the Science of Meaning* (New York: Barnes & Noble, Inc., 1962), 193–235.

historical context of the Song. Next, it will discuss some preliminary matters, such as the delimitation of the Song and its structure, in preparation for the examination of the divine metaphors.[5] The chapter will end with an English translation of the Song along with the Hebrew text.

## Historical Context of the Song of Moses

J. W. Watts rightly observes, "In the wider context of Deuteronomy in its present form, the Song serves as a climactic, concluding hymn that sums up in a memorable, emphatic way the message of the entire book."[6] Olson shares a similar idea when he states, "The Song of Moses in chapter 32 presents a summary of Deuteronomy's version of the book of the *torah*."[7] This is not an exaggeration. Similar to the book of Deuteronomy, the Song calls the Israelites to remember their covenant with the sovereign God who has provided for his faithless people (Israel) and who plans to continue his ongoing care for them in the future.

Deuteronomy mainly consists of messages from Moses to the second generation of Israelites in contemplation of their imminent entry into the Promised Land, since the first generation had been banned from the Promised Land for their unfaithfulness. Although God led them from Egypt to the edge of the Promised Land and told them to conquer it, the Israelites refused. God then judged the first generation by decreeing that the Israelites' fate would be as they had spoken: every person twenty years old and upward would die in the wilderness (Num 14:28–29). Now that all those decreed to die in the wilderness were dead, God is preparing the second generation to enter the land.

Hence, by the eleventh month of the fortieth year of Israel's wandering since the Exodus (Deut 1:3), the first generation had died and the death of their leader, Moses, was imminent (1:34–35). Therefore, it was significant for

---

5. As stated earlier, critical issues such as the date and authorship of the Song will not be discussed in this study. The focus here is on the divine metaphors to see how they contribute to the theology of the poem.

6. James W. Watts, *Psalm and Story: Inset Hymns in Hebrew Narrative* (Sheffield, UK: JSOT Press, 1992), 73–80.

7. Dennis T. Olson, *Deuteronomy and the Death of Moses: A Theological Reading* (Eugene, OR: Wipf & Stock Publishers, 1994), 138.

God to renew his covenant with the new generation of Israel to ensure they knew and understood their obligations.[8] In renewing the covenant, God reminded his people of his faithfulness and loyal love and urged them to obey him wholeheartedly in order that it might go well with them in the land they were about to possess (Deut 4:40; 6:1–3). God promised to bless his people if they would trust and obey him. In contrast, his punishment would fall on them if they were disobedient. Therefore, to ensure the people understood their requirements, God used Moses as a mediator (cf. Deut 5:22–33).

Following God's lead, Moses began his sermon by rehearsing the past to the new generation of Israelites to remind them of how they reached the boundary of the Promised Land (Deut 1:1–25). While reminding the Israelites of their history, Moses urged them to be courageous and strong to take possession of the land promised to them. He articulated this encouragement with these words, "See, Yhwh your God has placed the land before you; go up, take possession, as Yhwh, the God of your fathers, has spoken to you. Do not fear or be dismayed" (1:21). Moses then recounted specific incidents related to Israel's failure and success. Their failures included their rebellion against the command of Yhwh to go up and possess the land of Canaan (Deut 1:26–33; Num 13), God's judgment on the first generation of Israel by preventing them from entering Canaan (Deut 1:34–40), and Israel's shameful tentative conquest of the Amorites due to their disobedience to God's command not to go up and fight (Deut 1:41–46). Their successes included their first act of obedience since they left Horeb, which led them to have victory over the Amorite kings Sihon and Og, as mentioned in Deut 2 and 3.

After the historical prologue (Deut 1–3), Moses taught the people of God the various precepts that must be obeyed in the land of Canaan in order to remain in it and to be blessed beyond measure (Deut 4). Then, Moses provided the Israelites with a restatement of the Ten Commandments (literally, Ten Words) to let them know what God required of them as a covenant nation (Deut

---

8. Peter C. Craigie, *The Book of Deuteronomy*, NICOT 5 (Grand Rapids: Eerdmans, 1976), 30–31. Craigie understands the renewal ceremony within two principal perspectives: "the matter of the succession in human leadership in the covenant community," and the "military conquest which lay in the immediate future of all the people assembled on the plains of Moab" (30).

# THE FIRST ROCK SONG:
## Contributions of Divine Metaphors to the Theology of the Song of Moses

5). Starting in Deut 6, Moses preached a sermon containing both the "general stipulations" (6:1–11:32) and the "specific stipulations" (12:1–26:15).[9] The general stipulations are a series of exhortations to Israel to be loyal to God by obeying him wholeheartedly (Deut 6–11). Here, Moses reminded the people of their past disobedience in order to encourage them to be faithful to God's covenant. The specific stipulations concern various topics such as loyal devotion to Yhwh (12:1–26:15), appointment of officials to rule over Israel (16:18–18:22), laws related to the citizens of Israel (19:1–22:8), laws of purity (22:9–23:18), laws regarding interpersonal relationships (23:19–25:19), and laws concerning covenant celebration and confirmation (26:1–15).

In Deut 27 and 28, Moses spelled out the blessings and curses that could follow, depending on Israel's behavior in the land.[10] Deuteronomy 29 and 30 gave the stipulations for the covenant in Moab, besides the covenant that God had made with the Israelites in Horeb (Deut 29:1). In Deut 31, Moses urged the Israelites to trust Yhwh, their God, and to obey all his commandments (vv. 1–8). He commissioned Joshua to be his successor and commanded the priests and Levites to read this "Torah" to the Israelites every seven years so that they might continue to fear Yhwh, observe all his commandments, and pass them on to their children (vv. 9–13).[11] In vv. 14–22, Yhwh summoned Moses and Joshua to present themselves at the tent of meeting to reveal to them an important prophetic word. The revelation given provides knowledge that after Moses' death, the Israelites will play the harlot and break God's covenant (v. 16). They will turn to other gods and forsake Yhwh, their creator and provider. Consequently, Yhwh will severely punish them, and the punishment will prompt them to inquire about his presence among them (v. 17). For this reason, God recited a song to Moses and Joshua so that they might teach

---

9. Eugene H. Merrill, *Deuteronomy*, NAC 4 (Nashville: Broadman & Holman Publishers, 1994), 30.

10. According to Marvin Pate, "Obedience to the words of Yahweh is central to becoming the people of God. The Deuteronomic blessings and curses highlight the central nature of their obedience." See C. Marvin Pate et al., *The Story of Israel: A Biblical Theology* (Downers Grove: InterVarsity Press, 2004), 23.

11. T. Desmond Alexander, *From Paradise to the Promised Land: An Introduction to the Pentateuch*, 3rd ed. (Grand Rapids: Baker Academic, 2012), 287. See also Brian Britt, "Deuteronomy 31–32 as a Textual Memorial," *BibInt* 8, no. 4 (2000): 358–74.

it to the Israelites (Deut 31:19-20). As Block explains, "YHWH commanded Moses to teach the Song to the Israelites from beginning to end, not only that they might take it with them across the Jordan into the Promised Land, but that it might be passed on to their descendants and never be forgotten from the lips of future generations."[12]

Moses then summoned the assembly to listen to the Song which he taught "verbatim to the people" (31:30; cf. 32:44).[13] He called the people to listen attentively to the message because he proclaimed the name of Yhwh—that is, his attributes (v. 3). Ultimately, the Song would function as didactic material to motivate certain behavior, to witness for God against his faithless people when they failed to follow him (vv. 19–26), and to teach them about the sovereignty of God over all creation and his just punishment of sins. Harold Fish summarizes the function of the poem well when he states,

> It will act as a mnemonic, an aid to memory, because during the intervening period it will have lived unforgotten in the mouth of the reader or hearer, ready to come to mind when the troubles arrive. Poetry is thus a kind of time bomb; it awaits its hour and then springs forward into harsh remembrance. ... It will live in their minds and mouths, bringing them back, whether they like it or not, to the harsh memory of the desert sojourn. Once learned it will not easily be forgotten. The words will stick, they will be importunate, they will not let us alone.[14]

# Delimitation of the Song of Moses

After establishing the historical context of the Song, the next logical step is to determine where it begins and ends. The Song is introduced in Deut 31:30,

---

12. Daniel I. Block, *How I Love Your Torah, O LORD!* (Eugene, OR: Wipf and Stock Publishers, 2011), 166.

13. Daniel I. Block, *The Gospel according to Moses: Theological and Ethical Reflections on the Book of Deuteronomy* (Eugene, OR: Cascade Books, 2012), 47.

14. Harold Fisch, *Poetry with a Purpose: Biblical Poetics and Interpretation* (Bloomington: Indiana University Press, 1988), 51.

# THE FIRST ROCK SONG:
## Contributions of Divine Metaphors to the Theology of the Song of Moses

"Then Moses spoke in the hearing of all the assembly of Israel the words of this הַשִּׁירָה 'song' until they were complete."[15] This introductory statement implies that the Song begins in Deut 32:1. Likewise, the statement, "Then Moses came and spoke all the words of this הַשִּׁירָה 'song' in the hearing of the people, he, with Joshua the son of Nun" in Deut 32:44 indicates that the Song ends in Deut 32:43. These two verses (Deut 31:30 and Deut 32:44) serve as markers for the Song and form an inclusio. As Watts declares, "Designations of genre mark many inset poems in narratives of the Hebrew Bible," most often with the nominal or verbal form of שִׁיר (sing) appearing in the narrative introduction.[16]

## Structure of the Song of Moses

Early biblical scholars had done little to find a structure in the Song of Moses because, as Lundbom explains, "they were consumed with questions of date, authorship, and provenance."[17] S. R. Driver was among the earliest scholars who took this matter under consideration, calling the first three verses of the Song an exordium, and taking the last verse as a conclusion.[18] Moreover, as the editor of Deuteronomy for the 1906 edition of *Biblia Hebraica*, Driver was probably the one who indented the lines of the Song at vv. 4, 7, 10, 15, 19, 23, 28, 34, 39, 43, thus suggesting indirectly that the poem contained an introduction, a body of eight stanzas, and a conclusion.[19]

---

15. Childs, in his comments on Exodus 15 states, "This type of superscription fits the poem into the narrative." Brevard S. Childs, *The Book of Exodus: A Critical, Theological Commentary* (Louisville: Westminster John Knox Press, 2004), 248. Childs also provides other parallel texts in the Old Testament such as Deut 31:30, Judg 5:1, and 1 Sam 2:1 where the same structure occurs.

16. James W. Watts, "'This Song' Conspicuous Poetry in Hebrew Prose," in *Verse in Ancient Near Eastern Prose*, AOAT 42, ed. Johannes C. de Moor and Wilfred G. Watson (Neukirchen-Vluyn: Neukirchen Verlag, 1993), 345.

17. See Jack R. Lundbom, *Deuteronomy: A Commentary* (Grand Rapids: Eerdmans, 2013), 858.

18. S. R. Driver, *A Critical and Exegetical Commentary on Deuteronomy* (New York: Charles Scribner's Sons, 1895), 348–49.

19. Ibid.

To date, no consensus has been reached on the structure of the Song. However, most scholars divide it according to the ancient Near Eastern covenant lawsuit genre known as the *rîb*-pattern, a lawsuit address in which a suzerain or ruler confronted his vassals for lack of loyalty.[20] For these scholars, the Song of Moses outlines the various controversies Yhwh (the suzerain) had with his vassals (Israel) because of covenant violation.[21] Thompson, one of the advocates of this genre, divides the Song into eight stanzas, which can be outlined as follows:

a. Introduction, the calling of heaven and earth and the declaration of the character of God (vv. 1–4); b. Interrogation and implied accusation (vv. 5, 6); c. Recollection of the mighty acts of God on Israel's behalf in years past (vv. 7–14); d. Direct indictment (vv. 15–18); e. The sentence (vv. 19–25).[22] However, after the "sentence" section (vv. 19–25), Thompson states, "At this point a new theme is introduced which is not found in the secular *rîb*-pattern, namely, a word of hope. The analysis of the chapter proceeds with f. The assurance of Israel's deliverance (26–38); g. Yahweh's own word promising deliverance (39–42); and finally, h. A call for Israel to worship God (43)."[23]

Thompson's structure has its weaknesses. For, although the Song does provide a certain formulation of the covenant lawsuit, this fact alone does not indicate that this was the original author's intent. The reason is that there are

---

20. J. A. Thompson, *Deuteronomy: An Introduction and Commentary* (Downers Grove: InterVarsity Press, 1974), 296. See also G. Ernest Wright, "The Lawsuit of God: A Form-Critical Study of Deuteronomy 32," in *Israel's Prophetic Heritage: Essays in Honor of James Muilenburg*, ed. Bernhard W. Anderson and Walter Harrelson (New York: Harper & Brothers, 1962), 26–67; Pierre Buis and Jacques Leclercq, *Le Deutéronome* (Paris: Librairie Lecoffre, 1963), 192; Merrill, *Deuteronomy*, 408. Edward J. Woods, *Deuteronomy*, TOTC 5 (Downers Grove: InterVarsity Press, 2011), 308; A. D. H. Mayes, *Deuteronomy* (Grand Rapids: Wm. B. Eerdmans, 1981), 380.

21. For example, Alday notes, "Vienen en primer lugar algunos textos clasificados como Gerichtsreden, Lawsuits, Procesos que Yahweh instituye contra su Pueblo por su falta de correspondencia." S. Carrillo Alday, *El Cántico de Moisés* (Dt 32) (Madrid: Instituto Francisco Suarez, 1970), 34. This quote is translated as follows: "First of all, some texts are classified as Gerichtsreden (lawsuits or court speeches), a process that Yhwh institutes against his people for their lack of correspondence."

22. Thompson, *Deuteronomy: An Introduction and Commentary*, 297.

23. Ibid.

# THE FIRST ROCK SONG:
## Contributions of Divine Metaphors to the Theology of the Song of Moses

sections that do not agree with the formulation in parallel examples where scholars define the genre.[24] Thompson admits this when he declares, "The chapter is not completely parallel to the standard covenant lawsuit."[25] He then gives two reasons for that. First, Moses introduces the Song as "teaching" in v. 2, thus giving it a didactic function.[26] Second, vv. 30-43, which express hope and confidence in God's deliverance, do not correspond to any component of the covenant lawsuit.[27] This means that one should not rely only on the covenant lawsuit genre to find the structure of the Song.[28]

It seems best to reconstruct the Song based on an analysis of its substance since it will help to see the flow of the text.[29] As Watson correctly observes, "The broad divisions of poetic texts can be fairly determined by seeing where the subject matter changes."[30] By the term "division," Watson is referring to *stanza*, a "major subdivision of a poem — which comprises one or more strophes."[31] As an illustration, he cites Gen 49 and Deut 33 in which "the

---

24. See De Roche who discusses four difficulties associated with designating the Song as a covenant lawsuit. M. de Roche, "Yahweh's *Rib* against Israel: A Reassessment of the So-Called 'Prophetic Lawsuit' in the Preexilic Prophets," *JBL* 102 (1983): 563-74.

25. Thompson, *Deuteronomy: An Introduction and Commentary*, 297.

26. Ibid.

27. Ibid.

28. Some scholars have demonstrated the ineffectiveness of assigning the Song to a covenant lawsuit genre. For these scholars, the Song displays features of various genres such as hymn, covenant lawsuit, wisdom, and praise. See Jeffrey H. Tigay, *Deuteronomy* (Philadelphia: Jewish Publication Society, 1996), 509. See also C. J. Labuschagne, "The Song of Moses: Its Framework and Structure," in *De Fructu Oris Sui: Essays in Honour of Adrianus van Selms*, ed. I. H. Eybers et al. (Leiden: E. J. Brill, 1971), 93.

29. Fokkelman divides the poem based on syllable count; he believes that the poem contains 11 stanzas arranged into 27 strophes. See J. P. Fokkelman, *Ex. 15, Deut. 32, and Job 3*, vol. 1 in *Major Poems of the Hebrew Bible at the Interface of Prosody and Structural Analysis*, Studia Semitica Neederlandica (The Netherlands: Van Gorcum & Company, 2000), 58-60.

30. Wilfred G. E. Watson, *Classical Hebrew Poetry: A Guide to Its Techniques* (London: T&T Clark International, 2005), 163.

31. Watson defines a strophe as "a group of one or more lines forming a subdivision of a stanza." See Watson, *Classical Hebrew Poetry*, 161-62.

stanza division coincides with the sequence of oracles concerning Reuben, Judah, Levi, Benjamin and so on."[32] Stated differently, each of these oracles constitutes a separate stanza in these two texts. The same is true for Ps 119, which contains a division of twenty-two stanzas based on the letters of the Hebrew alphabet.[33]

As far as the Song of Moses is concerned, the change of speaker from narrator to Yhwh and vice-versa (or a change of speech) seems to be the stanza-marker because with this change comes a shift in focus. This marker divides the Song into eight major stanzas (vv. 1–6; 7–18; 19–27; 28–31; 32–35; 36–38; 39–42; 43).[34] The first stanza begins with the voice of the narrator (Moses) invoking heaven and earth as witnesses against the Israelites when they fail to obey God's precepts (vv. 1–2). The narrator also calls Israel to ascribe greatness to Yhwh (v. 3). In doing so, he spells out the first major theme of the poem: Yhwh is faithful and just (v. 4). This is followed immediately by the second major theme of the poem, namely that Israel is faithless and corrupt (vv. 5–6).

The second stanza begins the narrator's second speech in which he calls the Israelites to consult their history to understand God's past dealings with the nation (vv. 7–18). Within this stanza, the narrator explains how Yhwh chooses Israel (vv. 7–9) and provides for and blesses them (vv. 10–14). The narrator does so as he elaborates on the first major theme of the Song: God's faithfulness and benefactions to Israel (vv. 7–14). Then, the shift in person (from Yhwh to Israel) by the narrator in v. 15 begins the elaboration of the second major theme, namely, Israel's rejection of Yhwh (vv. 15–18).

In the third stanza, there is a shift in person (from Israel to Yhwh) where the narrator introduces Yhwh's first speech (v. 19). Yhwh addresses the Israelites to explain his decision to judge them as well as his decision to limit their judgment to ensure his actions are not misunderstood by the enemy (vv. 20–27). Yhwh says he will reject his chosen people (vv. 19–21), judge them (vv. 22–25), and limit their judgment (vv. 26–27).

32. Watson, *Classical Hebrew Poetry*, 161–62.
33. Ibid., 163–64.
34. Labuschagne has a structure similar to this one with only one exception: he breaks the sixth stanza after verse 39 whereas this dissertation breaks it after verse 38. His main reason is that verse 39 does not belong to the seventh stanza but to what precedes. See Labuschagne, "The Song of Moses," 94–98.

# THE FIRST ROCK SONG:
## Contributions of Divine Metaphors to the Theology of the Song of Moses

In the fourth stanza, the narrator speaks again in the third person, commenting on God's rationale for judging Israel (vv. 28–31). The fifth stanza, introduced with the כִּי particle, marks the beginning of the second speech of Yhwh in which he announces judgment upon the adversaries (vv. 32–35). In the sixth stanza, the narrator comments on the second speech of Yhwh (vv. 36–38). He tells the Israelites that Yhwh will have compassion on them (v. 36). This is followed by a downfall of the adversaries. The narrator says that Yhwh will bring judgment upon the enemy (vv. 37–38).

The seventh stanza describes the third speech of Yhwh. It shifts back to the first person as Yhwh addresses his people to describe his authority as the only sovereign God, the one who will use his weapons to punish his foes (vv. 39–42). Finally, the eighth stanza returns to the voice of the narrator, inviting the people to rejoice because of God's justice (v. 43). This stanza is marked by a mood change (from indicative to imperative), which moves from justice to celebration (v. 43). Thus, the outline of the poem is as follows:

I. The narrator invokes heaven and earth to hear his teaching on God's faithfulness and Israel's faithlessness (vv. 1–6)
   A. The narrator invokes heaven and earth as witnesses to hear his teaching (vv. 1–3)
   B. The narrator contrasts Yhwh's faithfulness with Israel's faithlessness (vv. 4–6)

II. The narrator elaborates on Yhwh's faithfulness and Israel's faithlessness (vv. 7–18)
   A. Yhwh chooses Israel (vv. 7–9)
   B. Yhwh provides for and blesses Israel (vv. 10–14)
   C. Israel abandons Yhwh (vv. 15–18)

III. Yhwh decides to judge Israel (vv. 19–27)
   A. Yhwh rejects Israel (vv. 19–21)
   B. Yhwh executes judgment on Israel (vv. 22–25)
   C. Yhwh limits Israel's judgment (vv. 26–27)

IV. The narrator comments on Yhwh's decision to judge Israel (vv. 28–31)
V. Yhwh speaks again to pronounce judgment on Israel's enemy (vv. 32–35)
VI. The narrator speaks to tell Israel that Yhwh will have compassion on them and will destroy the enemy (vv. 36–38)
  A. Yhwh will have compassion on Israel (v. 36)
  B. Yhwh will destroy Israel's enemy (vv. 37–38)
VII. Yhwh speaks to describe his authority as the sovereign God (vv. 39–42)
VIII. The narrator speaks to invite the Israelites to celebrate their deliverance (v. 43)

# The Song of Moses: Text and Translation[35]

A הַאֲזִינוּ הַשָּׁמַיִם וַאֲדַבֵּרָה
B וְתִשְׁמַע הָאָרֶץ אִמְרֵי־פִי׃

¹ Listen, O heavens, and let me speak!
And let the earth hear the words of my mouth!

A יַעֲרֹף כַּמָּטָר לִקְחִי
B תִּזַּל כַּטַּל אִמְרָתִי
A כִּשְׂעִירִם עֲלֵי־דֶשֶׁא
B וְכִרְבִיבִים עֲלֵי־עֵשֶׂב׃

² May my teaching drop like the rain,
My speech distill like the dew
Like showers on new grass
And like soft rains on green plants.

---

35. This translation reflects this writer's understanding of the poem. The A B pattern helps to see the poetic lines and facilitates the identification of the divine metaphors.

# THE FIRST ROCK SONG:
## Contributions of Divine Metaphors to the Theology of the Song of Moses

A כִּי שֵׁם יהוה אֶקְרָא
B הָבוּ גֹדֶל לֵאלֹהֵינוּ:

³ For the name of Yhwh I will proclaim;
Ascribe greatness to our God!

A הַצּוּר תָּמִים פָּעֳלוֹ
B כִּי כָל־דְּרָכָיו מִשְׁפָּט
A אֵל אֱמוּנָה וְאֵין עָוֶל
B צַדִּיק וְיָשָׁר הוּא: א

⁴ The rock: perfect is his work
For all his ways are just;
A God of faithfulness and without injustice
Righteous and upright is he.

A שִׁחֵת לוֹ לֹא בָּנָיו מוּמָם
B דּוֹר עִקֵּשׁ וּפְתַלְתֹּל:

⁵ They have acted corruptly toward him,
they are not his children, (it is) their blemish;
A generation twisted and perverse.

A הֲ־לַיהוה תִּגְמְלוּ־זֹאת
B עַם נָבָל וְלֹא חָכָם
A הֲלוֹא־הוּא אָבִיךָ קָּנֶךָ
B הוּא עָשְׂךָ וַיְכֹנְנֶךָ:

⁶ Do you thus repay Yhwh?
A people foolish and unwise!
Is not he your father who acquired you?
He himself made you and established you.

A זְכֹר יְמוֹת עוֹלָם
B בִּינוּ שְׁנוֹת דּוֹר־וָדוֹר
A שְׁאַל אָבִיךָ וְיַגֵּדְךָ
B זְקֵנֶיךָ וְיֹאמְרוּ לָךְ:

*The Song of Moses in Context*

⁷ Remember the days of old!
Consider the years of generation and generation!
Ask your father and let him tell you;
Your elders and they will say to you:

A בְּהַנְחֵל עֶלְיוֹן גּוֹיִם
B בְּהַפְרִידוֹ בְּנֵי אָדָם
A יַצֵּב גְּבֻלֹת עַמִּים
B לְמִסְפַּר בְּנֵי יִשְׂרָאֵל׃

⁸ When the Most High gave inheritance to the nations,
When he separated the sons of man,
He established the boundaries of the peoples,
According to the number of the sons of Israel.

A כִּי חֵלֶק יהוה עַמּוֹ
B יַעֲקֹב חֶבֶל נַחֲלָתוֹ׃

⁹ For the allotment of Yhwh is his people;
Jacob is the lot (region) of his inheritance.

A יִמְצָאֵהוּ בְּאֶרֶץ מִדְבָּר
B וּבְתֹהוּ יְלֵל יְשִׁמֹן
A יְסֹבְבֶנְהוּ יְבוֹנְנֵהוּ
B יִצְּרֶנְהוּ כְּאִישׁוֹן עֵינוֹ׃

¹⁰ He found him in a land, a desert,
Even in a wasteland, a howling wilderness;
He encircled him, cared for him,
Guarded him like the pupil of his eye.

A כְּנֶשֶׁר יָעִיר קִנּוֹ
B עַל־גּוֹזָלָיו יְרַחֵף
A יִפְרֹשׂ כְּנָפָיו יִקָּחֵהוּ
B יִשָּׂאֵהוּ עַל־אֶבְרָתוֹ׃

¹¹ Like an eagle rouses its nest,
Over its young it hovers;
He spread out his wings, sheltered him
Lifted him on his pinion.

# THE FIRST ROCK SONG:
## Contributions of Divine Metaphors to the Theology of the Song of Moses

A יהוה בָּדָד יַנְחֶנּוּ
B וְאֵין עִמּוֹ אֵל נֵכָר:

12 Yhwh alone led him;
And there was not with him a foreign god.

A יַרְכִּבֵהוּ עַל־בָּמוֹתֵי אָרֶץ
B וַיֹּאכַל תְּנוּבֹת שָׂדָי
A וַיֵּנִקֵהוּ דְבַשׁ מִסֶּלַע
B וְשֶׁמֶן מֵחַלְמִישׁ צוּר:

13 He made him ride on the heights of the land,
And he ate the crops of the field;
And he made him suckle honey from stone,
And oil from flinty rock.

A חֶמְאַת בָּקָר וַחֲלֵב צֹאן
B עִם־חֵלֶב כָּרִים וְאֵילִים בְּנֵי־בָשָׁן וְעַתּוּדִים
A עִם־חֵלֶב כִּלְיוֹת חִטָּה
B וְדַם־עֵנָב תִּשְׁתֶּה־חָמֶר:

14 Curds from the cow, and milk from the flock,
With fat from lambs, and rams bred from Bashan and goats,
With fat kernels of wheat;
And blood from the grape, you drank foaming wine.

A וַיִּשְׁמַן יְשֻׁרוּן וַיִּבְעָט
B שָׁמַנְתָּ עָבִיתָ כָּשִׂיתָ
A וַיִּטֹּשׁ אֱלוֹהַּ עָשָׂהוּ
B וַיְנַבֵּל צוּר יְשֻׁעָתוֹ:

15 But Jeshurun fattened and kicked;
You were fattened, thickened, engorged;
And he abandoned God who made him,
And disdained the rock of his salvation.

A יַקְנִאֻהוּ בְּזָרִים
B בְּתוֹעֵבֹת יַכְעִיסֻהוּ:

16 They made him jealous with strange things;
With abominable things they provoked him.

| | |
|---:|:---|
| A | יִזְבְּחוּ לַשֵּׁדִים לֹא אֱלֹהַּ |
| B | אֱלֹהִים לֹא יְדָעוּם |
| A | חֲדָשִׁים מִקָּרֹב בָּאוּ |
| B | לֹא שְׂעָרוּם אֲבֹתֵיכֶם׃ |

¹⁷ They sacrificed to demons, not God;
Gods they had not known;
New ones, who recently came,
Whom your fathers did not dread.

| | |
|---:|:---|
| A | צוּר יְלָדְךָ תֶּשִׁי |
| B | וַתִּשְׁכַּח אֵל מְחֹלְלֶךָ׃ |

¹⁸ The rock who begot you, you neglected;
And forgot the God who birthed you.

| | |
|---:|:---|
| A | וַיַּרְא יהוה וַיִּנְאָץ |
| B | מִכַּעַס בָּנָיו וּבְנֹתָיו׃ |

¹⁹ And Yhwh saw and spurned,
Because of the provocation of his sons and his daughters.

| | |
|---:|:---|
| A | וַיֹּאמֶר אַסְתִּירָה פָנַי מֵהֶם |
| B | אֶרְאֶה מָה אַחֲרִיתָם |
| A | כִּי דוֹר תַּהְפֻּכֹת הֵמָּה |
| B | בָּנִים לֹא־אֵמֻן בָּם׃ |

²⁰ And he said, "Let me hide my face from them;
I will see what their end will be;
For they are a perverse generation;
Sons, there is no faithfulness in them.

| | |
|---:|:---|
| A | הֵם קִנְאוּנִי בְלֹא־אֵל כִּעֲסוּנִי בְּהַבְלֵיהֶם |
| B | וַאֲנִי אַקְנִיאֵם בְּלֹא־עָם בְּגוֹי נָבָל אַכְעִיסֵם׃ |

²¹ They themselves made me jealous with a non-god;
Provoked me with their vanities;
So I myself will make them jealous with a non-people;
With a foolish nation I will provoke them.

# THE FIRST ROCK SONG:
## Contributions of Divine Metaphors to the Theology of the Song of Moses

| | |
|---:|:---|
| A כִּי־אֵשׁ קָדְחָה בְאַפִּי | |
| B וַתִּיקַד עַד־שְׁאוֹל תַּחְתִּית | |
| A וַתֹּאכַל אֶרֶץ וִיבֻלָהּ | |
| B וַתְּלַהֵט מוֹסְדֵי הָרִים׃ | |

²² For fire is kindled by my anger,
And burns to Sheol below,
And eats the land and its produce,
And flames the foundations of mountains.

A אַסְפֶּה עָלֵימוֹ רָעוֹת
B חִצַּי אֲכַלֶּה־בָּם׃

²³ I will gather upon them disasters;
My arrows I will use up on them.

A מְזֵי רָעָב
B וּלְחֻמֵי רֶשֶׁף
C וְקֶטֶב מְרִירִי
A וְשֶׁן־בְּהֵמוֹת אֲשַׁלַּח־בָּם
B עִם־חֲמַת זֹחֲלֵי עָפָר׃

²⁴ Weakened through famine
And consumed by flame
And bitter plague;
And the tooth of beasts I will turn loose on them;
With the venom of crawlers in the dust.

A מִחוּץ תְּשַׁכֶּל־חֶרֶב
B וּמֵחֲדָרִים אֵימָה
A גַּם־בָּחוּר גַּם־בְּתוּלָה
B יוֹנֵק עִם־אִישׁ שֵׂיבָה׃

²⁵ From outdoors the sword will bereave;
And from indoors, terror!
Both young man and young woman,
Infant with the man of gray hair.

| | |
|---:|:---|
| A אָמַרְתִּי אַפְאֵיהֶם | |
| B אַשְׁבִּיתָה מֵאֱנוֹשׁ זִכְרָם: | 26 I would have said, 'I will cut them to pieces! Let me remove from mankind their memory!' |
| A לוּלֵי כַּעַס אוֹיֵב אָגוּר | |
| B פֶּן־יְנַכְּרוּ צָרֵימוֹ | |
| A פֶּן־יֹאמְרוּ יָדֵינוּ רָמָה | |
| B וְלֹא יהוה פָּעַל כָּל־זֹאת: | 27 Except that provocation from the enemy I feared, Lest their adversaries would misjudge; Lest they would say, 'our hands reached high!' And not, 'Yahweh did all this.'" |
| A כִּי־גוֹי אֹבַד עֵצוֹת הֵמָּה | |
| B וְאֵין בָּהֶם תְּבוּנָה: | 28 For they are a nation wandering from counsel; And there is not understanding in them. |
| A לוּ חָכְמוּ יַשְׂכִּילוּ זֹאת | |
| B יָבִינוּ לְאַחֲרִיתָם: | 29 If only they would be wise, would understand this, Would consider their end! |
| A אֵיכָה יִרְדֹּף אֶחָד אֶלֶף | |
| B וּשְׁנַיִם יָנִיסוּ רְבָבָה | |
| A אִם־לֹא כִּי־צוּרָם מְכָרָם | |
| B וַיהוה הִסְגִּירָם: | 30 How could one chase a thousand, And two cause ten thousand to flee, Unless their rock had sold them, And Yhwh had handed them over? |
| A כִּי לֹא כְצוּרֵנוּ צוּרָם | |
| B וְאֹיְבֵינוּ פְּלִילִים: | 31 For not like our rock is their rock, Even our enemies are judges. |

# THE FIRST ROCK SONG:
## Contributions of Divine Metaphors to the Theology of the Song of Moses

| | |
|---:|---:|
| A | כִּי־מִגֶּפֶן סְדֹם גַּפְנָם |
| B | וּמִשַּׁדְמֹת עֲמֹרָה |
| A | עֲנָבֵמוֹ עִנְּבֵי־רוֹשׁ |
| B | אַשְׁכְּלֹת מְרֹרֹת לָמוֹ׃ |

<sup>32</sup>"For the vine of Sodom is their vine,
And from the fields of Gomorrah;
Their grapes are grapes of poison,
Clusters of bitterness are theirs.

| | |
|---:|---:|
| A | חֲמַת תַּנִּינִם יֵינָם |
| B | וְרֹאשׁ פְּתָנִים אַכְזָר׃ |

<sup>33</sup> Venom of serpents is their wine;
And cruel poison of asps.

| | |
|---:|---:|
| A | הֲלֹא־הוּא כָּמֻס עִמָּדִי |
| B | חָתֻם בְּאוֹצְרֹתָי׃ |

<sup>34</sup> Is not this stored up with me,
Sealed in my storehouses?

| | |
|---:|---:|
| A | לִי נָקָם וְשִׁלֵּם |
| B | לְעֵת תָּמוּט רַגְלָם |
| A | כִּי קָרוֹב יוֹם אֵידָם |
| B | וְחָשׁ עֲתִדֹת לָמוֹ׃ |

<sup>35</sup> Mine is vengeance and recompense
For the time their foot slips;
For near is the day of their calamity,
And prepared (doom) things rush on them.

| | |
|---:|---:|
| A | כִּי־יָדִין יהוה עַמּוֹ |
| B | וְעַל־עֲבָדָיו יִתְנֶחָם |
| A | כִּי יִרְאֶה כִּי־אָזְלַת יָד |
| B | וְאֶפֶס עָצוּר וְעָזוּב׃ |

<sup>36</sup> For Yhwh will judge his people,
And to his servants he will show compassion;
When he sees that the hand is gone,
And there is nothing, bound or free.

| | |
|---:|---:|
| A | וְאָמַר אֵי אֱלֹהֵימוֹ |
| B | צוּר חָסָיוּ בוֹ׃ |

37 And he will say, "Where are their gods,
The rock they took refuge in.

| | |
|---:|---:|
| A | אֲשֶׁר חֵלֶב זְבָחֵימוֹ יֹאכֵלוּ |
| B | יִשְׁתּוּ יֵין נְסִיכָם |
| A | יָקוּמוּ וְיַעְזְרֻכֶם |
| B | יְהִי עֲלֵיכֶם סִתְרָה׃ |

38 Which ate the fat of their sacrifices,
Drank the wine of their libation?
Let them arise and help you;
Let it be for you a refuge!"

| | |
|---:|---:|
| A | רְאוּ עַתָּה |
| B | כִּי אֲנִי אֲנִי הוּא |
| A | וְאֵין אֱלֹהִים עִמָּדִי |
| B | אֲנִי אָמִית וַאֲחַיֶּה |
| A | מָחַצְתִּי וַאֲנִי אֶרְפָּא |
| B | וְאֵין מִיָּדִי מַצִּיל׃ |

39 See now,
That I, I am he!
And there are no gods with me!
I myself kill and bring to life,
I wound and I myself heal,
And there is no one who can rescue from my hand.

| | |
|---:|---:|
| A | כִּי־אֶשָּׂא אֶל־שָׁמַיִם יָדִי |
| B | וְאָמַרְתִּי חַי אָנֹכִי לְעֹלָם׃ |

40 For I raise my hand to heaven;
And say, "Alive am I forever!

| | |
|---:|---:|
| A | אִם־שַׁנּוֹתִי בְּרַק חַרְבִּי |
| B | וְתֹאחֵז בְּמִשְׁפָּט יָדִי |
| A | אָשִׁיב נָקָם לְצָרָי |
| B | וְלִמְשַׂנְאַי אֲשַׁלֵּם׃ |

# THE FIRST ROCK SONG:
## Contributions of Divine Metaphors to the Theology of the Song of Moses

⁴¹ If I sharpen my flashing sword,
And my hand seizes in justice;
I will return vengeance on my enemies,
And to those who hate me I will repay.

A אַשְׁכִּיר חִצַּי מִדָּם
B וְחַרְבִּי תֹּאכַל בָּשָׂר
A מִדַּם חָלָל וְשִׁבְיָה
B מֵרֹאשׁ פַּרְעוֹת אוֹיֵב:

⁴² I will make my arrows drunk from blood,
And my sword will eat flesh;
From the blood of the slain and the captive,
From the long-haired heads of the enemy.

A הַרְנִינוּ גוֹיִם עַמּוֹ
B כִּי דַם־עֲבָדָיו יִקּוֹם
A וְנָקָם יָשִׁיב לְצָרָיו
B וְכִפֶּר אַדְמָתוֹ עַמּוֹ:

⁴³ Rejoice, O nations, with his people!
For the blood of his servants, he will avenge.
And vengeance he will return on his enemies,
And he will atone for his land and people.

*Chapter Three*

# Metaphor: God Is a Rock

Although the almighty God has no physical form (Deut 4:12; John 1:18; John 4:24), the Hebrew Bible often depicts him through various imageries. One such image is a "rock." In the Song of Moses alone, the term צוּר (*ṣûr*; "rock") occurs eight times.[1] As a metaphor for the true God (Yhwh), צוּר (*ṣûr*; "rock") occurs in vv. 4, 15, 18, 30, and 31. The term also occurs in v. 37 for the pagan gods. The frequency of the word צוּר (*ṣûr*; "rock") demonstrates that it plays an important role in the meaning of the Song.

## Identification and Interpretation of the Metaphor God Is a צוּר "Rock"

To understand how Yhwh can figuratively be portrayed as a rock for his people, it is fundamental to look at the meaning of the word in its literal sense. As Ryken remarks, "Metaphor and simile first demand that we take the time to let the literal situation sink in. Then we must make a transfer of meaning(s)

---

1. The term סֶלַע "rock" is synonymous with the term צוּר and occurs once in the Song (Deut 32:13), although the former is not used here as a divine metaphor. Elsewhere, they are used interchangeably as divine metaphors in the Hebrew Bible. See Jerome F. D. Creach, *Yahweh as Refuge and the Editing of the Hebrew Psalter*, JSOT 287 (Sheffield, UK: Sheffield Academic Press, 1996), 28.

# THE FIRST ROCK SONG:
## Contributions of Divine Metaphors to the Theology of the Song of Moses

to the topic or experience the poem is talking about."[2] Letting the literal situation sink in entails looking at lexicons and dictionaries for definitions and surveying certain biblical texts to see how the term is used.

## Literal Meaning of the term צוּר "Rock"

Theological lexicons and dictionaries define the word צוּר (ṣûr) as a "rocky ground," a "rock," a "rocky mountain," or a "boulder."[3] It is also defined as a rocky wall or a cliff.[4] In other words, צוּר (ṣûr) can be characterized as a rugged cliff of the geographical terrain (Jer 18:14; 21:13). According to King and Stager, the principal צוּר (ṣûr) in ancient Israel was "limestone, a sedimentary rock consisting mostly of calcium carbonate."[5] It was one of the most popular building materials in Israel.[6] It was also used as weight for olive oil presses and measurement standards.[7]

צוּר (ṣûr) appears in the Hebrew Bible in various geographical contexts. The rock is designated by צוּר (ṣûr) when it is : (1) a place of refuge (Exod 33:18–23); (2) a high place which provides safety for people (Num 23:1–9); (3) a hard rock not easily broken up (Nah 1:5–8); (4) a place of sacrifice or altars (Judg 13:19–20); and (5) a hard boulder providing sustaining water (Exod 17:3–7; Deut 8:11–16).[8] Because rocks were durable and were often structured as caves, they sometimes served as shelters or places of refuge for God's people in ancient times (Gen 19:30; Ezek 33:27; Judg 6:2). As Basson observes, "Because of its hardness, צוּר (ṣûr) conveys the idea of stability and immovability. It provides a solid foundation, protection and security."[9] But

---

2. Leland Ryken, *How to Read the Bible as Literature* (Grand Rapids: Zondervan, 1984), 95.

3. *HALOT*, 3:1016. See also *NIDOTTE*, 3:793.

4. BDB, 849. While the term צוּר (or its synonym סֶלַע) usually refers to a large boulder (rock), the term אֶבֶן usually refers to small stones or rocks (Gen. 28:11).

5. See Philip J. King and Lawrence E. Stager, *Life in Biblical Israel* (Louisville: Westminster John Knox Press), 21.

6. Ibid., 21–22.

7. Ibid., 195–98.

8. For more information, see *HALOT*, 3:1016.

9. Alec Basson, "'You Are My Rock and Fortress.' Refuge Metaphors in Psalm

the term "rock" was not peculiar to Israel. In fact, although there is no exact cognate of צוּר (ṣûr) in the ancient Near Eastern languages, scholars successfully make some connections. According to Fabry, the Ugaritic term *gʻr* "occurs in the meaning 'mountain', which with ṣwr may derive from a common linguistic basis."[10] In Aramaic the cognate term for צוּר (ṣûr) occurs a few times in extrabiblical literature as "mountain."[11] For instance, in the story of Ahiqar, which focuses on the court of the Assyrian kings Sennacherib (704–681 B.C.) and Esarhaddon (680–669 B.C.), an officer received instructions from King Esarhaddon to kill Ahiqar "between these two mountains" (*byn ṭwry ʾ*).[12]

## Figurative Meaning of the Term צוּר "Rock"

Although the term "rock" as a designation for a deity has its first appearance in the Song of Moses, such an idea was probably not new to Israel. Two points support this claim. First, according to Walton, Matthews, and Chavalas, "It [the term 'rock'] is used in Israelite names both as a metaphor for God (Zuriel, Num 3:35, 'God is my Rock') and as a divine name (Pedahzur, Num 2:20, 'Rock is my redeemer')."[13] Second, the term "rock" was often used for pagan deities in the ancient Near East. According to Driver, the term "Great Rock" was a title for Assur and Bel in Assyrian texts.[14] Knowles shares a similar idea when he says that mountain imagery was widely used in the ancient Near East "in the naming of gods."[15] This phenomenon prompts Albright to conclude, "Since 'mountain' was often a synonym for 'god' in Syria and Anatolia, it is not surprising to find that *ṣûr* is simply a synonym of *El* in early Hebrew literature. *šadday*, 'He of the mountains', though a more obviously secondary

---

31. A Perspective from Cognitive Metaphor Theory," *AcT* 25, no. 2 (2005): 12.

10. H. J. Fabry, "צוּר," *TDOT*, 12:312.

11. Ibid.

12. See *ANET*, 428.

13. John Walton, Victor H. Matthews, and Mark W. Chavalas, *The IVP Bible Background Commentary: Old Testament* (Downers Grove: InterVarsity Press, 2012), 205.

14. S. R. Driver, *A Critical and Exegetical Commentary on Deuteronomy* (New York: Charles Scribner's Sons, 1895), 351.

15. Michael P. Knowles, "The 'Rock', His Work Is Perfect: Unusual Imagery for God in Deuteronomy 32," *VT* 39, no. 3 (Jul 1989): 315.

# THE FIRST ROCK SONG:
## Contributions of Divine Metaphors to the Theology of the Song of Moses

appellation, belongs semantically with *ṣûr*."[16] As Albright explains, ancient Near Eastern gods were often characterized as rocks and mountains. This is clear from Ugaritic myths where both El and Baal—two predominant deities in the Ugaritic pantheon—were linked with mountains. El (the head of the pantheon) who oversaw humanity had a mountain as his place of residence.[17] Baal—a young, dynamic warrior god—was often linked with a mountain called "Zaphon," which later was equated with the Greek god Zeus.[18] This background shows that the concept was well known in the ancient Near East. Thus, Israel could also use the term "rock" without borrowing it from the other surrounding nations.

## צוּר (*ṣûr*) as a Metaphor for God in the Song of Moses

The first occurrence of the term צוּר in the Song is found in v. 4, but prior to the occurrence of the term, Moses calls on the heavens and earth to hear his teaching (v. 1). It was a common practice in the ancient Near Eastern treaties to call heaven and earth along with the gods as supreme authorities to punish those who violate the covenant stipulations.[19] In Deuteronomy, however, Moses invokes heaven and earth as witnesses to hear and testify on God's behalf when he inflicts his just discipline on his disobedient children (Deut 4:26; Deut 31:28). As Tigay correctly notes, heavens and earth function "as objective onlookers who witness the justice of the poem's charges and the fairness of Israel's punishment."[20] In v. 2, Moses uses a set of similes to sustain the interest of the reader with the hope that his audience will listen with sympathy to the message of the Song.[21] The reason the poet wants his audience to pay attention to his speech is expressed in the next verse, which begins with

---

16. William F. Albright, *Yahweh and the Gods of Canaan: A Historical Analysis of Two Contrasting Faiths* (Winona Lake, IN: Eisenbrauns, 1994), 188–89.

17. See *ANET*, 130–35.

18. See Albright, *Yahweh and the Gods of Canaan*, 125.

19. See *ANET*, 200–1.

20. Jeffrey H. Tigay, *Deuteronomy* (Philadelphia: Jewish Publication Society, 1996), 299.

21. Robert G. Bratcher and Howard A. Hatton, *A Handbook on Deuteronomy* (New York: United Bible Societies, 2000), 533.

an emphatic particle כִּי (v. 3).²² It is because he proclaims the name of Yhwh and ascribes greatness to him. In other words, the poet wants his audience to listen attentively to his speech because he declares God's qualities and acknowledges his greatness by recounting his wondrous deeds (v. 3; cf. Exod 33:19, 34:5–6). The poet's hope is that all who hear the public proclamation of God's name can acknowledge his majesty and righteousness.²³ Thus, these three verses set the tone for the metaphor because they show that the subject to be praised is Yhwh. As Olson states, "This word of divine praise sets up the introduction of the song's overall theme in 32:4–6: the contrast between the justice, mercy, and faithfulness of YHWH and the foolishness, apostasy, and rebellion of God's people, Israel."²⁴

## Deut 32:4: God is a צוּר: Identification and Interpretation

A הַצּוּר תָּמִים פָּעֳלוֹ
B כִּי כָל־דְּרָכָיו מִשְׁפָּט
A אֵל אֱמוּנָה וְאֵין עָוֶל
B :א צַדִּיק וְיָשָׁר הוּא

The rock: perfect is his work
For all his ways are just;
A God of faithfulness and without injustice
Righteous and upright is he.

*Identification of the Metaphor*

The examination of the metaphor begins properly with its parallelism. Berlin defines parallelism as "a linguistic phenomenon" which uses elements of language such as "words, phonemes, grammar in a variety of interesting ways."²⁵ She rightly understands the importance of parallelism in poetry

---

22. David L. Petersen and Kent Harold Richards, *Interpreting Hebrew Poetry* (Minneapolis: Fortress Press, 1992), 72.

23. Eugene H. Merrill, *Deuteronomy*, NAC 4 (Nashville: Broadman & Holman Publishers, 1994), 410.

24. Dennis T. Olson, "God for Us, God against Us: Singing the Pentateuch's Songs of Praise in Exodus 15 and Deuteronomy 32," *ThTo* 70 (2013): 57.

25. Adele Berlin, *The Dynamics of Biblical Parallelism*, rev. and exp. (Grand Rapids: Eerdmans, 2008), 2.

when she writes, "It is parallelism more than anything else that creates the perception of 'couplets' in biblical poetry."[26] Berlin is worth quoting at length:

> There are several benefits to be derived from the study of biblical parallelism. One is to increase our understanding of biblical Hebrew, its elasticity, the possibilities for its expressive permutations. Parallelism activates all levels of language, and what better way is there to observe these levels than to see them at work in parallelism. Second, through the study of parallelism we come to a better understanding of poetic texts. If, indeed, parallelism is the constructive device of poetry, then we cannot comprehend a poem's structure, its unity, until we have discovered which things it equates and which it contrasts. And related to the unity of a poem is its message, its meaning.[27]

Berlin's statements not only help to see the importance of parallelism in biblical poetry in terms of connectedness but also in terms of meaning. In other words, parallelism structures the poetic verses in such a way as to show an interaction between all the elements of a poem. Therefore, it is imperative that the study of the divine metaphors in the Song of Moses begins with parallelism.

Deuteronomy 32:4 contains two bicola arranged chiastically. Lines A and B in the first bicolon are parallel lexically. The adjective "perfect" in line A corresponds with the adjective "just" in line B. The phrase "his work" corresponds with "all his ways." These lines are also parallel grammatically, but in an inverted order: predicate-subject versus subject-predicate. Line B completes line A by providing an explanation of its statement.

Lines A and B in the second bicolon are also parallel lexically. The first line starts with "God" and the second ends with "he." Similarly, "a God of faithfulness" parallels "righteous," and "without injustice" parallels "upright." Line B serves to complete the thought in line A by intensifying that God is righteous and upright. Thus, he is a God of faithfulness and without injustice.

On a macro level, the two bicola are parallel with each other. The term צור, used for God in the first bicolon, corresponds with God in the third line

---

26. Berlin, *The Dynamics of Biblical Parallelism*, 6.
27. Ibid., 17.

of the second bicolon. Similarly, "perfect" in the first bicolon goes with "a God of faithfulness and without injustice," whereas "just" in the first bicolon corresponds with "righteous" and "upright" in the second. Lines A and B of the second bicolon serve to expand on God's actions in lines A and B in the first by associating these moral attributes to him.

In this verse, the author begins with the word הַצּוּר "the rock."[28] In the Bible, צוּר can be used either positively or negatively. On the one hand, the word is often used to refer to a place of refuge and security for people, as in the case of Moses hidden in the cleft of the rock to be protected from the glory of God (Exod 33:21–22). On the other hand, the term "rock" can signal a danger or something impenetrable because of its hardness (Job 14:18). This shows that the term "rock" can literally have different connotations depending on the context, but the picture of the physical boulder is still in view. According to Kittay, this literal meaning of the term is called "the first-order meaning."[29]

However, in the fourth verse of the poem, the term "rock" is not used as a physical place of refuge or a solitary boulder because the context, especially the third verse, suggests that it is used metaphorically for Yhwh.[30] Furthermore, the poet attributes divine characteristics to הַצּוּר: perfect, a God of faithfulness, and without injustice. This language does not fit a physical boulder or stone because it is an inanimate object. Rather, the context suggests that הַצּוּר is used as a metaphor for Yhwh. Therefore, since Yhwh has the selection-restriction of *deity, spirit*, whereas rock has the selection-restriction of *inanimate object, solid*, the utterance is incongruent. In other words, "Yhwh" and "rock" belong to two different semantic fields. This is, according to Kittay, the second order meaning.[31] God is the tenor and rock is the vehicle.

---

28. According to the textual apparatus of the BHS, the LXX translators understood that the word הַצּוּר "rock" is a metaphor for Yhwh. However, they did not retain the metaphorical term. They substituted it with θεός in every occurrence. See for instance, Henry Barclay Swete, *The Old Testament in Greek: According to the Septuagint* (Cambridge, UK: Cambridge University Press, 1909), 1:410.

29. See Eva Feder Kittay, *Metaphor: Its Cognitive Force and Linguistic Structure* (Oxford: Clarendon Press, 1991), 16–18.

30. Knowles, "The 'Rock', His Work Is Perfect," 322; Creach, *Yahweh as Refuge*, 28.

31. Kittay, *Metaphor*, 70.

# THE FIRST ROCK SONG:
## Contributions of Divine Metaphors to the Theology of the Song of Moses

### Interpretation of the Metaphor

In crafting his poem, Moses uses the term הַצּוּר in v. 4 as *casus pendens*, a noun or a pronoun "placed at the head of a clause in such a way as to stand aloof from what follows, and then resumed by means of a retrospective pronoun."[32] As Nielsen states, הַצּוּר is "ein Vokativ, als solcher durch den bestimmten Artikel angegeben."[33] In other words, the term "rock" stands as a nominative absolute and has the definite article ה affixed to the noun to mark the focus of the Song. As such, it points directly toward God, especially since it is followed by the word אֵל "God" and the pronoun הוּא "He" (v. 4).[34]

Elaborating on the character of God as rock, the poet says תָּמִים פָּעֳלוֹ "perfect is his work." The adjective תָּמִים describes the quality of what is sound, whole, and unimpaired.[35] This adjective is often used in the Hebrew Bible to describe animals without blemish, as in Exod 29:1 and Lev 4:3.[36] In this poem, it is used to describe the deeds of God [פָּעֳלוֹ] as reliable and upright.[37] The word פָּעֳלוֹ "his works" can be used in a literal sense to refer to one's daily labors or accomplishments.[38] However, it is used here to refer to God's providence, that is, his perfect governance by which he cares for and directs all things in the universe.[39] Not only is God's work perfect, כָּל־דְּרָכָיו מִשְׁפָּט "all his ways are just." The word דֶּרֶךְ translated as "way" can literally refer to a road or path.[40] However, in this context, it is used figuratively for Yhwh to describe

---

32. Paul Joüon, *A Grammar of Biblical Hebrew*, vol. 1 & 2 (Rome: Editrice Pontificio Istituto Biblico, 2003), 2:586. See also Alviero Niccacci, *The Syntax of the Verb in Classical Hebrew Prose*, trans. W. G. E. Watson, JSOTSup 86 (Sheffield, UK: JSOT Press, 1990), 148.

33. Eduard Nielsen, *Deuteronomium*, HAT (Tübingen: Mohr, 1995), 287. This quote is translated, "הַצּוּר is a vocative, as indicated by the particular article."

34. The LXX substitutes the pronoun הוּא with Κύριος. See Swete, *The Old Testament in Greek*, 1:410.

35. BDB, 1071.

36. See *DCH*, 8:643.

37. Tigay, *Deuteronomy*, 300.

38. *HALOT*, 4:951.

39. BDB, 821.

40. For a full lexical study of the word דֶּרֶךְ, see especially T. Muraoka, ed., *Semantics of Ancient Hebrew*, AbrNSup 6 (Louvain: Peeters Louvain, 1998), 11–33.

his moral administration.⁴¹ So, Ellman is right when she says, "To live according to God's law in Deuteronomy is to walk in God's way (5:33; 8:2, 6; 9:12; 10:12; 11:22, 28; 13:6; 19:9; 26:17; 28:9; 30:16; 31:29)."⁴² Furthermore, the noun מִשְׁפָּט translated as "just" is frequently used in Deuteronomy to refer to God's covenantal laws, especially when used in conjunction with the term חֻקִּים "ordinances" (Deut 4:1; 5:1). In the Song, it refers to God's fairness and justice as he deals with humans. Lundbom conveys the idea well when he states, "God's rule in the world that he created is just and right."⁴³ Therefore, once the Israelites hear the words of this first bicolon, they will immediately remember the mighty acts God made known to them. They will also remember the precepts and ordinances of Yhwh who is absolutely fair in his dealings.⁴⁴ As Block says, "Everything he [God] does serves the cause of justice."⁴⁵

The rock's perfect nature or character is further amplified by four distinct moral attributes: אֵל אֱמוּנָה וְאֵין עָוֶל צַדִּיק "A God of faithfulness and without injustice, righteous and upright is he." The first attribute אֱמוּנָה can mean "firmness," "dependability, faithfulness," "honesty."⁴⁶ As such, the term describes God as someone whose words match his actions. God is trustworthy; he will always keep his promises. Therefore, his people can rely on him. The phrase וְאֵין עָוֶל "and without injustice" denotes the quality of someone who shows no partiality in judgment, as in Lev 19:15. As such, it describes Yhwh as impartial, a God who remains faithful to his character. He does no wrong. Furthermore, the poet describes Yhwh as צַדִּיק "righteous." This pertains to what is just. It de-

---

41. BDB, 203.

42. Barat Ellman, *Memory and Covenant: The Role of Israel's and God's Memory in Sustaining the Deuteronomic and Priestly Covenants* (Minneapolis: Fortress Press, 2013), 99.

43. Jack R. Lundbom, *Deuteronomy: A Commentary* (Grand Rapids: Eerdmans, 2013), 873.

44. See Gary H. Hall, *Deuteronomy*, The College Press NIV Commentary (Joplin, MO: College Press, 2000), 469.

45. Daniel I. Block, *Deuteronomy*, The NIV Application Commentary (Grand Rapids: Zondervan, 2012), 750.

46. *TLOT*, 147.

# THE FIRST ROCK SONG:
## Contributions of Divine Metaphors to the Theology of the Song of Moses

scribes the quality of someone who has good conduct and character.[47] Finally, Moses says that Yhwh is יָשָׁר, that is, he is "straightforward" in all his dealings with humanity.[48] The piling up of these descriptive terms serves to enrich the picture of God as a rock. All in all, they describe him as the God whose character, works, and ways are inherently good, immutably faithful, and complete in justice, firmly unable in his own nature to countenance wrong.

## Deut 32:15 Identification and Interpretation

A וַיִּשְׁמַן יְשֻׁרוּן וַיִּבְעָט
B שָׁמַנְתָּ עָבִיתָ כָּשִׂיתָ
A וַיִּטֹּשׁ אֱלוֹהַ עָשָׂהוּ
B וַיְנַבֵּל צוּר יְשֻׁעָתוֹ׃

But Jeshurun fattened and kicked;
You were fattened, thickened, engorged;
And he abandoned God who made him,
And disdained the rock of his salvation.

### *Identification of the Metaphor*

The second occurrence of the term צוּר for God is found in v. 15. While the preceding section (vv. 12–14) describes some of Yhwh's deeds to his people, which include his provision of milk, honey, oil, fats of lambs, and rams, v. 15 describes Israel's rebellious nature toward their creator and provider. The people of God do not care about the perfect and faithful צוּר. So, they provoke him to anger by following other gods who are not even gods. There are several textual notes worth mentioning here. The first textual variant in this verse relates to the word "Jeshurun." The LXX substitutes "the beloved" [ὁ ἠγαπημένος] for it in the second colon, probably because the word Jeshurun was not a familiar term.[49] But the term "Jeshurun" seems to suit the context better because it is a poetic name for Israel.[50] Since the word occurs elsewhere

---

47. BDB, 843.

48. BDB, 449.

49. Apart from the use of the word here in Deut 32:15, it only occurs in Deut 33:5, 26, and Isa 44:2 as a designation for Israel.

50. BDB, 449.

in the Hebrew Bible as a poetic name for Israel, and since it fits the context of the poem nicely, the MT reading is thus retained.

The second textual variant relates to the use of the pronouns. The LXX changes the verbs from the second person to the third person. Thus, instead of reading, "You were fattened, thickened, engorged," as in the MT, the LXX reads, "He was fattened, thickened, engorged." This change is probably to retain the third person of the first line. However, the MT reading is most likely a shift in person added for rhetorical effect. In fact, rhetorical shifts are quite common in the Hebrew Bible (Gen 23:16; Job 13:4; Prov 14:20; Isa 42:20; Jer 29:19). This rhetorical device is called "énallage," an exchange of one word (e.g., part of speech, tense, mood, person, or number) for another.[51] The poem itself contains other instances of such a shift (see vv. 17–18, 38). Therefore, there is no need to change the MT.

Structurally, lines A and B are parallel lexically with the use of the same root verb to begin both lines שָׁמֵן and with the synonymous words "fattened, were fattened, were thickened, and were engorged" in line B. With the énallage (shift in person) and the addition of these verbs, line B serves to intensify line A. Moreover, lines A and B in the second bicolon are parallel lexically as this pattern shows: "abandoned, disdained;" "God, the rock;" and "made him, his salvation." Line B of the second bicolon intensifies the action of abandonment in line A with the act of disdain.

The poet explains the rebellion of Jeshurun, a poetic name for Israel.[52] Jeshurun fattened, kicked, thickened, and engorged. All these terms express the disobedience of Jeshurun who behaves "like an unruly beast fattened up on rich pasture."[53] Jeshurun is then accused of having forsaken the God who made him and of having rejected the rock of his salvation (v. 15b). The synonymous parallelism in the second bicolon helps to identify the metaphor. In the first line,

---

51. Ethelbert William Bullinger, *Figures of Speech Used in the Bible, Explained and Illustrated* (Grand Rapids: Baker Book House, 1968), 490. Bullinger made it clear that such changes can involve part of speech, tense, mood, person, number, or case; but never of one noun for another.

52. Peter C. Craigie, *The Book of Deuteronomy*, NICOT 5 (Grand Rapids: Eerdmans, 1976), 382.

53. J. A. Thompson, *Deuteronomy: An Introduction and Commentary* (Downers Grove: InterVarsity Press, 1974), 327.

# THE FIRST ROCK SONG:
## Contributions of Divine Metaphors to the Theology of the Song of Moses

Jeshurun abandoned the God who made him and in the second, he disdained the rock of his salvation. The term "God" then parallels the term "rock." Simply stated, God is the one called "rock" in this verse. This parallelism contains a semantic anomaly because God has the selection restrictions of *deity, spirit*, while rock has the restrictions of *inanimate object, solid*. Hence, the language is deviant to produce a metaphor. God is thus the tenor and rock is the vehicle.

## Interpretation of the Metaphor

Gile is correct when he writes, "Because of YHWH's upbringing, Israel prospers."[54] Verses 13 and 14 of the Song confirm this statement because they metaphorically describe Yhwh's care and provision for his people. Yhwh has blessed the Israelites to the point of excess. He has provided milk, honey, fats of lamb, rams, fruits, and oil for his people (vv. 13–14). But the imagery suddenly changes in v. 15 to describe Israel's negative attitude toward his provider. The Israelites display rebellion and disobedience toward God. Thus, the imagery of abundance changes abruptly in v. 15 from excessive divine provision to excessive human rebellion. As Wikander observes, "Now Israel is no longer the eater of animals, but is itself represented as one—and a rather stubborn animal."[55]

The poet says that Jeshurun וַיִּשְׁמַן "fattened." The poetic name יְשֻׁרוּן, a term meaning "Upright one," is here used ironically to mock Israel.[56] As Hall correctly says, "Israel was supposed to be the 'upright one' because she belonged to God who was upright (v. 4b). But she was anything but upright."[57] The term thus describes a rebellious people who provoke their God to anger and jealousy.[58] The verb שָׁמֵן "to grow fat" normally refers to prosperity and abundance, as in Neh 9:25, which explains how the Israelites lived in abundance after Yhwh had redeemed them and allowed them to possess the Promised Land. In the Song, however, the verb is used ironically to describe Israel's negative behavior toward Yhwh. Block correctly points out that the verb de-

---

54. Jason Gile, "Ezekiel 16 and the Song of Moses: A Prophetic Transformation?" *JBL* 130, no. 1 (2011): 92.
55. Ola Wikander, "Ungrateful Grazers: A Parallel to Deut. 32:15 from the Hurrian/Hittite Epic of Liberation," *SEA* 78 (2013): 138.
56. BDB, 449.
57. Hall, *Deuteronomy*, 474.
58. *ABD*, 3:771.

scribes Jeshurun as being "fat of mind," i.e., stupid.[59] The Israelites, who were supposed to be upright like their rock failed to live up to their expected moral character.[60] Not only did Jeshurun become fat, וַיִּבְעָט "he kicked." The verb "to kick" is a zoomorphism, which represents an entity in animal form.[61] But not just any animal, because, as Hall notes, "Usually the fat animal is docile and lazy, but Israel kicked."[62] So, the poet compares the nation of Israel to an unruly animal, one that is not amenable to discipline.[63] Israel has become unmanageable like an overgrown animal. Christensen concludes, "In short, Israel behaved like a spoiled ox fattened on rich pasture."[64]

The second line of the first bicolon addresses Israel directly using the pronoun "you." The énallage or the shift in person enhances the accusation reported in the verse. The effect is to personify the nation Israel as someone stuffing himself with food.[65] It reads, שָׁמַנְתָּ עָבִיתָ כָּשִׂיתָ "You are fattened, thickened, and engorged." The poet uses the term for "fat" in both lines, probably to emphasize the rebellion of Israel. The verb עָבָה "to become thick" parallels the first verb שָׁמֵן "to become fat." Figuratively, the verb עָבָה describes the rebellion of Jeshurun who has been highly fed like a beast.[66] The verb כָּשָׂה "to be sated," "to be gorged with food," "to be engorged," seems to be a cognate of the Arabic verb *kašiʿa* which means "to be filled with food."[67] In the context of the Song, it means "to become obstinate."[68] All these verbs describe Jeshurun's unwillingness to follow Yhwh's commands. Instead of becoming docile and obedient, the Israelites re-

---

59. Block, *Deuteronomy*, 755.

60. Tigay, *Deuteronomy*, 306.

61. Michael S. Mills, *Concise Handbook of Literary and Rhetorical Terms* (USA: Estep-Nichols Publishing, 2010), 212.

62. Hall, *Deuteronomy*, 474.

63. Carl Friedrich Keil and Delitzsch Franz, *Biblical Commentary on the Old Testament* (Edinburgh: T & T Clark, 1873), 1:992.

64. Duane L. Christensen, *Deuteronomy 21:10–34:12*, WBC 6B (Nashville: Thomas Nelson, 2002), 806.

65. Lynell Zogbo and Ernst R. Wendland, *Hebrew Poetry in the Bible: A Guide for Understanding and for Translating* (New York: United Bible Societies, 2000), 52.

66. BDB, 716.

67. BDB, 449.

68. *HALOT*, 1:502.

# THE FIRST ROCK SONG:
## Contributions of Divine Metaphors to the Theology of the Song of Moses

volted against their provider like an unruly animal (Deut 9:4-6). Thompson is thus correct when he says that the Israelites refuse to give "undivided allegiance and exclusive loyalty to Yahweh."[69] As Bergey writes, "Israël est devenu « gras », c'est-à-dire ingrat (v.15). Il a méprisé le Rocher de son salut (v. 15), ceci en se détournant de Dieu, en se tournant vers les idoles, un « non-Dieu »."[70]

Soon after Jeshurun increased, וַיִּטֹּשׁ "he abandoned" the God who made him. Material possessions and physical comfort can easily lead to self-congratulation, which in turn leads to forsaking Yhwh, a warning Moses clearly spelled out in Deut 8:11-16. The verb נָטַשׁ means "to forsake," "to abandon" "to discontinue performing a specific action."[71] In the Hebrew Bible, the verb usually revolves around the covenant relationship that Yhwh has established with the Israelites.[72] In other words, to forsake or to abandon Yhwh is tantamount to forgetting his covenant relationship as well as his mighty deeds, which include his acts of redeeming Israel from slavery in Egypt. In this case, Jeshurun violated the terms of the covenant by failing in their continuing duty to honor Yhwh, by performing according to its provisions. The verb עָשָׂה is often used for God in various contexts. It may refer to God making specific things such as heavens and earth (Isa 44:24), the stars (Ps 104:19), etc. It may also refer to God causing something to happen, such as when he declares that he will make (עָשָׂה) Abraham a great nation (Gen 12:2). Here in verse 15b, the verb is used to describe God as making Israel a nation, such as when he invited Israel into a covenant relationship after their exodus from Egypt.[73]

---

69. Thompson, *Deuteronomy: An Introduction and Commentary*, 327.

70. Ronald Bergey, "Le Cantique de Moïse — Son Reflet dans le Prisme du Canon des Ecritures," *RRef* 223, no. 3 (2003): 4. This quote is translated as follows: "Israel is fattened, that is, ungrateful. He despised the Rock of his salvation (v. 15), this by turning away from God, by turning to idols, a 'non-God.'"

71. Leland Ryken, James C. Wilhoit, and Tremper Longman III, eds., *Dictionary of Biblical Imagery: An Encyclopedic Exploration of the Images, Symbols, Motifs, Metaphors, Figures of Speech and Literary Patterns of the Bible* (Downers Grove: InterVarsity Press, 1998), 303.

72. Ibid., 303-4.

73. Edward J. Woods, *Deuteronomy*, TOTC 5 (Downers Grove: InterVarsity Press, 2011), 312.

Moreover, the verb נבל translated as "to disdain" means "to treat as a fool" or "to treat with contumely."[74] The Israelites treated God with contempt, meaning that they ignored God's covenantal precepts. As Block says, "Instead of honoring Yahweh their father and generous divine benefactor, they despise him."[75] Such a treatment is an affront to Yhwh who is the perfect and righteous God (v. 4). Israel also וַיְנַבֵּל צוּר יְשֻׁעָתוֹ "disdains the rock of his salvation." The noun יְשׁוּעָה translated here as "salvation" comes from the verb יָשַׁע. BDB lists the basic meaning of this verb as "to deliver."[76] In the Song, the poet boldly reminded the Israelites that God was their savior and deliverer. The Israelites disdained God who served as a place of refuge to protect them from Pharaoh and his Egyptian army as well as from all the other adversaries.

## Deut 32:18 Identification and Interpretation

A צוּר יְלָדְךָ תֶּשִׁי
B וַתִּשְׁכַּח אֵל מְחֹלְלֶךָ׃

The rock who begot you, you neglected;
And forgot the God who birthed you.

### *Identification of the Metaphor*

The third occurrence of the term צוּר for God is found in v. 18. Here, the poem charges the Israelites directly for having forgotten their own parent.[77] One textual issue that needs to be addressed in this verse pertains to the final word of the first poetic line, תֶּשִׁי. According to BDB, this verb is probably from שָׁיָה.[78] If so, the verb is a hapax legomenon, occurring only here. It seems plausible, however, that the verb is from נָשָׁה, another more common verb meaning "to forget," in the sense of showing neglect.[79] This meaning fits the parallelism well since the verb in the second line שָׁכַח also means "to forget."[80]

---

74. BDB, 614.
75. Block, *Deuteronomy*, 756.
76. BDB, 446.
77. Tigay, *Deuteronomy*, 307.
78. BDB, 1009.
79. BDB, 886.
80. BDB, 1013.

# THE FIRST ROCK SONG:
## Contributions of Divine Metaphors to the Theology of the Song of Moses

This verse is chiastically arranged with the object-modifier-verb versus verb-object-modifier. The chiasm shows that the focus is on the unfaithfulness of the people who, by virtue of idolatry, forgot and neglected their creator. These lines are also parallel lexically with "the rock, God," "begot, birthed," and "neglected, forgot." Line B serves to expand line A by adding or clarifying the maternal imagery. This parallelism shows that the language is deviant, and this deviance can be seen from two angles. First, a rock cannot bear children because it is an inanimate object. Second, the chiasm demonstrates that the term צוּר "rock" who bears the children is God, treating him as if he were a physical parent. In other words, God is depicted as the צוּר, although he is not a physical rock or boulder. Thus, there is a violation of the semantic domain. As noted above, God has the restrictions *deity, spirit*, and צוּר "rock" has the restrictions *inanimate object, solid, physical*. Therefore, the language is metaphorical. God is the tenor and rock is the vehicle.

### Interpretation of the Metaphor

The term צוּר "rock" stands at the beginning of v. 18, as in v. 4 to parallel the divine name אֵל "God" here in the second colon. The author refers to Israel directly using the pronoun "you." This emphasizes the accusation leveled against the people of Israel. In the first relative clause, the verb יָלַד "to beget" or "to bring forth" modifying צוּר "rock" is most often used in its literal sense for a female mother (human or animal) giving birth to her child (Gen 3:16, 4:1; Jer 14:5).[81] However, in some instances, it can refer to a male as in Gen 4:18 where Mehujael יָלַד (begot) Methushael, or in Gen 10:8 where Cush יָלַד (begot) Nimrod.

There is some disagreement as to which figure is implied by the usage of יָלַד in this poem since it is used in conjunction with the verb חוּל which always refers to a female giving birth to children. Thompson, for example, believes that "God is here pictured both as father (*begot you*) and as mother (*who gave you birth*)."[82] Ollenburger agrees with Thompson and says quite emphatically, "The first verb refers to the paternal role in begetting, and the second refers to

---

81. BDB, 408.
82. Thompson, *Deuteronomy: An Introduction and Commentary*, 300. See also Woods, *Deuteronomy*, 313.

the maternal role of birthing."[83] For these scholars, v. 18 contains a metaphor for God as father and a metaphor for God as mother. This is a possibility since the poet could use these two verbs (יָלַד and חוּל) as word pairs to contrast each other in order to complete the thought about a parent.[84] On the other hand, other scholars think the poet simply wanted to portray God as mother. For instance, regarding יָלַד and חוּל, Tigay states, "The first is used far more often for giving birth than for fathering, and the second refers literally to the mother's labor pains."[85] For Tigay, only the maternal imagery is in view. Bratcher and Hatton share a similar idea: "Some suggest that the writer deliberately used a male figure and a female figure; but it seems more reasonable to suppose that the two parallel lines have the same meaning, in both of them God being compared to a mother."[86] Both options are plausible. The poet could have meant to convey the paternal imagery as well as the maternal one, in which case the verbs are contrasting each other to complete the thought about a parent. However, since the poetic lines are parallel, the poet could have used the verbs to emphasize the idea of a mother giving birth. Although there can be no certainty regarding which figure the author had in mind, this dissertation will treat יָלַד as referring to the paternal role in begetting and חוּל as referring to the maternal role in birthing. The reason for this choice is because the verbs seem to be used as word pairs contrasting each other to convey the idea that the rock (God) is the sole parent of Israel.

It is important to note, at the outset, that the Bible never calls God a mother directly and never uses feminine titles for Yhwh.[87] Even Deut 32:18,

---

83. Ben C. Ollenburger, *Old Testament Theology: Flowering and Future* (Winona Lake, IN: Eisenbrauns, 2004), 317.

84. See Berlin, *The Dynamics of Biblical Parallelism*, 41.

85. Tigay, *Deuteronomy*, 306.

86. Bratcher and Hatton, *A Handbook on Deuteronomy*, 546.

87. In his book, *Our Father in Heaven*, Cooper does a good job examining various biblical passages in which feminine metaphors for God's activity are used. He rightly concludes that feminine metaphors are used to illustrate the tenderness of God without attributing any female titles to God. He writes, "Linguistically, all the clear and plausible instances of feminine reference to God are imagery or figures of speech: similes, analogies, metaphors, and personification.... There are no cases in which feminine terms are used as names, titles, or invocation of God, and thus there

# THE FIRST ROCK SONG:
## Contributions of Divine Metaphors to the Theology of the Song of Moses

which describes God in motherly terms, does not make that claim. This is perhaps to avoid the notion of a female God, as was common in the ancient Near East.[88] The Hebrew scriptures merely use feminine imagery for God to display qualities often associated with women, like tenderness and gentleness. The purpose of attributing such qualities to God is likely to demonstrate to the Israelites that Yhwh, their covenant partner, cares for them. Thus, the goal of this project is not to prove that God has gender (whether male or female) because the Bible explicitly states that God has no physical form (Deut 4:12). Rather, the goal is to show that God, in his covenant relationship with Israel, is depicted through anthropomorphic terms to help his people understand who he is and what he represents for them.

Hence, the poet says that the צוּר who begot Israel, he neglected. The verb נָשָׁה translated as "to neglect" can also be translated as "to forget."[89] It is used here to describe Israel's lack of commitment to God.[90] The poet implies that the Israelites show no concern for the rock who begot them. Instead of following Yhwh, the faithful and perfect צוּר who begot them, the Israelites have neglected him in favor of other gods who had not created them (v. 15). As Thompson says, "So unspeakable was Israel's ingratitude that she preferred such new deities to the *Rock* that bore her and the God who gave her birth."[91]

In the relative clause of the second line, the poet says that Israel שָׁכַח the God who birthed him. Here again, the verb שָׁכַח "to forget" serves to emphasize that the Israelites lived their lives in such a way as to deny Yhwh. The verb חוּל "to give birth" also modifies God. In its literal sense, this verb is used to refer to a mother who writhes in travail; that is, a mother giving birth to a child in pain

---

are no feminine pronouns for God. There are no instances where God is directly identified by a feminine term, even a metaphorical predicate noun. In other words, God is never directly said to be a mother, a mistress, or female bird in the way he is said to be a father, king, judge, or shepherd." John W. Cooper, *Our Father in Heaven: Christian Faith and Inclusive Language for God* (Grand Rapids: Baker Books, 1999), 89.

88. For example, the Babylonian creation myth elevates Tiamat (the sea goddess) as the mother of all creation. See *ANET*, 60.

89. BDB, 674.

90. Merrill, *Deuteronomy*, 416.

91. Thompson, *Deuteronomy: An Introduction and Commentary*, 328.

(Isa 45:10; 51:2).⁹² Figuratively, the use of the verb חול for God here suggests that the Israelites are dear to God, because he was the one who created them as a nation. Yhwh alone caused Israel to exist. Yet the Israelites abandoned their sole parent. Therefore, Israel's indictment is complete. God will pronounce judgment on his people. As Hall rightly says, "Despite Moses' earlier warning Israel did forget God. She had lost memory of him and abandoned him… The Song now would become a witness to later Israel. It would explain the reason for her devastation and provide another opportunity to learn from the past."⁹³

## Deut 32:30 Identification and Interpretation

A אֵיכָה יִרְדֹּף אֶחָד אֶלֶף
B וּשְׁנַיִם יָנִיסוּ רְבָבָה
C אִם־לֹא כִּי־צוּרָם מְכָרָם
D וַיהוה הִסְגִּירָם׃

How could one chase a thousand,
And two cause ten thousand to flee,
Unless their rock had sold them,
And Yhwh had handed them over?"

### *Identification of the Metaphor*

The word אֵיכָה "how" introduces the rhetorical question.⁹⁴ Lines A and B are parallel not so much in terms of equivalence but in terms of "an assertion of *a fortiori*, 'how much more so.'"⁹⁵ As Berlin explains, אֶחָד "one" and שְׁנַיִם "two" are natural pairs in biblical Hebrew poetry.⁹⁶ The mathematical pattern is: n=n+1.⁹⁷ These lines (A and B) are also grammatically parallel with an

---

92. BDB, 297.

93. Hall, *Deuteronomy*, 474.

94. The Samaritan Pentateuch reads אֵיךְ instead of אֵיכָה in the first line and omits the כִּי particle in the third line. However, these changes are not necessary because they do not make the translation smoother or better. Therefore, the MT is retained as it stands.

95. Robert Alter, *The Art of Biblical Poetry*, rev. and upd. (New York: Basic Books, 2011), 11.

96. Berlin, *The Dynamics of Biblical Parallelism*, 45.

97. Wilfred G. E. Watson, *Classical Hebrew Poetry: A Guide to Its Techniques* (London: T&T Clark International, 2005), 145.

# THE FIRST ROCK SONG:
## Contributions of Divine Metaphors to the Theology of the Song of Moses

inverted pattern: verb-subject-object versus subject-verb-object. Line B intensifies line A with the mathematical addition for dramatic effect.

In the second bicolon, lines A and B are lexically parallel with "their rock," "Yahweh," "sold," and "handed over." Line B specifies Yhwh as the one referred to as "rock" in line A. Thus, Yhwh is the one who could by his natural right as the Lord of their covenant sell and hand his people over to the adversaries.

As stated earlier, v. 30 is in the form of a rhetorical question: How could one [enemy] soldier put to rout one thousand [Israelites] soldiers? And two [enemies] soldiers cause a myriad to flee? (v. 30a). The answer to the rhetorical question is provided in the second bicolon. This cannot happen unless "their rock had sold them; and Yhwh had handed them over" (v. 30b). Once again, the parallelism in this bicolon shows that the term rock is not used for a physical boulder or a stone. It is used for Yhwh who has the restrictions of *deity, spirit*, whereas rock has the restrictions *inanimate, solid*. Therefore, this incongruity in the language tells the reader that it is metaphorical. God is the tenor and rock is the vehicle.

## Interpretation of the Metaphor

The particle אֵיכָה "how" at the beginning of the verse is followed by the verb יִרְדֹּף meaning "to chase," or "to put to flight."[98] Then two cardinal numbers אֶחָד אֶלֶף "one and thousand" immediately follow. The second line וּשְׁנַיִם יָנִיסוּ רְבָבָה "and two ten thousands to flee" serves to strengthen the first "how can one chase a thousand." Together, the first bicolon reads, "How can one chase a thousand; and two cause ten thousand to flee?" The rhetorical question is a statement of incredulity, and its function is twofold. First, it displays the folly of the enemies who think their power has caused them to defeat Israel (v. 27). Tigay states it well, writing, "If the enemy were wise it would realize that its victory was not due to its own power: its small numbers could not have defeated thousands of Israelites without the Lord's help. The rout of Israel will be so great as to be explicable only by supernatural causes."[99] Second, the rhetorical question helps the Israelites to see their defeat as a direct consequence of their unfaithfulness to Yhwh. In doing so, they will remember

---

98. BDB, 922.

99. Tigay, *Deuteronomy*, 310.

God's promises to them. For, in the book of Leviticus, God says to the Israelites, "Five of you shall chase a hundred, and a hundred of you shall chase ten thousand, and your adversaries shall fall before you by the sword" (Lev 26:8). This would happen if the Israelites walk according to God's precepts and keep his commandments because God is the one who would fight for them (Lev 26:3; cf. Josh 23:10). However, failure to observe God's covenant stipulations would result in God handing the Israelites over to the adversaries (Lev 26:17). Thus, the message would have been clear to the Israelites once they heard the rhetorical question. One enemy can chase a thousand Israelites, and two can cause ten thousand of them to flee because they have disobeyed their rock.

Therefore, the Israelites would have understood the meaning of this verse. With the use of the two cardinal numbers (one and thousand), the poet is looking for a logical explanation for Israel's rout. A superior army should not be defeated by an army smaller and weaker.[100] The second bicolon points the reader to the right answer using the metaphor "rock" for Yhwh. It tells the reader that this can only happen when the army's rock has sold them into the hands of the enemy. The bicolon begins with the negative conditional clause אִם־לֹא "unless" followed by the causal clause כִּי־צוּרָם "because their rock." Literally, the whole construction could be rendered "if not because their rock."[101] The verb מָכַר "to sell" signifies that the rock has delivered them because, as Tigay explains, "Mere abandonment wouldn't have produced a rout of such proportions."[102] The second line of the second bicolon clarifies that the rock in the first colon is יהוה. Israel's rock has sold them for covenant violation. The name יהוה is followed by the verb סָגַר translated as "to deliver over" in the Hiphil.[103] Thus, this colon explains that Yhwh has played an active role in Is-

---

100. This question helps to remind the Israelites of the defeat they had experienced by enemy armies much smaller than theirs, such as the Amalekites and Canaanites at Hormah (Num 14:39–45). See Bratcher and Hatton, *A Handbook on Deuteronomy*, 554.

101. For more information on this construction, see Bruce K. Waltke and Michael Patrick O'Connor, *An Introduction to Biblical Hebrew Syntax* (Winona Lake, IN: Eisenbrauns, 1990), 636–38.

102. Tigay, *Deuteronomy*, 310.

103. BDB, 688.

# THE FIRST ROCK SONG:
## Contributions of Divine Metaphors to the Theology of the Song of Moses

rael's defeat. Thus, Tigay declares, "God must have actively aided the enemy."[104] In short, the metaphor describes God's power as one who had in his sovereignty given up and weakened his people so that the enemies would overcome them.[105] While the rock (Yhwh) can provide security, protection, and care for his people (vv. 4, 18), he can also use the enemy as his agent to carry out his plan of judgment on his disobedient people.

## Deut 32:31 Identification and Interpretation

A כִּי לֹא כְצוּרֵנוּ צוּרָם
B וְאֹיְבֵינוּ פְּלִילִים׃

For not like our rock is their rock,
Even our enemies are judges.

### *Identification of the Metaphor*

In this verse, the word "rock" occurs twice in the same poetic line. The first לֹא כְצוּרֵנוּ refers to Yhwh, and the second צוּרָם "their rock" refers to the heathen gods.[106] As such, the poet uses the same vehicle (rock) to display two different tenors: "God as rock" and "a heathen god as rock." The purpose is to contrast Israel's God and the enemy's god. The second line "Even our enemies are judges" confirms the turnabout in the first line. As noted above, since Yhwh is not a physical boulder, the language is incongruent.

### *Interpretation of the Metaphor*

The poet juxtaposes "God as rock" with heathen gods to describe Israel's lack of wisdom in following useless idols. He begins with the כִּי particle. The כִּי is explanatory and refers to the statement made in v. 30, namely that Israel's God is the one who has handed them over to the enemy. The simile כְצוּרֵנוּ is used with the negation לֹא to make a comparison between the God of Israel (the solid rock) and the god(s) of the enemy. It specifically says לֹא כְצוּרֵנוּ צוּרָם "not like our rock is their rock." Thus, it contrasts the weakness of the false gods with the strength and power of the God of Israel.

---

104. Tigay, *Deuteronomy*, 310.

105. Pierre Van Hecke, *The Metaphor in the Hebrew Bible* (Leuven: University Press, 2005), 268.

106. See Tigay, *Deuteronomy*, 310.

Israel's opponents are weak and powerless. However, because of Israel's rebellion, Yhwh has decided to give them up so that the enemy might defeat them. Such a victory does not show the power of the army of Israel's enemy. Rather, it shows the power of the true God of Israel, in contrast to the weakness of the false gods to whom Israel has turned. Such an observation is made by Israel's enemy, as the poet says וְאֹיְבֵינוּ פְּלִילִים. As Merrill comments regarding these false gods, "Even their worshipers were forced to concede that their gods ('their rock') were vastly inferior to the God ('our Rock') of Israel not only in power but in quality. The idea here is not so much that the nations blatantly confessed the weakness of their gods but that they were forced to face the facts when confronted by the awesomeness of Israel's God."[107]

The metaphor "rock" suggests that Yhwh is powerful and can deliver his people when they live in obedience to him.[108] In contrast, the god of the enemy to whom Israel has turned is powerless and insignificant, due to being a created object, an inanimate rock. The God of Israel is a king or warrior who can fight for his people to give them victory over the enemy. However, the god (or gods) of the enemy is not dependable. The contrast is to distinguish the covenant God from the insignificant gods to whom the Israelites have turned.[109]

## Deut 32:37 Identification and Interpretation

A וְאָמַר אֵי אֱלֹהֵימוֹ
B צוּר חָסָיוּ בוֹ:

And he will say, "Where are their gods,
The rock they took refuge in.

### Identification of the Metaphor

The previous verse (v. 36) sets the context for this metaphor. It explains Yhwh's plan to judge his people (v. 36a). However, when the Israelites reach the point of total helplessness, God will stand up and have compassion on them (v. 36b). In so doing, he will point out how the rock/gods in whom they

---

107. Merrill, *Deuteronomy*, 421.

108. See Paul Sanders, *The Provenance of Deuteronomy 32* (Leiden: Brill, 1996), 215.

109. Knowles, "The 'Rock', His Work is Perfect," 322.

# THE FIRST ROCK SONG:
## CONTRIBUTIONS OF DIVINE METAPHORS TO THE THEOLOGY OF THE SONG OF MOSES

trusted were powerless by asking, "Where are their gods, the rock they took refuge in?"[110] The verb וְאָמַר "and he will say" introduces the question: אֵי אֱלֹהֵימוֹ "where are their gods?" It is followed by the statement צוּר חָסָיוּ בוֹ "the rock they took refuge in."

The noun צוּר is an irony; it is used for the false gods that the Israelites follow when they reject Yhwh.[111] Structurally, lines A and B are parallel lexically with "gods," and "rock" in chiasm. There is also a staircase parallelism with the progression of thought which serves to expand line A by mentioning the security and trust the people of God place in the demons (false gods). Hence, it suggests that the heathen gods are those being called "rock." Since the other gods would have the selection restrictions *deity, spirit,* and rock has the restrictions *inanimate object,* the language is metaphorical. Therefore, the tenor is "gods" and the vehicle is "rock."

*Interpretation of the Metaphor*

As stated above, the verbal form וְאָמַר "and he will say" in v. 37 introduces the question about the pagan deities. The epithet צוּר is used ironically since the false gods were unable to help Israel.[112] The rhetorical question אֵי אֱלֹהֵימוֹ "where are their gods?" (literally, "where are his gods?") suggests that the heathen gods are unable to come to Israel's aid. Thus, the question is asked to mock the Israelites for their wrong choices.

Furthermore, the poet adds, צוּר חָסָיוּ בוֹ "the rock they took refuge in." Dictionaries list the basic meanings of חָסָה as "to seek refuge," "to flee for protection."[113] As such, it denotes the confident seeking of security rather than a

---

110. While the MT simply has וְאָמַר "and he will say," other ancient manuscripts such as the Qumran and the LXX supply יהוה as the subject.

111. Watson, *Classical Hebrew Poetry*, 311.

112. Ibid. See also Tigay, *Deuteronomy*, 312.

113. See for instance, BDB, 340. This Hebrew word has several words that are derivatives of the verb. One of them is the feminine noun חָסוּת "refuge," as in Isa 30:3. Another more common cognate word is מַחְסֶה "refuge," "shelter," and it occurs, for instance, in Job 24:8, Ps 46:2 (2x), Isa 28:7, Isa 4:6. In all of these usages, the basic meaning of seeking refuge is in view. The verb חָסָה is attested in Arabic (hašiya) where it means "to set apart," "to go aside," "apart." The noun (hašan) essentially means "shelter," or "protection," as in Hebrew. In Akkadian, the verb means "to cover," "to con-

flight of desperation.¹¹⁴ This idea of taking refuge was common in the ancient Near East as men of war used to run to the hills to hide themselves behind the rocks for safety and protection.¹¹⁵ In the Song, the verb is used to describe one of the qualities of a צוּר "rock." Moses ironically invites the Israelites to call on the false gods for help because he knows the pagan gods are powerless. Currid makes the point, "The gods of the nations are not like Yhwh. They cannot deliver. They give no aid. They are of no help at all! Yhwh employs divine sarcasm by calling pagan gods 'the rock'. That is a term rightfully belonging only to Yhwh (see 32:4), and thus he mocks the idols because they truly have no substance and they are undependable."¹¹⁶ Thus, the poet uses this verb here to explain what level of deliverance the false gods were supposed to offer Israel. That is, if they were powerful, they would have saved the Israelites from Yhwh's judgment. But they cannot do so, being incapable of offering refuge.

# Function of the Metaphor God is a צוּר

This section will survey the rhetorical function of the metaphor God is a צוּר in the Song of Moses to see how the author intended to persuade his audience.¹¹⁷ As McGinniss says regarding the Song of Songs, "Because the Song is the product of an author (or, as some suggest, an artistic compiler), it is meant to somehow influence its audience."¹¹⁸ McGinniss' observation regarding the Song of Songs is also true for the Song of Moses, which according to Gordley, is

---

ceal." In the Ethiopic language, it means "to cover," "to hide." All these meanings in the cognate languages parallel the usage of the Hebrew word. *TLOT*, 464.

114. *TLOT*, 464.

115. *TLOT*, 464.

116. John D. Currid, *A Study Commentary on Deuteronomy* (Darlington: Evangelical Press, 2006), 510.

117. For more information on rhetoric, see Phyllis Trible, *Rhetorical Criticism: Context, Method, and the Book of Jonah* (Minneapolis: Fortress Press, 1994), 7; Wayne C. Booth, *The Rhetoric of RHETORIC: The Quest for Effective Communication* (Malden, MA: Blackwell Publishing, 2004), 17–22.

118. Mark McGinniss, *Contributions of Selected Rhetorical Devices to a Biblical Theology of the Song of Songs* (Eugene, OR: Wipf & Stock, 2011), 11.

"essentially a summary of the teaching of Deuteronomy in the form of a song."[119] Thus, the metaphors in the Song were purposely used by Moses to produce a rhetorical effect on the Israelites. To quote McGinniss again, "It is vitally important to the exposition of the theology of the text to be able to ascertain the intended effect that the text is thought to have on its original audience."[120]

## Deuteronomy 32:4

The main function of the metaphor "God is a rock" is representational.[121] That is, Moses uses the metaphor "to transfer something familiar to what is less well known, though of more importance."[122] The poet uses the term "rock" to describe the moral character of Yhwh as well as his perfect deeds to Israel. By using a term common to the people of God, the poet allows the reader to have a greater understanding of the concept and of the character of God. The צוּר imagery creates a beautiful and profound image in the mind of the Israelites. According to Knowles, the metaphor "God is a rock" in this verse serves to "draw both on the associations it conveys by virtue of the natural imagery of the metaphor (the 'strength', 'refuge', 'stability', 'steadfastness', etc., of a literal rock) and on the associations it acquires from being paired with the Hebrew God of the covenant ('holiness', 'uprightness', 'perfection', and so on)."[123] As Van Hecke correctly suggests, "God is not only righteous, like for instance a king or a judge, he is of eternity like a rock, he is unshakable like a rock, he is reliable like a rock."[124]

---

119. Matthew E. Gordley, *Teaching Through Song in Antiquity: Didactic Hymnody among Greeks, Romans, Jews, and Christians* (Tübingen, DE: Mohr Siebeck, 2011), 168.

120. McGinniss, *Contributions of Selected Rhetorical Devices*, 11.

121. Watson classifies the function of metaphor in two categories: representational and presentational. Representational occurs when a "poet uses metaphor to transfer something familiar to what is less well known, though of more importance. Presentational, on the other hand, pertains to the poet's description of "something which is, in a way, made present" while the poet also mentions the main subject. See Watson, *Classical Hebrew Poetry*, 270.

122. Watson, *Classical Hebrew Poetry*, 270.

123. Knowles, "The 'Rock', His Work is Perfect," 322.

124. Van Hecke, *Metaphor in the Hebrew Bible*, 26.

Such a representation also serves to establish a sharp contrast between Yhwh and his people. This is made explicit in the next verse where Moses says that the Israelites have acted corruptly toward Yhwh. They are not his children; it is their blemish. They are a generation twisted and perverse (v. 5; cf. Phil 2:15). As Craigie rightly states, "The epithet or name, Rock, emphasizes the stability or permanence of the God of Israel. It is one of the principal themes of the Song stressing the unchanging nature of the God of the covenant and contrasting it with the fickle nature of the covenant people."[125]

## Deuteronomy 32:15

Rhetorically, the poet parallels the divine title "God" with the term "rock" to reactivate some of the previous metaphorical connections in the mind of the audience (cf. v. 4). This can be seen even in the choice of verbs used. In v. 4, the author uses the verb פָּעַל meaning "to do" or "to make." In v. 15, he uses the synonymous verb עָשָׂה "to do" or "to make."[126] Furthermore, the poet states that Jeshurun disdains the rock which saves and continues to protect him from danger.[127] The idea is that God, as rock, is not only a provider but also a savior or deliverer. Israel was enslaved and oppressed for approximately four hundred years under Pharaoh and the Egyptians (Gen 15:13; Exod 12:40–41). But God performs signs and wonders to deliver his people. According to Goldingay, "The signs indicate that the God who delivers Israel from Egypt has sovereign power in the natural world and is prepared to exercise it. They suggest no disjunction between political events and events in the natural realm. Yhwh is sovereign in both. They also hold together the inanimate, the animal and the human realm."[128] The God who delivered Israel from Egypt still serves as a place of refuge to protect them from the enemies. As such, he is dependable and solid. However, the Israelites are hostile toward their savior and protector. They forsake and disdain him.

---

125. Craigie, *The Book of Deuteronomy*, 12.
126. These verbs are also parallel in Ps 92:5 and Ps 143:5 in the Hebrew Bible.
127. Tigay, *Deuteronomy*, 306.
128. John Goldingay, *Israel's Gospel*, vol. 1 of *Old Testament Theology* (Downers Grove, IL: InterVarsity Press, 2003), 315.

According to Van Hecke, this metaphor highlights two important ways of describing God in the Hebrew Bible: "God as the saving God who acts in history and God as the creating and blessing God."[129] Thus, Block is right when he says, "Although rocks are normally associated with defense, by going on the offensive, this Rock created a people for himself by choosing them, providing for them in the desert, and granting them prosperity in his land (vv. 8–14)."[130]

## Deuteronomy 32:18

Rhetorically, the metaphor combined with the two verbs in v. 18 (begot and birthed) suggests a strong familial bond between Yhwh and the nation, Israel. Yhwh redeemed the Israelites from bondage in Egypt "with a strong hand and an outstretched arm" (Ps 136:12) and led them through "the great and terrible wilderness, with its fiery serpents and scorpions" (Deut 8:15). He also drove out many great nations before the Israelites and settled them in their place. All these mighty acts demonstrate God's power over his created universe as well as his love for Israel's ancestors, yet the Israelites have forgotten their root and acted ungratefully. They have not been loyal to their parent. As Van Hecke rightly states, "The relationship between parents and children is so strong that they should neither desert nor forget each other. The parent-child metaphor underlines the strong bond between Yahweh and Israel."[131] Here, the parent is faithful, righteous, and loving. However, the child is rebellious and ungrateful.

## Deuteronomy 32:30

The function of this metaphor is threefold. First, it reminds the Israelites of Yhwh's role in their prior victories (Deut 2:32–37; Deut 3:1–11). In some way the Song sums up the people's history with God, and here Moses uses irony to remind them of the source of their victories. On various occasions, Yhwh told the people that he is the one who delivers the enemy into Israel's hands (Num 21:34; Deut 2:24, 31; 3:2; 21:10). Second, the metaphor also reminds the

---

129. Van Hecke, *Metaphor in the Hebrew Bible*, 267.
130. Block, *Deuteronomy*, 756.
131. Van Hecke, *Metaphor in the Hebrew Bible*, 267.

Israelites of their defeat when Yhwh has handed them over to the enemy. For instance, in Deut 1, Moses reminds the disobedient Israelites of the time when they decided to go up and fight with their enemies against the will of God, thus causing their tentative conquest to be unsuccessful and shameful (Deut 1:41–46; Numbers 14). Third, the metaphor serves to invite the Israelites to return to Yhwh their rock and to live in obedience to him to receive his blessings.

## Deuteronomy 32:31

Rhetorically, the metaphor functions to urge the Israelites to reconsider their choice. They have rejected their covenant God in favor of the heathen gods, who are nothing but idols (v. 21). They have provoked Yhwh to anger and have acted corruptly toward him (vv. 5–6). Thus, upon hearing the first colon of this verse, the Israelites will reflect upon their choice of the pagan gods as they recognize the uniqueness of Yhwh. They will realize their mistakes when they remember prior wonderful acts of God in which he delivered them and rescued them from danger without assistance from other deities. Moreover, upon hearing the second colon, the Israelites will fully realize their insecurity, having abandoned a powerful God for powerless ones. As they realize the fragility of their lives, they will see the necessity of turning back to Yhwh for their security and provision.

## Deuteronomy 32:37

Rhetorically, this metaphor serves a twofold purpose. First, it teaches the Israelites that the other gods are unable to rescue Israel. This is supported by the rhetorical question, "Where are their gods?" The implication is that, if the other gods cannot help the people in times of need, they are powerless and therefore not deserving of worship. Yhwh alone is God because he is all-powerful. Second, the metaphor serves to influence the attitude of the Israelites to remind them that God is their rock, the only one who can provide refuge and protection for them. As such, they ought to restore their relationship with him.

THE FIRST ROCK SONG:
CONTRIBUTIONS OF DIVINE METAPHORS TO THE THEOLOGY OF THE SONG OF MOSES

# Theological Contributions of the Metaphor "God is a צוּר"

Moses uses the term "rock" metaphorically in his Song to communicate a theological message to his audience. Several theological points are born from the author's use of the metaphor "rock" in the Song. Thus, it is necessary to articulate such points. As Rosner emphatically points out, "The books of the Bible are first and foremost religious texts. To ignore this dimension is forgivable, if one's interests lie elsewhere."[132] Rosner warns the exegetes against treating the biblical books as mere intellectual enterprise or academic books. The books of the Bible were shaped to communicate a timeless theological message.[133] Therefore, it is not appropriate to stop at the exegetical level in the study of the divine metaphors of the Song. However, Rosner is worth quoting at length again regarding this matter:

> Without questioning the legitimacy of the Bible as an object of academic study for a wide range of disciplines, biblical theology urges that the interpretation of the text cannot be left there. Biblical theology is not just one of a number of ways to read the Bible, as if there is theologically motivated interpretation alongside historically, aesthetically or ideologically motivated interpretation. Not to attend to theological interpretation is to stop short of interpretation, to ignore the interests of the texts themselves. If not to misinterpret, at best it is to engage in incomplete interpretation. Biblical study is incomplete until biblical theology has been done.[134]

Rosner's observation is sound and needed for the study of the metaphors in the Song because the poet uses the power of imagery to constantly remind the Israelites of who their rock/God is and what he has done for them as they

---

132. Brian S. Rosner, "Biblical Theology," in *New Dictionary of Biblical Theology*, ed. T. Desmond Alexander and Brian S. Rosner (Downers Grove, IL: InterVarsity, 2000), 4.

133. See Lim, "Toward a Final Form Approach to Biblical Interpretation," 6–7.

134. Rosner, "Biblical Theology," 4.

## Metaphor: God Is a Rock

sing this Song. But a word of caution is needed here. The metaphors do not communicate a theological message in and of themselves; rather, they contribute to the overall theological message of the Song. As Osborne succinctly declares, "Theology rarely stems from the metaphor itself but rather from the whole context of which it is a part."[135] Therefore, this section will articulate the theological contributions of truths that derive from the author's use of the metaphor צוּר in the context of the Song.

The first theological observation that arises from the metaphor צוּר pertains to the goodness of Yhwh, which is here described by his various attributes. The rock of Israel is תָּמִים perfect (v. 4a). According to Grudem, "God's perfection means that God completely possesses all excellent qualities and lacks no part of any qualities that would be desirable for him."[136] God is morally pure and clean. All his knowledge is perfect. As such, his work or his law is also perfect, unimpaired, and reliable. Because God is תָּמִים, he commands his people to be like him. That command is clearly spelled out in Deut 18 where Yhwh told them not to imitate the superstitious practices of the surrounding nations (Deut 18:9–14). The Israelites were called to be set apart for God's service. They were to be devoted to God alone. They were not to obey anyone who practiced magic and divination to get what they wanted because their lives were supposed to be wholly dedicated to God, the one who is wholly unimpaired.

Not only is the rock of Israel perfect, he is also just (v. 4b). Yhwh commands only what is just and right. He never commits wrong. He executes justice with fairness and equity as part of his very nature; in his aseity the loving God is immutably just. That is why, in recounting Israel's history from Mount Sinai to the plains of Moab, Moses reminds the people that he called upon the judges to conduct their legal procedures with equity, knowing that every judgment belongs to Yhwh (Deut 1:16–18; cf. Exod 18). Yhwh is trustworthy and stable, but he is also וְאֵין עָוֶל "without injustice" (Deut 32:4). He punishes sin because it is not in conformity to his standard (Deut 7:10). Because Yhwh is impartial, he urges his people to be impartial toward one another

---

135. Osborne, *Hermeneutical Spiral*, 188.

136. Wayne Grudem, *Systematic Theology: An Introduction to Biblical Doctrine* (Grand Rapids: Zondervan, 1994), 218.

# THE FIRST ROCK SONG:
## Contributions of Divine Metaphors to the Theology of the Song of Moses

(Lev 19:15). As Erickson succinctly puts it, "God expects his followers to emulate his righteousness and justice. We are to adopt as our standard his law and precepts. We are to treat others fairly and justly (Amos 5:15, 24; James 2:9) because that is what God himself does."[137]

The rock of Israel is also faithful. The poet says that Yhwh אֵל אֱמוּנָה is a God of faithfulness (Deut 32:4c). That means, Yhwh is "faithful to his word."[138] He made unconditional promises to Israel through Abram (and later to Isaac and Jacob), making the people of Israel his own people and granting them title to the land (Gen 12, 26, and 28). It was such a commitment and love that caused God to redeem the Israelites from slavery so that they could enjoy the benefits of the land (Deut 7). As Moses said to the Israelites earlier in Deuteronomy, "Know therefore that Yahweh your God, he is God, the faithful God, who keeps his covenant and his steadfast love to a thousandth generations with those who love him and keep his commandments" (Deut 7:9). To use the words of Balaam which he spoke to Balak, "God is not a man, that he should lie, nor a son of man, that he should repent" (Num 23:19). Because Yhwh is faithful, he urged his covenant people to be faithful in order to reflect his character.

The rock of Israel is perfect, just, faithful. But he is also צַדִּיק וְיָשָׁר "righteous and upright" (Deut 32:4d). He has good conduct in everything and is straightforward in all his dealings with humanity. To quote Goldingay, "All Yhwh's deeds and ways involve making decisions that have integrity."[139] Because of his righteousness, God calls his people to live a righteous life. For instance, Yhwh asked Israel to protect the less fortunate of the Israelite society. He warned them against perverting justice due to the alien and the orphan and forbade taking a widow's garment in pledge (Deut 24:17–18). Similarly, Yhwh asked owners of fields and orchards to avoid going back to their field and reaping their crops a second time. Whatever was left after the first reap belonged to the alien, the orphan, and the widow, since these people groups

---

137. Millard J. Erickson, *Christian Theology*, 2nd ed. (Grand Rapids: Baker Books, 1998), 315.

138. Daniel I. Block and Richard L. Schultz, *Sepher Torath Mosheh: Studies in the Composition and Interpretation of Deuteronomy* (Peabody, MA: Hendrickson Publishers, 2017), 366.

139. John Goldingay, *Israel's Life*, vol. 3 of *Old Testament Theology* (Downers Grove: InterVarsity Press, 2009), 60.

were often landless and poor (Deut 24:19–22). Thus, leaving a portion of the crops for them would enable them to participate in the blessings of the land which God had given to his people.

The second theological observation that arises from the metaphor צוּר is that Yhwh was Israel's provider (v. 15a). He provided for his people in abundance. An example of God's provision is seen in how he fed the Israelites in the wilderness. After their deliverance from Egyptian servitude, the Israelites wandered in the wilderness of Sinai for forty years. During that time, they experienced hunger because they were not able to carry enough bread with them for the journey. But Yhwh miraculously provided for them (Exod 16; Deut 8:2–6). God afflicted his people by allowing them to experience hunger; then he fed them with manna, a previously unknown food coming directly from heaven (Exod 16:4). Thus, God was the provider for his covenant people (Israel). Yet Israel's obligations toward their covenant partner (God) were basic and simple. The people of God were simply commanded to fear him, walk in his ways, love him, and serve him wholeheartedly (Deut 10:12). Sadly, Israel failed to live up to that expected standard.

The third theological truth is that the צוּר is Israel's deliverer (v. 15d). The God of Israel saved his people who were enslaved in Egypt under the dominion of Pharaoh (Exod 3:13–15; Exod 6:6–7; Deut 4:31–34). Yhwh is the all-powerful God who divided (parted) the Red Sea so that his people could pass through it on dry land, while causing the sea to return to its normal state to overthrow the Egyptians in the midst of it (Exod 14:21–28). Despite all that Yhwh had done for the Israelites, they were unwilling to obey him. Israel's history was one of continuous rebellion against their covenant God. They had been unfaithful to God on numerous occasions. In fact, the people provoked Yhwh to wrath in the wilderness, soon after He had redeemed them from slavery in Egypt (Deut 9:7–14).

The fourth theological truth revealed by the metaphor צוּר in the context of the Song is that Yhwh is the ultimate judge of his people (v. 30). Because God is righteous, he must judge sin. The book of Deuteronomy makes it clear that God punishes sin. That is why Moses repeatedly called Israel to covenant obedience. Yhwh chose Israel "among all the peoples" to be his "own possession" (Exod 19:5). His choice was not based upon Israel's merits because they had none.

# THE FIRST ROCK SONG:
## Contributions of Divine Metaphors to the Theology of the Song of Moses

Rather, God's choice was an act of divine grace. As God's people, the Israelites could enjoy the blessings of God. However, complete obedience was needed to enjoy the blessings. Failure to obey would result in curses, which could be in the form of death or removal from the land. Like the Canaanite nations that Yhwh expelled from the land, Israel would perish because they would not listen to Yhwh's voice, that is, to obey all his commandments (Deut 8:17–20).

The fifth theological truth revealed in the Song through its metaphor צוּר is that Yhwh is unique (v. 31). Since Yhwh alone is God, he requires an undivided love and loyalty from his people (Deut 6:4–5). Yhwh is not a plurality of gods; he is unique. The other gods are nothing but idols (Deut 32:21). God is unique in that he alone is the author of the entire creation; he is "God in heaven above and on the earth below" (Deut 4:39).

The sixth theological statement derived from the use of the metaphor צוּר pertains to God's protective ability for his people (v. 37). Yhwh alone can provide protection and security. This truth is implied in the connection between the rhetorical question in the metaphor צוּר in verse 37. Yhwh—not the powerless gods—is able to provide shelter (refuge) for his people. Yhwh carried Israel in the wilderness, just as a man carries his son (Deut 1:31), and he is still able to carry his people when they follow his commandments. Therefore, the Israelites were commanded to remain faithful to Yhwh because he could meet all their needs.

In short, through the rock imagery, the poet communicates several important attributes of God. As a rock, God is perfect in all his ways. He is just and faithful. He is upright and righteous (v. 4). As a rock, Yhwh delivers Israel (v. 18). He is the only one who provides shelter for them (v. 37). Yet, despite God's goodness to Israel, they respond with ungratefulness. They ignore God's word and reject him as their rock (vv. 15, 18, 30–31). Instead of seeking refuge in Yhwh who is the solid rock, the Israelites seek refuge in powerless rocks (v. 37).

Nevertheless, since Yhwh is a faithful rock, he does not abandon his faithless people. He calls the disobedient Israelites to change their wicked ways and to acknowledge him as their rock. Through this Song, God communicates all these attributes to his chosen people so that they might emulate them. Obedience to these commands would cause the Israelites to reflect the character of their God, the one who called them to be a "kingdom of priests" to represent him on earth as a holy nation (Exod 19:4–6). The next chapter will examine the metaphor "God is a Father" to see which characteristics the poet wanted to reveal about God in this Song.

*Chapter Four*

# Metaphor: God Is a Father

The Song of Moses not only depicts God as a "rock," but also as a "father," a term which denotes the "male parent" acting in "a complementary relationship" to a female parent.[1] The Hebrew Bible refers to God as אָב (*'ābh* "father") eighteen times in at least three different ways.[2] First, in five of the eighteen occurrences of the word, Yhwh is said to be the father of David and his descendants. For instance, in 2 Sam 7 David consulted the prophet Nathan concerning building a lasting structure to house the ark of Yhwh. Nevertheless, while David thought he was the one to build a house for Yhwh, it was Yhwh who would first build a house for David (a dynasty) "through which Israel would become secure."[3] God promised to raise up David's descendants after him in order that he might establish the Davidic royal line forever (2 Sam 7:12–13).[4] It is in this context that God said to David regarding his son, "I will be a אָב 'father' to him and he will be a son to me" (2 Sam 7:14).[5]

Second, two of these occurrences simply involve comparing God's love to the love of a human father for his children. For example, in Ps 103 the

---

1. *TLOT*, 2.

2. BDB, 3. This does not account for implicit statements where Israel is said to be God's first born or son (e.g. Exod 4:22).

3. J. Robert Vannoy, *1–2 Samuel*, Cornerstone Biblical Commentary 4a (Carol Stream, IL: Tyndale House Publishers, 2009), 307.

4. Robert D. Bergen, *1, 2 Samuel*, NAC 7 (Nashville: Broadman & Holman Publishers, 1996), 340.

5. The word אָב is used in this way again in 1 Chr 17:13; 22:10; 28:6; and Ps 89:27.

psalmist David declares, "Just as a father has compassion on his children, so Yhwh has compassion on the ones who fear him" (Ps 103:13).[6] Here, God is not explicitly stated as a father, but he is comparable to a human father. He acts like a human father to the ones who fear him. As Longman states, "God is like a Father to his people. He shows compassion towards them, knowing their weakness."[7]

Finally, eleven of the occurrences refer to God as the father of Israel.[8] A prime example is found in the Song of Moses. Thus, this section will examine the metaphor "God is a father" in the Song to see what the poet meant to communicate to his audience. The literal meaning of the vehicle will be examined first to evaluate how it was used in ancient Israel and/or in the ancient Near Eastern neighboring nations. The purpose of this section is not to import the ancient Near Eastern view of fatherhood into the meaning of the metaphor in the Song. Rather, this section serves to enhance the literary analysis of the divine metaphor by providing a historical and geographical context for the biblical text. This will pave the way for the examination of the metaphor, which will be completed in three steps: a) identification and interpretation of the metaphor; b) function of the metaphor; and c) theological observation regarding the metaphor.

## Identification and Interpretation of the Metaphor God is a אָב "Father"

Before beginning with the identification and interpretation of the metaphor proper, it is essential to understand the literal meaning of the term אָב to see how Yhwh can be portrayed as a father to Israel.

---

6. The word for father is used in the same way in Prov 3:12.

7. Tremper Longman III, *Psalms*, TOTC 15–16 (Downers Grove: InterVarsity Press, 2014), 357.

8. Deut 32:6; 1 Chr 29:10; Ps 68:6; Isa 63:16 (x2); 64:8; Jer 3:4, 19; 31:9; Mal 1:6; 2:10.

## Literal Meaning of the Term אָב

According to Mounce, the term אָב denotes the biological male parent.[9] This meaning can be illustrated throughout the Hebrew Bible as early as the book of Genesis. In Gen 4, Lamech had relations with his wife Adah, and she gave birth to Jabal (Gen 4:19). Furthermore, the Bible says that Jabal was the אָב "father" of those who dwell in tents (Gen 4:20). Thus, אָב clearly denotes the biological male parent of a child. However, the term can also refer to a grandfather, as in Gen 32:9, where Jacob called Yhwh the God of his אָב Abraham and of his אָב Isaac.[10] Or, it can even apply to a more distant ancestor, as in 1 Kgs 19:4. By extension, the term אָב can refer to persons in authority, as in Judg 17:10 where Micah asked the Levite from Bethlehem in Judah to dwell with him and be a אָב "father" to him (see also 1 Sam 24:11).

It is noteworthy to mention that Israel's society was patriarchal.[11] The male parent was very important in ancient Israel as he was the one assigned most of the responsibilities.[12] According to King and Stager, in ancient Israel the father was the "head of the family" and had authority over his household.[13] The father was responsible to protect and provide for his wife and children.[14] He was responsible for teaching God's laws to his children. For example, Abraham was supposed to teach his children to observe God's commandments so that God's promises with him might be fulfilled (Gen 18:19; Deut 6:6–9). Elwell summarizes the role of the father in ancient Israel as follows:

---

9. William D. Mounce, *Complete Expository Dictionary of Old & New Testament Words* (Grand Rapids: Zondervan, 2006), 241.

10. See *HALOT*, 1:1.

11. This word is intended to describe societal practices over three thousand years ago, not bearing on today's discussion of the matter.

12. See Walter A. Elwell, *Evangelical Dictionary of Biblical Theology* (Grand Rapids: Baker Books, 1996), 243.

13. Philip J. King and Lawrence E. Stager, *Life in Biblical Israel* (Louisville: Westminster John Knox Press, 2001), 38.

14. Ibid.

# THE FIRST ROCK SONG:
## CONTRIBUTIONS OF DIVINE METAPHORS TO THE THEOLOGY OF THE SONG OF MOSES

> In the everyday affairs of a Hebrew household, it was the father's responsibility to maintain the family fortune and to be the provider. He might work in the fields, most probably with crops of flax, barley, or wheat. Or he would work at a trade, possibly as a weaver, builder, potter, dyer, fuller, or a worker in copper or bronze. If he lived near the shore, he might be a fisherman. The father was also responsible for the religious well-being of the family. It was his duty to take over his sons' education from the mother at an early age, teaching them the tenets of Hebrew religion (Ex 10:2; 12:26; Dt 4:9; 6:7). He also explained all the facets of the Law and the interwoven history of the nation.[15]

This summary helps to see the importance of the concept *father* in ancient Israel. But the term was not peculiar to the Israelites. The ancient Near Eastern neighboring nations also had fathers in similar roles and used the term in similar ways. Ringgren notes that the Egyptian word *it* translated as "father" was used for an earthly father but could also denote an ancestor or even forefather.[16] As in Israel so in Egypt, the father was responsible to educate his children to make sure they became useful to society.[17] Likewise in Mesopotamia, the term "father" denoted the head of the family, the male parent who was responsible to teach his children.[18] In addition to teaching the children, the father was responsible to protect and provide for his family.[19] Thus, the concept of fatherhood had the same basic literal meaning in nearly every ancient Near Eastern society.

The above section has presented the term אָב in its literal sense in the Hebrew Bible and has shown that the term denotes a biological male parent acting complementary to a female parent. It has been shown that the male parent (father) was the one who protects and provides for his family as well as providing education for his children. Now it remains to show how אָב "father" can be used metaphorically for God in the Song.

---

15. *BEB*, 1:771–72.
16. *TDOT*, 1:2.
17. Ibid.
18. *TDOT*, 1:4.
19. Ibid.

## אָב as a Metaphor for God in the Song of Moses

The word אָב occurs in the second strophe of the poem (vv. 4–6). This strophe begins the body of the poem and presents the thesis, namely, "YHWH is faithful to his people; but inexplicably, they rebel."[20] Verse 4 describes the fidelity of Yhwh using the epithet "rock" as a metaphor. As stated above in the analysis of the metaphor "rock," that rock is Yhwh, the God of Israel. He is blameless and perfect in all his ways. Verse 5 stands in contrast with v. 4 and describes the unfaithfulness of Israel: "Yahweh abruptly declares Israel as no longer being his children due to their corruption and idolatry."[21] In v. 6, the Song shifts from the third person to the second plural to address the Israelites directly, charging them with "answering God's fatherly benefactions with ingratitude and rebellion."[22] In short, the Israelites have been unfaithful to the אָב who acquired them, the one who made and established them (v. 6).

### Identification of the Metaphor: Deut 32:6

A הֲ־לַיהוה תִּגְמְלוּ־זֹאת
B עַם נָבָל וְלֹא חָכָם
A הֲלוֹא־הוּא אָבִיךָ קָּנֶךָ
B הוּא עָשְׂךָ וַיְכֹנְנֶךָ׃

Do you thus repay Yhwh?
A people foolish and unwise!
Is not he your father who acquired you?
He himself made you and established you.

The examination of the metaphor begins with a study of its parallelism, for as Berlin notes, "The poetic function—the 'focus on the message for its own sake'—is achieved through parallelism; and so parallelism becomes our

---

20. Mark E. Biddle, *Deuteronomy*, SHBC (Macon, GA: Smyth & Helwys, 2003), 472.

21. Jeffrey G. Audirsch, *The Legislative Themes of Centralization: From Mandate to Demise* (Eugene, OR: Pickwick Publications, 2014), 60.

22. Jeffrey H. Tigay, *Deuteronomy* (Philadelphia: Jewish Publication Society, 1996), 301.

# THE FIRST ROCK SONG:
## Contributions of Divine Metaphors to the Theology of the Song of Moses

entrée into the message. Through the relationships which parallelism creates we are shown the poem's meaning."[23]

Structurally, v. 6 begins with the interrogative particle הֲ to introduce a positive rhetorical question addressing the twisted and perverse Israel mentioned in v. 5. That interrogative particle is also repeated in the third line to introduce a negative rhetorical question. Lines A and B of the first bicolon are parallel with the use of the negative לֹא in line B to reinforce line A.[24]

Lines A and B of the second bicolon are parallel lexically where the clause "he, your father acquired you" corresponds to "he himself made you and established you." The third person pronoun הוּא is placed in both lines to emphasize that it is Yhwh who is Israel's אָב.[25] Thus, the parallelism shows that Yhwh is the one who made and established Israel, a language reminiscent to a physical אָב "father." Therefore, since Yhwh has the selection restrictions of *deity, spirit,* and Israel has the restrictions of *human, physical,* the language is incongruent.

It is important to note at the outset that while the metaphor is identified in v. 6, it does not end until v. 14. This kind of metaphor is what Watson calls "extended metaphor," where the poet explains the metaphor in detail in order to "drive home a particular message."[26] In v. 6, the poet states that Yhwh is Israel's father. Then he explains to his audience how Yhwh values his people (vv. 7-9). Lastly, the poet explains how God provides for his people (vv. 10-14). Brueggemann is worth quoting here because he captures the idea well:

---

23. Adele Berlin, *The Dynamics of Biblical Parallelism*, rev. and exp. (Grand Rapids: Eerdmans, 2008), 17.

24. James L. Kugel, *The Idea of Biblical Poetry: Parallelism and Its History* (Baltimore: Johns Hopkins University Press, 1981), 14.

25. The LXX substitutes the emphatic pronoun הוּא with καὶ ("and") in the second bicolon and reads the entire bicolon as one long question: οὐκ αὐτὸς οὗτός σου πατὴρ ἐκτήσατό σε, καὶ ἐποίησέν σε; —"Is not he your father who acquired you, made you and created you?" However, it is best to follow the MT since both lines show clear parallelism. Henry Barclay Swete, *The Old Testament in Greek: According to the Septuagint* (Cambridge, UK: Cambridge University Press, 1909), 1:410. See also John William Wevers, *Notes on the Greek Text of Deuteronomy*, SBLSCS 39 (Atlanta: Scholars Press, 1995), 511-12.

26. Wilfred G. E. Watson, *Classical Hebrew Poetry: A Guide to Its Techniques* (London: T&T Clark International, 2005), 269.

In Deut 32:6, a very old poem, the role of Yahweh as father of Israel is taken as fundamental and orienting for Israel's identity in the world: "Is not he your father, who created you, who made you and established you?" The following verses speak of Yahweh's peculiar valuing of Israel (vv. 7–9) and Yahweh's peculiar attentiveness to Israel in need (vv. 10–14). In these verses the nurture of the sojourn tradition is cited as evidence of Yahweh's fatherliness.[27]

Brueggemann is correct that the metaphor "father" is first cited in v. 6 and then expanded in the following verses (vv. 7–14). Moses makes the claim that Yhwh is Israel's father and then explains the content of Yhwh's role as a father to Israel. Therefore, any examination of the metaphor must include the verses which spell out the deeds of Yhwh to Israel. For this reason, this analysis will begin with the metaphor proper in v. 6 and then tackle the other sections related to the metaphor, as shown above.

### Interpretation of the Metaphor

The poet begins this verse (v. 6) with a rhetorical question to address the disobedient Israel in these terms, הֲ־לַיהוה תִּגְמְלוּ־זֹאת "Do you thus repay Yhwh?" The personal name יהוה "Yhwh" is placed at the beginning for emphasis. Thus the clause can be read, "Is it to *Yhwh* you repay thus?"[28] This rendering captures the essence of Moses' message as it "underscores the shocking nature of Israel's unfilial behavior."[29] The verb גָּמַל which basically means "to deal fully" or "to deal adequately with" can also mean "to recompense" or "to repay" in a bad sense, as if here asking, Is this how you repay your father?.[30] The poet accuses the Israelites of dealing unfaithfully with Yhwh. In the second line of the first bicolon, the poet calls Israel עַם נָבָל וְלֹא חָכָם "a people foolish and unwise." The adjective נָבָל usually refers to someone who has no "perception

---

27. Walter Brueggemann, *Theology of the Old Testament: Testimony, Dispute, Advocacy* (Minneapolis: Fortress Press, 1997), 245.

28. Jack R. Lundbom, *Deuteronomy: A Commentary* (Grand Rapids: Eerdmans, 2013), 874.

29. Tigay, *Deuteronomy*, 301.

30. BDB, 168.

# THE FIRST ROCK SONG:
## Contributions of Divine Metaphors to the Theology of the Song of Moses

of ethical and religious claims."[31] Here, it specifically applies to Israel as being "unappreciative" of all benefits of Yhwh.[32] Lundbom explains that "in biblical thought foolishness stands next to godlessness. People are foolish when they deal corruptly with a good and righteous God."[33] Lundbom's observation aligns well with Moses' accusation that the Israelites have acted corruptly toward the righteous God, Yhwh (v. 5). For this reason, Moses also says that Israel is וְלֹא חָכָם "unwise." That means, the Israelites did not act in a godly way. They did not show any evidence of having the fear of Yhwh. Moses poses a rhetorical question to the Israelites and expects a "yes" answer from them. He states, הֲלוֹא־הוּא אָבִיךָ קָּנֶךָ "Is not he your father who acquired you?"

The imagery of a god acting as "father" was not uncommon in the ancient Near Eastern societies. Countries such as Mesopotamia, Egypt, and Canaan frequently used the metaphor when referring to members of their pantheons. For instance, one of the most important deities of the Sumerian pantheon known as *Enlil* was thought to be "the father of the gods," "king of heaven and earth," and "king of all lands."[34] In the appointment of Lipit-Ishtar as the fifth king of the First Dynasty of Isin (ruling around 1934–1924 BCE), it is stated,

> [When] great [god An, father of the gods], and the god Enlil, [king of the lands, the lord who determines] destinies, gave a favorable reign and the kingship of the lands of Sumer and Akkad to the goddess Ninisina, child of An, pious lady, for whose reign [...] rejoicing, for whose brilliant glance..., in the city of Isin, her treasure house (?), established by the god An, at that time, the gods An and Enlil called Lipit-Ishtar to the princeship of the land — Lipit-Ishtar, the wise shepherd, whose name has been pronounced by the god Nunamnir — in order to establish justice in the land, to eliminate cries for justice, to eradicate enmity and armed violence, to bring well-being to the lands of Sumer and Akkad.[35]

---

31. BDB, 614.

32. BDB, 168.

33. Lundbom, *Deuteronomy*, 875.

34. Samuel Noah Kramer, *History Begins at Sumer: Thirty-nine Firsts in Man's Recorded History* (Philadelphia: University of Philadelphia Press, 1981), 88.

35. COS, 2:411.

## Metaphor: God Is a Father

This god Enlil was responsible for the productivity of the Sumerian land. In fact, according to Kramer, the god Enlil was regarded as a "friendly, fatherly deity who watches over the safety and well-being of all humans, particularly the inhabitants of Sumer."[36] Similarly, as Tasker notes, the Canaanite creator god named *El* was often spoken of as "father" in relation "to both gods and humanity."[37] Tasker further says, "El is portrayed not only as clansman-protector of Kirta, the earthly king, but also as the one to have dominion over all humanity."[38] By the same token, Moses says to the Israelites regarding Yhwh, הֲלוֹא־הוּא אָבִיךָ קָּנֶךָ "Is not he your אָב who acquired you?" This statement would have been understood by Moses' audience immediately when they heard it. They would be reminded of how Yhwh has acted as a father to help them. These divine acts are described by a group of three verbs: קָנָה "to acquire," עָשָׂה "to make," and כּוּן "to establish."

The verb קָנָה means "to get," "to acquire," or "to produce."[39] The verb can relate to childbirth (e.g., Gen 4:1) or to creation (e.g., Ps 139:13). Sometimes the verb connotes the idea of paying a price to someone to buy something, as in Gen 25:10 where Abraham קָנָה a field from the sons of Heth.[40] However, the verb also occurs in reference to Yhwh acquiring the Israelites in the context of the Exodus deliverance (Exod 15:16). In the present context of the Song, the verb refers to Yhwh's bringing the Israelites into existence as a people.[41] This specifically means that Israel has been brought into sonship by Yhwh.[42] Moreover, Moses says, הוּא עָשְׂךָ וַיְכֹנְנֶךָ "he himself made you and established you." The verb עָשָׂה connotes the idea of doing something with hands. Here in the poem,

---

36. Kramer, *History Begins at Sumer*, 89.

37. David R. Tasker, *Ancient Near Eastern Literature and the Hebrew Scriptures about the Fatherhood of God*, StBibLit 69 (New York: Peter Lang, 2004), 67. See also John D. Currid, *Against the Gods: The Polemical Theology of the Old Testament* (Wheaton: Crossway, 2013), 133.

38. Tasker, *Ancient Near Eastern Literature*, 68.

39. BDB, 888.

40. The sons of Heth refer to the Hittites. According to Genesis, Heth was the son of Canaan and great-grandson of Noah (Gen 10:15).

41. Lundbom, *Deuteronomy*, 875.

42. Peter C. Craigie, *The Book of Deuteronomy*, NICOT 5 (Grand Rapids: Eerdmans, 1976), 379.

# THE FIRST ROCK SONG:
## Contributions of Divine Metaphors to the Theology of the Song of Moses

it specifically refers to God making (constituting) Israel as a national entity, a people of his own possession (Exod 19:4–6).⁴³ Finally, the verb כּוּן literally means "to be firm."⁴⁴ The idea is that Israel's father, Yhwh, made them "secure" and "strong."⁴⁵ The poet's point is clear in this verse: Yhwh has caused Israel to exist as a nation. As Tigay rightly declares, "The Bible is quite conscious of the fact that Israel had not existed from time immemorial but owed its national existence to God."⁴⁶

## God as אָב Elects Israel (vv. 7–9): Identification and Interpretation

This strophe provides details about some of the deeds of Yhwh, as Israel's father. Here the poem invites the Israelites to go to their physical fathers and ask them about what their spiritual father (God) has done for them.

### Identification of the Metaphor: Deut 32:7–9

A זְכֹר יְמוֹת עוֹלָם
B בִּינוּ שְׁנוֹת דּוֹר־וָדוֹר
A שְׁאַל אָבִיךָ וְיַגֵּדְךָ
B זְקֵנֶיךָ וְיֹאמְרוּ לָךְ׃

⁷Remember the days of old!
Consider the years of generation after generation!
Ask your father and let him tell you;
Your elders and they will say to you:

A בְּהַנְחֵל עֶלְיוֹן גּוֹיִם
B בְּהַפְרִידוֹ בְּנֵי אָדָם
A יַצֵּב גְּבֻלֹת עַמִּים
B לְמִסְפַּר בְּנֵי יִשְׂרָאֵל׃

---

43. See Robert G. Bratcher and Howard A. Hatton, *A Handbook on Deuteronomy* (New York: United Bible Societies, 2000), 536.
44. BDB, 465.
45. Bratcher and Hatton, *A Handbook on Deuteronomy*, 536.
46. Tigay, *Deuteronomy*, 302.

⁸When the Most High gave inheritance to the nations,
When he separated the sons of man,
He established the boundaries of the peoples,
According to the number of the sons of Israel.

A כִּי חֵלֶק יהוה עַמּוֹ
B יַעֲקֹב חֶבֶל נַחֲלָתוֹ׃

⁹For the allotment of Yhwh is his people;
Jacob is the lot (region) of his inheritance.

In v. 7, lines A and B are parallel grammatically. They contain two parallel verbs with different numbers: זְכֹר (Qal imperative singular) with בִּינוּ (Qal imperative plural).⁴⁷ Also the phrase יְמוֹת עוֹלָם (days of old) parallels דּוֹר־וָדוֹר (generation after generation). דּוֹר־וָדוֹר "generation after generation" occurs in the singular to give the line a distributive sense (see also Deut 15:20).⁴⁸ However, the pattern is the same in both lines: verb-direct object-construct chain. The second line serves to intensify the first line where Moses urges the people to remember their history.

Lines A and B of the second bicolon are also parallel lexically with אָבִיךָ (your father) and זְקֵנֶיךָ (your elders) as its traditional, logical, or natural pairs.⁴⁹ Additionally, the verb וְיַגֵּדְךָ parallels וְיֹאמְרוּ לָךְ with a contrast in number. Line B intensifies line A and is regarded as a "double application" implying that "the days become years, the father is accompanied by the elders (plural)."⁵⁰

In v. 8, the first bicolon is parallel lexically: "gave inheritance" corresponds to "separated," whereas "nations" corresponds to "sons of man." Line B functions to complete the thought of line A. Thus, the giving of the inheritance was a separation of the sons of man (v. 8a). Furthermore, in the second bicolon, God divides the sons of man and assigns to them their geographical allotments (v. 8b). There is one important textual issue that needs to be ad-

---

47. Adele Berlin, *The Dynamics of Biblical Parallelism*, rev. and exp. ed. (Grand Rapids: Eerdmans, 2008), 47.

48. Christo H. J. van der Merwe, Jackie A. Naudé, and Jan H. Kroeze, *A Biblical Hebrew Reference Grammar*, Biblical Languages: Hebrew 3 (London: Sheffield Academic Press, 2006), 184.

49. Berlin, *The Dynamics of Biblical Parallelism*, 45.

50. J. P. Fokkelman, *Reading Biblical Poetry: An Introductory Guide* (Louisville: Westminster John Knox Press, 2001), 82.

# THE FIRST ROCK SONG:
## Contributions of Divine Metaphors to the Theology of the Song of Moses

dressed at this point. In the MT, line B of the second bicolon reads, לְמִסְפַּר בְּנֵי יִשְׂרָאֵל "according to the number of the sons of Israel."[51] However, the Septuagint reads, κατὰ ἀριθμὸν ἀγγέλων θεοῦ meaning "according to the number of the angels of God."[52] Moreover, Tov mentions two Greek manuscripts, 846 and 106c, which read υἱῶν θεοῦ "sons of God" and thinks this reading reflects the original reading.[53] The reading of the two Greek manuscripts 846 and 106c is also attested to in the Qumran text of 4QDeut͡ʲ as it contains the phrase בְּנֵי־הָאֱלֹהִים instead of בְּנֵי יִשְׂרָאֵל that the MT has.[54] This prompts some scholars to believe that בְּנֵי יִשְׂרָאֵל is likely a scribal error. For example, Chisholm writes, "A scribe might have assumed that the phrase 'sons of God' was a reference to the Israelites on the basis of Hos 1:10 [2:1]."[55] Over the years, scholars have debated as to which reading could be the original, but no consensus has been reached.[56] Those who believe the phrase should be translated as "sons of God" think it refers to some other divine beings. In this case, the variant reading בְּנֵי־הָאֱלֹהִים would suggest that "each people was allotted a land, and a god."[57] Tigay goes as far as saying, "This means that when God was allotting nations to the divine beings, he made the same number of nations and territories as there were such beings. Verse 9 implies that He then assigned the other nations to those divine beings, and states explicitly that He kept Israel for

---

51. This dissertation agrees with Stevens that the MT reading is the correct one and that the LLX reading "sons of God" is an intentional error. David E. Stevens, "Does Deuteronomy 32:8 Refer to 'Sons of God' or 'Sons of Israel'?," *BSac* 154, no. 614 (1997): 137–38.

52. Swete, *The Old Testament in Greek*, 1:410.

53. Emmanuel Tov, *Textual Criticism of the Hebrew Bible* (Minneapolis: Fortress Press, 1992), 269.

54. Eugene Ulrich et al., *Qumran Cave 4.IX: Deuteronomy, Joshua, Judges, Kings*, DJD XIV (Oxford: Clarendon, 1995), 90.

55. Robert B. Chisholm Jr., *From Exegesis to Exposition: A Practical Guide to Using Biblical Hebrew* (Grand Rapids: Baker Books, 1998), 27.

56. For a full treatment of the textual critical issue, see especially Michael S. Heiser, "Deuteronomy 32:8 and the Sons of God," *BSac* 158 (2001): 52–74.

57. Jan Joosten, "A Note on the Text of Deuteronomy xxxii 8," *VT* 57, no. 4 (2007): 549; Emmanuel Tov, *Textual Criticism of the Hebrew Bible*, 3rd ed., rev. and exp. (Minneapolis: Fortress Press, 2012), 248.

Himself."⁵⁸ However, this teaching is not consistent with the rest of Scripture, which teaches that there is one God (Deut 4:35; 6:4; Isa 43:10–11; 46:9). All the so-called gods are merely idols with no real power (Isa 44:10; Ps 115:1–5). Therefore, this paper adopts the MT reading, which fits the context here as it highlights Israel's role in Yhwh's redemptive program. Thus, lines A and B of the second bicolon make a smooth parallel lexically with "peoples" in the first line corresponding to "sons of Israel" in the second. Line B serves to expand line A by stating the principle of the partition of the inheritance. On a macro level, the bicola form a parallel where "nations" in the first bicolon correspond to "peoples" in the second, and "sons of man" in the first bicolon corresponds to "sons of Israel" in the second.

In v. 9, lines A and B are parallel grammatically with the subject-object parallelism (עַמּוֹ "his people with יַעֲקֹב "Jacob"). They are also parallel lexically with חֵלֶק יהוה "allotment of Yhwh" and חֶבֶל נַחֲלָתוֹ "region of his inheritance." There is a repetition of sound (phonology) that occurs at the end of each line with the third person pronominal suffix masculine singular וֹ. Line B gives emphasis to line A by using synonymous terms in an inverted order. Finally, the root נָחַל meaning "to take as a possession" forms an *inclusio* for vv. 8 and 9. It occurs at the beginning of v. 8 and at the end of v. 9. This inclusio suggests that the focus of this section is on the giving of the inheritance/allotment by Yhwh to his people.

## Interpretation of the Extended Metaphor

Moses begins v. 7 with an imperative. He asks the Israelites to take a close look at history to understand what Yhwh has done for them. He states, זְכֹר יְמוֹת עוֹלָם "remember the days of old." To remember זָכַר is to call to mind the things of the past in order to better live in the present. As Merrill rightly argues, "Those who forget their history are doomed to repeat it, and with that sentiment in mind Moses urged the people to remember bygone days in order to be informed and inspired by them."⁵⁹ Moses further says, בִּינוּ שְׁנוֹת

---

58. Tigay, *Deuteronomy*, 303.

59. Eugene H. Merrill, *Deuteronomy*, NAC 4 (Nashville: Broadman & Holman Publishers, 1994), 412.

# THE FIRST ROCK SONG:
## Contributions of Divine Metaphors to the Theology of the Song of Moses

דּוֹר־וָדוֹר "consider the years of generation and generation!" This colon serves to emphasize the first by calling the Israelites to consider their history to be reminded of the deeds of Yhwh for them (cf. Deut 4:32). In the second bicolon, Moses says to Israel, שְׁאַל אָבִיךָ וְיַגֵּדְךָ "ask your father and he will tell you." He further says, זְקֵנֶיךָ וְיֹאמְרוּ לָךְ "your elders and they will say to you." In a predominantly oral culture, fathers and elders represent the custodians of historical tradition.[60] For this reason, the Israelites are encouraged to consult with them to understand their history.[61] The author piles up the imperative of the verbs *remember*, *consider* and *ask* (v. 7) to suggest an urgency for the people to reflect on their history. Once they remember their history, (e.g., how God redeemed them from the hand of Pharaoh), their hearts will be moved, and they will turn to Yhwh.

In v. 8, Moses begins with the clause בְּהַנְחֵל עֶלְיוֹן גּוֹיִם "when the Most High gave inheritance to the nations." The term עֶלְיוֹן (Most High) is a title for Yhwh (Gen 14:17–20). It is often used in the book of Psalms to emphasize God's supremacy over the universe (Psa 7:17[18], 9:2[3], 18:13[14], 21:7[8] etc. Here in the Song, it refers to Yhwh's universal action in an early era.

The next colon reads, בְּהַפְרִידוֹ בְּנֵי אָדָם "when he separated the sons of man." The עֶלְיוֹן "Most High" separated the sons of man. This separation seems to refer to the "division of the human race after the Flood," as outlined in Gen 10.[62] Yhwh יַצֵּב "established" the boundaries of the peoples according to the number of the בְּנֵי יִשְׂרָאֵל. This likely refers to the seventy people of the house of Jacob who settled in Egypt (Gen 46:27). This demonstrates that the God of Israel was the one who controlled the affairs of the whole world. Although Yhwh chose Israel as his covenant people, he showed that he cared for the other nations as well. Merrill captures this idea well: "God from the beginning carved out a geographical inheritance for his elect people and arranged the allotments of all other nations, especially those of Canaan, to accommodate that purpose."[63]

---

60. Tigay, *Deuteronomy*, 301.
61. Ibid.
62. Ibid., 302.
63. Merrill, *Deuteronomy*, 412.

In v. 9, the poet introduces Israel as חֵלֶק יהוה (the allotment of Yhwh) to emphasize the centrality of the Israelites in the salvific purpose of God.[64] As Hall succinctly states, "Out of all the nations God had chosen Israel as his allotted inheritance. God had planned it from the beginning. Her special place in his purpose was secure. Her current situation was proof as well. She was ready to take the land, which was her heritage. But prior to that was the fact that she was God's heritage."[65] The second line is more specific. It states Jacob as the חֶבֶל "region" of God's inheritance. Here, Jacob is regarded as the father of the family and stands for all the Israelites. Moreover, חֶבֶל (region or lot) stands for the measured land. The Israelites have a special privilege to be in a covenant relationship with the true God.

## God as a אָב Provides for His Children (vv. 10–14): Identification and Interpretation

The father who values his children also provides for them. Yhwh delivered the Israelites from a threatening situation and provided for their physical comfort. The Israelites have every reason to trust and obey their spiritual father because he has always been faithful to them.

### Identification of the Metaphor: Deut 32: 10–14

A יִמְצָאֵהוּ בְּאֶרֶץ מִדְבָּר
B וּבְתֹהוּ יְלֵל יְשִׁמֹן
A יְסֹבְבֶנְהוּ יְבוֹנְנֵהוּ
B יִצְּרֶנְהוּ כְּאִישׁוֹן עֵינוֹ׃

¹⁰He found him in a land, a desert,
Even in a wasteland, a howling wilderness;
He encircled him, cared for him,
Guarded him like the pupil of his eye.

---

64. Merrill, *Deuteronomy*, 413.
65. Gary H. Hall, *Deuteronomy*, The College Press NIV Commentary (Joplin, MO: College Press, 2000), 471.

# THE FIRST ROCK SONG:
## Contributions of Divine Metaphors to the Theology of the Song of Moses

A כְּנֶ֙שֶׁר֙ יָעִ֣יר קִנּ֔וֹ  
B עַל־גּוֹזָלָ֖יו יְרַחֵ֑ף  
A יִפְרֹ֤שׂ כְּנָפָיו֙ יִקָּחֵ֔הוּ  
B יִשָּׂאֵ֖הוּ עַל־אֶבְרָתֽוֹ׃

¹¹Like an eagle rouses its nest,
Over its young it hovers;
He spread out his wings, sheltered him
Lifted him on his pinion.

A יְהוָ֖ה בָּדָ֣ד יַנְחֶ֑נּוּ  
B וְאֵ֥ין עִמּ֖וֹ אֵ֥ל נֵכָֽר׃

¹²Yhwh alone led him;
And there was not with him a foreign god.

A יַרְכִּבֵ֙הוּ֙ עַל־*בָּמֳתֵי* אָ֔רֶץ  
B וַיֹּאכַ֖ל תְּנוּבֹ֣ת שָׂדָ֑י  
A וַיֵּנִקֵ֤הֽוּ דְבַשׁ֙ מִסֶּ֔לַע  
B וְשֶׁ֖מֶן מֵחַלְמִ֥ישׁ צֽוּר׃

¹³He made him ride on the heights of the land,
And he ate the crops of the field;
And he made him suckle honey from stone,
And oil from flinty rock.

A חֶמְאַ֨ת בָּקָ֜ר וַחֲלֵ֣ב צֹ֗אן  
B עִם־חֵ֤לֶב כָּרִים֙ וְאֵילִ֤ים בְּנֵֽי־בָשָׁן֙ וְעַתּוּדִ֔ים  
A עִם־חֵ֖לֶב כִּלְי֣וֹת חִטָּ֑ה  
B וְדַם־עֵנָ֖ב תִּשְׁתֶּה־חָֽמֶר׃

¹⁴Curds from the cow, and milk from the flock,
With fat from lambs, and rams bred from Bashan and goats,
With fat kernels of wheat;
And blood from the grape, you drank foaming wine.

In v. 10, lines A and B are lexically parallel as each contains two nouns. Line B completes the thought of line A by adding more descriptions of the land where Yhwh found Israel. The verb is elided from line B to allow the poet to add further description in the second line.⁶⁶ The function of lines A and B

---

66. This section contains a group of imperfect or YIQTOL verbs used in the past tense. According to Alviero, this phenomenon is quite common in archaic poetry of the Pentateuch. Niccacci Alviero, *The Syntax of the Verb in Classical Hebrew Prose*, trans. W. G. E. Watson, JSOTSup 86 (Sheffield, UK: Sheffield Academic Press, 1990),

## Metaphor: God Is a Father

(first bicolon) is to describe the desperate situation of the people, while lines A and B (second bicolon) describe the greatest care of God for that desperate people. Thus, the second bicolon completes the thought of the first one. The lines in the second bicolon are semantically parallel and contain together three verbs used for protection (to encircle, to fortify, and to protect). These verbs are parallel phonetically with the alliteration of the sound הו. On a macro level, the first bicolon parallels the second phonetically. Together, the two bicola contain six initial י and five words ending in הו.

In v. 11, lines A and B are parallel lexically where the verb "rouses" corresponds to "hovers," and "nest" corresponds to "young." There is an inverted order grammatically with the pattern preposition-subject-verb-object versus preposition-object-verb. Line B completes line A by specifying the protective actions of the eagle toward its nest.

Lines A and B (second bicolon) are parallel both lexically and phonologically. Lexically, the words "wings," "feather," "sheltered," and "lifted" are parallel. Phonologically, the sound הו (hu) is in both lines, and the third person masculine singular pronominal suffix ו (his) appears in the whole quatrain. Thus, line B here extends the activities of line A by showing that it is Yhwh who cares for and protects his people.

In v. 12, the words "Yhwh alone" corresponds to "foreign god, not with him." Lines A and B are parallel lexically. "Yhwh alone" corresponds to "foreign god, not with him." The second line emphasizes the first one and the two describe the superiority of Yhwh. He alone, with no help, led his people.

In v. 13, lines A and B are parallel lexically where "land" corresponds to "fields." Line B gives the results of line A. In the second bicolon, lines A and B are also parallel lexically with "honey," "oil," "stone," and "flinty rock." They are also parallel syntactically as the following pattern demonstrates: verb-object-preposition versus elliptic verb-object-preposition. The verb that is elided is וַיֵּנִקֵהוּ from line A in the second bicolon.

In v. 14, lines A, B of the first bicolon and line A of the second bicolon form a chiastic gender pattern that occurs within construct chains: f-m-m-f.[67] Line B of the second bicolon is different as indicated by the introductory con-

---

194.

67. Watson, *Classical Hebrew Poetry*, 125.

# THE FIRST ROCK SONG:
## Contributions of Divine Metaphors to the Theology of the Song of Moses

junction וֹ and its verbal form. That difference signals where the list in lines A, B (first bicolon), and A (second bicolon) reaches its climax, especially as indicated by the shift from the third person singular forms of vv. 10–13 to the second person verb in line B of this verse (14d).

## Interpretation of the Extended Metaphor

In this strophe, Moses begins recounting some of the works of Yhwh who has served as a shepherd, protector, and as father for his unfaithful people. The Israelites have every reason to trust and obey their spiritual father because he has always been faithful to them. Moses recounts the deeds of Yhwh using terms related to animals (vv. 13–14). He describes how Yhwh, as a faithful father, blesses his people. He provides milk, honey, the fat of lamb, rams, fruits, and oil for his people. In other words, he takes good care of his children.

Starting in v. 10, Moses states, יִמְצָאֵהוּ בְּאֶרֶץ מִדְבָּר "He found him in a land, a desert." The verb מָצָא has the idea of attaining something that was sought.[68] In the Song, it specifically pictures an abandoned child or an exposed infant in the wild (Gen 21:16–17).[69] The verb מָצָא is followed by the phrase בְּאֶרֶץ מִדְבָּר to suggest that the Israelites were lost as they wandered in the desert and that Yhwh מָצָא them in a precarious condition.[70] The first line of the second bicolon emphasizes that God found Israel וּבְתֹהוּ "even in a wasteland," an "empty, trackless waste."[71] That place was regarded as a יְלֵל יְשִׁמֹן "howling wilderness" an onomatopoeia, emphasizing "the horrible howling of the beasts of the desert, especially in the early part of the night."[72] According to Merrill, what is in view here is "Israel's postexodus experience in the Sinai desert, the 'barren

---

68. BDB, 592.

69. See Stephen K. Sherwood, *Leviticus, Numbers, Deuteronomy*, Berit Olam: Studies in Hebrew Narrative and Poetry (Collegeville, MN: The Liturgical Press, 2002), 280. See also Stephen A. Geller, "The Dynamics of Parallel Verse: A Poetic Analysis of Deut 32:6–12," *HTR* 75, no. 1 (1982): 51.

70. See Lundbom, *Deuteronomy*, 879.

71. BDB, 1062.

72. John Peter Lange, Philip Schaff, and Wilhelm Julius Schröeder, *A Commentary on the Holy Scriptures: Deuteronomy* (Bellingham, WA Logos Bible Software, 2008), 213.

## Metaphor: God Is a Father

and howling waste' where the Lord made covenant with them and through which he guided them to the present moment."[73] This does not mean that Yhwh's relationship with his people first began in the wilderness because Yhwh had cared for them before that time. For example, while the Israelites were enslaved in Egypt, Yhwh sent ten plagues to Pharaoh and the Egyptians so that they might release his people (Exod 7–11). During the night that preceded Israel's liberation, Yhwh killed all the firstborn of the Egyptians during the tenth plague but spared all the firstborn of Israel (Exod 12:12–13) in God's Passover. Lundbom's comment is helpful:

> It is striking that the Song makes no mention of the exodus, the defining event in Israelite history. The verb מָצָא suggests that Israel was a lost wanderer and that Yahweh "found" her in this precarious state.... In the Song we were told a few verses earlier that Yahweh chose Israel soon after creation (vv. 8–9). The two ideas can exist without contradiction, for Yahweh could certainly have "chosen" Israel before "finding" her.[74]

Hall is even more specific in his comments: "God's election of Israel is placed in the wilderness period (he **found him in a barren and howling waste**). God's history with her predates the wilderness period, but the Song is outlining her precarious position and God's loving care. The contrast was between her previous poverty and current plenty."[75]

Not only did Israel's father מָצָא him, he also יְסֹבְבֶנְהוּ "encircled him," which means God encompassed Israel with protection.[76] God also יְבוֹנְנֵהוּ "cared for him." The verb בִּין means "to discern," "to understand," or "to consider" in the Qal.[77] However, its use here in the Polel means to consider someone or something in an attentive way.[78] Israel's father attentively cared for him in the wilderness: יִצְּרֶנְהוּ כְּאִישׁוֹן עֵינוֹ "guarded him like the pupil of his eye." The verb נָצַר

---

73. Merrill, *Deuteronomy*, 414.
74. Lundbom, *Deuteronomy*, 879.
75. Hall, *Deuteronomy*, 472.
76. BDB, 686.
77. BDB, 106.
78. Ibid.

# THE FIRST ROCK SONG:
## Contributions of Divine Metaphors to the Theology of the Song of Moses

means "to watch," "to keep," or "to guard."[79] The metaphorical "father" is here intensified by a simile כְּאִישׁוֹן עֵינוֹ "like the pupil of his eye." According to Brown, "The pupil of the eye is a most sensitive part of the human body and, if we are in physical danger, the defense-mechanism which shields the eye is immediately at work. The Lord guards his uniquely treasured people with that kind of instant help."[80] This emphasizes the level of protection that God offers to his people and shows the preciousness of Israel in the eyes of Yhwh. God protects his people as a person protects his/her precious and sensitive eye.[81] As Israel's father, Yhwh has done everything a father is supposed to do.

To further enhance the role of Yhwh as Israel's father, Moses uses the imagery of נֶשֶׁר "an eagle." According to Lundbom, the נֶשֶׁר is more likely a male bird, not the female.[82] This makes sense because Moses is here expanding on the father metaphor to explain how Yhwh protects his children (Israel). So, the male figure is still in view here. Moses says, כְּנֶשֶׁר יָעִיר קִנּוֹ "like an eagle rouses its nest." The verb עוּר in the Hiphil stem means "to rouse," or "to stir up (to activity)."[83] The idea is of a parent bird that stirs up the nest in order to aid the nestlings to fly.[84] To encourage the flying process, the eagle עַל־גּוֹזָלָיו יְרַחֵף "hovers over its young." The verb רָחַף translated as "to hover," as attested in the Syriac (raḥep), means "to move gently," or "to cherish."[85] The verb also occurs in the creation account where it is said that the spirit of God מְרַחֶפֶת was hovering over the face of the waters (Gen 1:2). Thus, the נֶשֶׁר "eagle" moves gently upon its young, trains and supports them to make sure they are capable of flying.[86] Like an eagle, Yhwh יִפְרֹשׂ כְּנָפָיו יִקָּחֵהוּ "spread out his wings, sheltered him [his children]," יִשָּׂאֵהוּ עַל־אֶבְרָתוֹ "He lifted him on his pinion" (in Exod 19:4). The idea of an eagle carrying and protecting someone was common in the ancient Near East. For example, in Mesopotamia, the *Tale of Etana* recounts how King Etana

---

79. BDB, 665.

80. Raymond Brown, *The Message of Deuteronomy: Not by Bread Alone* (Leicester, UK: Inter-Varsity Press, 1993), 297.

81. Tigay, *Deuteronomy*, 304.

82. Lundbom, *Deuteronomy*, 880.

83. BDB, 735.

84. See Lundbom, *Deuteronomy*, 880.

85. BDB, 934.

86. BDB, 676.

ascends to heaven on an eagle's back.⁸⁷ The eagle carries the king, lets him go from time to time and uses its wings to catch him.⁸⁸ The language of the story contains words like "wings" and "carry" that are quite similar to the language of the Song. For instance, in the Tale, the eagle declared to King Etana,

> Come, my friend, let me carry you up [to the sky],
> [Let us meet] with Ishtar, the mistress [of birth].
> Beside Ishtar the mistress [of birth let us].
> Put your arms over my sides,
> Put your hands over the quills of my wings.⁸⁹

Applied to Yhwh, the eagle imagery implies that God manifested love and care towards Israel during their wilderness trek (cf. Ps 36:8). God trained and supported his children to make sure they could safely make their way through the wilderness. As Brown rightly explains, the imagery serves to "highlight God's protective guidance through the hostile wilderness."⁹⁰

In v. 12, the poet "shifts back to language concerning Yhwh and the object of his affection and attention."⁹¹ He says, יהוה בָּדָד יַנְחֶנּוּ "Yhwh alone led him." The word יהוה is placed first for emphasis. The verb נָחָה means "to lead," or "to guide." Yhwh alone did that for Israel. No אֵל נֵכָר "foreign god" was with Yhwh when he rescued Israel from the hand of Pharaoh and led them through the wilderness, a land full of "fiery serpents and scorpions" (Deut 8:15–16). Yhwh only protected his chosen people all the way through the wilderness to lead them to the Promised Land.

---

87. According to Sparks, King Etana is remembered in this way: "Etana, a shepherd, the one who ascended to heaven." Kenton L. Sparks, *Ancient Texts of the Study of the Hebrew Bible: A Guide to the Background Literature* (Peabody, MA: Hendrickson Publishers, 2005), 285–86.

88. *COS*, 1:452–56.

89. *COS*, 1:456.

90. William P. Brown, *Seeing the Psalms: A Theology of Metaphor* (Louisville: John Knox Press, 2002), 22.

91. David L. Petersen and Kent Harold Richards, *Interpreting Hebrew Poetry* (Minneapolis: Fortress Press, 1992), 76.

## THE FIRST ROCK SONG:
### Contributions of Divine Metaphors to the Theology of the Song of Moses

In v. 13, the poet reminds the Israelites that although the wilderness trek was difficult, their father, Yhwh, led them through it successfully. Now, as Merrill explains, the scene is no longer in the wilderness of Sinai, but in "the more fertile lands of Transjordan."[92] There, Yhwh יַרְכִּבֵהוּ "made him ride" on the heights of the land. The verb רָכַב "to ride" is "typically used to describe someone riding an animal" i.e., the "steed upon which the individual is mounted."[93] The context of this verb suggests that, if the individual rides on the heights of the land, he will have a frame of reference that enables him to survey the countryside.[94] After the survey of the land, Israel וַיֹּאכַל תְּנוּבֹת שָׂדָי "ate the crops of the field." The wayyiqtol form of the verb אָכַל "to eat" implies that the eating is subsequent to the riding. This implies that Yhwh causes the individual to ride on the heights so that he can survey the land and eat from it. Furthermore, Yhwh וַיֵּנִקֵהוּ דְבַשׁ מִסֶּלַע "made him suckle honey from stone." The verb יָנַק "to suck" has the idea of a woman nursing her babe.[95] As Tigay rightly notes, "God fed Israel with virtually no effort on its part."[96] God caused Israel to suckle שֶׁמֶן "oil" or olive oil from flinty rock.[97] A flinty rock is not a hospitable place for an olive grove. However, Israel's father caused him to drink olive oil in "rocky limestone soils."[98]

Verse 14 contains no verb. Nielsen is correct when he asserts, "Syntaktisch als Objekte für das Verb הֵינִיק werden ferner Butter und Milch, Fett und Fleisch des Viehs, Weizen und Wein als köstliche Gaben Jahwes an sein Volk aufgezählt."[99] While Nielsen is right, it is best to replace the verb "to suckle" with the verb "to feed" since people do not normally suck curds, milk, and

---

92. Merrill, *Deuteronomy*, 415.
93. Petersen and Richards, *Interpreting Hebrew Poetry*, 77.
94. Ibid.
95. BDB, 413.
96. Tigay, *Deuteronomy*, 305.
97. See Merrill, *Deuteronomy*, 415.
98. Tigay, *Deuteronomy*, 305.
99. Eduard Nielsen, *Deuteronomium*, HAT (Tübingen: Mohr, 1995), 289. This quote is translated, "Syntactically, as objects for the verb קינה, butter and milk, fat and meat from cattle, wheat and wine are also given to his people as precious gifts from Yhwh."

fat of lambs.¹⁰⁰ Thus, the poet says that Yhwh fed Israel with חֶמְאַת בָּקָר וַחֲלֵב צֹאן "curds from the cow and milk from the flock." The word חֶמְאַת "curds" is often described as "curdled milk."¹⁰¹ It had the appearance of yogurt and was "prepared by churning fresh milk."¹⁰² In the Bible, the word חֶמְאַת "curds" often appears with חָלָב "milk" (as seen here and in Judg 5:25). It was served with milk to the three guests who visited Abraham and Sarah at the oaks of Mamre (Gen 18:8). The word חֵלֶב (fat) indicates that the individual has the best things to eat.¹⁰³ The words בְּנֵי־בָשָׁן literally "sons of Bashan" is an idiom which stands for Bashan, "the northern district of Transjordan," a rich and fertile land located in what is now the Golan Heights, east of the Sea of Galilee.¹⁰⁴ וְדַם־עֵנָב is a reference to wine (Gen. 49:11). Thus, the Song progresses from milk products to best meats, and to best grains. The piling up of these nouns serves to emphasize the incredible variety of foodstuffs Yhwh provided for Israel.¹⁰⁵

# Function of the Metaphor "God is a Father"

The fatherhood metaphor is embedded in two rhetorical questions and an *énallage* (a shift in person). Such imagery serves to foster the development of the metaphor. Thus, it is important to understand how the imagery functions to see how the fatherhood metaphor is developed. From a rhetorical standpoint, the question in the first bicolon of v. 6 functions to provoke thoughts and encourage reflection within the listener as to allow a person to feel the emotion of the poem. Through the metaphor of fatherhood, the first question encourages the Israelites (and us) to reflect on what the implied answer to the

---

100. Bratcher and Hatton capture the meaning of the verb "to suckle" well. They suggest three ways in which the verse should begin: "He fed them with," "He sustained them with," or "He provided them with." See Bratcher and Hatton, *A Handbook on Deuteronomy*, 541.

101. BDB, 326.

102. King and Stager, *Life in Biblical Israel*, 102.

103. BDB, 77.

104. Yohanan Aharoni, *The Land of the Bible: A Historical Geography*, rev. and enl. ed., transl. Anson Rainey (Philadelphia: The Westminster Press, 1979), 37.

105. Petersen and Richards, *Interpreting Hebrew Poetry*, 78.

question might be. In retrospect, the Israelites will remember God's wonders and deeds toward them and will feel the shock expressed by this rhetorical question. They will remember that they were not a people, but God (their father) established them as such. Therefore, they needed to be loyal to God.

The second rhetorical question serves as a self-assessment/evaluation to probe the mind of the Israelites to urge them to act wisely toward their God. It serves to reinforce the first one. By answering the negative question in the positive, the Israelites may come into contact or even empathize with the author's viewpoint that God demands faithfulness. As "father," he is faithful and upright in all his ways, and his people have a responsibility to respond to his work on their behalf. As Block notes, "These rhetorical questions highlight the folly of Israel's response to Yahweh's work on her behalf."[106] But in addition to what Block says, the rhetorical questions also launch an urgent call to Israel to repent from their evil ways in order to follow their father, the one who made and established them.

Third, the shift in person in v. 6 serves to draw the audience into greater engagement with the song as it charges them with "answering God's fatherly benefactions with ingratitude and rebellion."[107] Using the second person, Moses directly calls each individual Israelite to personal reflection on his or her mistakes. Through the fatherhood metaphor, the Israelites will stop and think about the various ways in which they have acted as if they are not God's children (v. 5). Such a reflection will cause the Israelites to feel their guilt and to act as true children of God, ones who obey his precepts and walk in his ways.

## Deuteronomy 32:7–9

Rhetorically, the metaphor "God is אָב" functions in at least three ways. First, through the extended metaphor God is אָב, the poet invites his listeners to think historically, to ask their physical fathers some questions regarding the deeds of their spiritual father (Yhwh) in order to live in complete obedience to him (v. 7). Such an attitude is one that brings multiple blessings to the peo-

---

106. Daniel I. Block, *Deuteronomy*, The NIV Application Commentary (Grand Rapids: Zondervan, 2012), 752.

107. Tigay, *Deuteronomy*, 301.

ple as it sets them apart as God's own inheritance (v. 8). Second, God's separation of the nations shows that he values human life in general, but that he especially cares for the lives of his chosen people (Israel). As Knight declares, "The quarrying of Moses' Song reveals the extreme importance of human life that is emphasized when Moses contemplates God's action in uniting himself in covenant with his chosen people."[108] Finally, the allotment/inheritance motif reminds the Israelites of two important events: the division of the nations and the Mount Sinai covenant. God divides the nations, giving each its own territory (Gen 10–11) to secure a special place for Israel. As Hall states, "Israel's God was the sovereign God who controlled the whole world. Each nation was the object of his care. His plan for Israel to become his chosen nation included preparing a place for her by assigning other nations to their place as well. This included establishing the boundaries for each nation."[109]

The allotment/inheritance motif also reminds the Israelites of God's covenant made at Mount Sinai after their liberation from Egypt (Exodus 19). Having been the dominant economic and military force of the world at that time, from a human perspective Egypt seemed nearly invincible. However, Yhwh powerfully defeated Egypt and rescued his people so that they might become his treasured possession among all the other nations (Exod 19:5; Deut 7:6).[110]

Israel was granted a special status. This privilege results from their unique covenant relationship with Yhwh, a relationship expressed in language reminiscent of the human nuclear family. The Israelites are called "the sons of Yhwh" (Deut 14:1), implying that Yhwh is their father. In other words, the Israelites are not strangers. The true God has adopted them as his own children, just as he would later adopt others "led by the Spirit of God" (Rom 8:14–17), and thus he is their father and their God, having given them the right to become his children (John 1:12). As such, Israel's life then (and the lives of faithful believers today) is not to reflect the culture and worship of the

---

108. George A. F. Knight, *The Song of Moses: Theological Quarry* (Grand Rapids: Wm. B. Eerdmans, 1995), 43.

109. Hall, *Deuteronomy*, 471.

110. See Merrill, *Deuteronomy*, 413.

## Deuteronomy 32:10–14

From a rhetorical perspective, the extended metaphor "God is אָב" intends to persuade the original audience in various ways. First, by reminding the Israelites that Yhwh מָצָא them in the wilderness, the poet invites them to turn their hearts toward Yhwh. This reminder pertains to Israel's experience in the wilderness. Although the journey was very difficult, Yhwh protected his people all the way through the wilderness to lead them to the Promised Land (vv. 15–16). Moses reminds the Israelites that God encompassed them with protection and guarded them like the pupil of his eye. This act served to teach the Israelites to depend on Yhwh alone. Thus, remembering "all the way of the wilderness" would serve as the foundation for obedience to God's ways in the land of Canaan (Deut 5:33; cf. on the parental promise, 5:16). The poet invites his listeners to have a spirit of gratitude toward God because he alone found them when they were lost in this precarious condition.[111]

Second, the fatherhood metaphor functions to remind Israel of God's provision for them in the wilderness, an experience of which the Israelites were not to lose sight. According to the account in Deut 8, during their journey in the wilderness, the Israelites experienced hunger because they were not able to carry enough bread with them for the journey. But Yhwh miraculously provided for them by feeding them with manna (Exod 16:4) created especially for them during their hardship in the wilderness when they no longer had any bread of their own (Josh 5:12). Thus, the hardship experience was brought about by Yhwh to make Israel understand that man does not live by bread alone, but by what proceeds from God's mouth (Deut 8:3; cf. Lk 4:4; Jn 6:25–29). In short, God's provision of manna substituted for the Israelites' leaning on their own ability to feed themselves.

Nevertheless, God's provision for Israel in the wilderness included more than just *manna*. God also provided clothes for his people and supernaturally protected these clothes from decay (Deut 8:4). While testing his chosen

---

111. Lundbom, *Deuteronomy*, 879.

people, God wanted to make sure their basic needs were met. He provided clothes for them that did not wear out and kept their feet from swelling. It was thus necessary for Israel to go through that learning experience so that they would learn to live by the Words of the Covenant. However, in case Israel did not understand God's purpose in humbling them, Moses made it clear, saying, "Thus you are to know in your heart that Yhwh your God was disciplining you just as a man disciplines his son" (Deut 8:5).

Third, the metaphor "father" serves to remind the Israelites of God's provision for them in Transjordan. After leading the Israelites through the wilderness journey, Yhwh provided for them in abundance on the edge of the Promised Land. This would serve to teach them a lesson that God's purpose was to humble them and test them "to do good" for them "in the end" (Deut 8:11–16). All in all, God was preparing his people to remain loyal to him and to trust him in every regard when they came to enjoy the riches of the Promised Land.

Fourth, the metaphor serves to teach the Israelites the omnipotence of God, as he was the "father" who led his children through the wilderness journey (v. 12). Israel was enslaved and oppressed for about four hundred years under Pharaoh and the Egyptians (Gen 15:13; Exod 12:40–41). But God was their liberator. He delivered them from their bondage in Egypt and redeemed them "with an outstretched arm" (Exod 3:13–15; 6:6–7). Even after redeeming the Israelites from slavery in Egypt, their father Yhwh did not leave them on their own. He acted as their leader. He נָחָה "led" them "through the great and terrible wilderness with its fiery serpents and scorpions and thirsty ground" (Deut 8:15). As Knight points out regarding vv. 12–13, "This exultant couple of verses point to the wonder that only Yhwh of all the gods of mankind, and of all the religions of the world—including those that have persisted to this day—could have adopted and actually did adopt a repulsive and vicious child and then 'led' him in the sense that a shepherd guards and leads his sheep (Ps 103:1–5; 136)."[112] Thus, with all these benefits in mind, the poet uses the metaphor "father" in the Song as motivation to move the Israelites away from their rebellion.

---

112, Knight, *The Song of Moses*, 53.

THE FIRST ROCK SONG:
CONTRIBUTIONS OF DIVINE METAPHORS TO THE THEOLOGY OF THE SONG OF MOSES

## Theological Contributions of the Metaphor "God is a אָב"

There are several theological observations that can be drawn from the metaphor God is a אָב. The first theological truth of the metaphor is that Yhwh is Israel's father (vv. 6–9). In times past, Yhwh created the world. He gave an inheritance to all the nations (Deut 32:8) but has chosen Israel as his allotted inheritance to have a special relationship with them. That relationship was established after the Exodus event in which Yhwh killed all the firstborn of the Egyptians and spared the firstborn of Israel (Exod 12:29–32). This mighty, divine act was done to redeem the Israelites from slavery in Egypt and to grant them a privilege of serving as a "kingdom of priests" and a "holy nation" (Exod 19:3–6). Such a privilege made Israel a special nation out of all the nations of the earth. But with this privilege came responsibilities. Israel must obey the precepts of Yhwh, their father. As Hall explains, Moses mixed the metaphors "father" and "creator" to establish "the basis of Israel's unique relationship with God. He was her maker and lord, but also her concerned father. God's action toward her was one of love, concern, and patience but also discipline and correction."[113] Second, Yhwh is a father who cares about his own family (vv. 6–9). Although Yhwh was the one who created all the nations of the earth, he sovereignly chose Israel as his own family. As Cook rightly observes, "Israel here becomes the Lord's personal offspring and charge, unique within the span of the ages and the expanse of the globe."[114] As God's personal offspring, the Israelites were commanded to ask their biological fathers about the deeds of God in order to better understand him and to live in complete obedience to him (v. 6). As a father who cares about his family, Yhwh also sustains them (vv. 8–9). He gave inheritance to the nations, separated the peoples, and established boundaries for them. This shows that Yhwh values other nations and people groups as well (v. 8). As MacDonald states, "YHWH's election of Israel is presented within a universal horizon. Israel was chosen by YHWH from amongst the nations. Israel, therefore, occupies

---

113. Hall, *Deuteronomy*, 470.
114. Stephen L. Cook, *Reading Deuteronomy: A Literary and Theological Commentary* (Macon, GA: Smyth & Helwys, 2015), 233.

a privileged place among the nations, and obedience of YHWH's laws will bring further blessing."[115] When Yhwh found Israel (Jacob) in his precarious condition, Yhwh encompassed him with his protection and guarded him like the pupil of his eye (v. 10). Yhwh provided an instant help to Jacob because, as a good father, God loves his children.

The third theological truth of this fatherhood metaphor is that God is the protector and teacher of his people (v. 11). Like an eagle that stirs up its nest, Yhwh trained Israel to ensure his people could safely make their way through the wilderness. As Israel's trainer, Yhwh caused them to spend about forty years in the wilderness to humble them by allowing them to experience hardship (Deut 8:2). During their desert experience, the Israelites were disciplined by their father Yhwh. His discipline was a learning experience in which attentive nurture or care was provided to protect the Israelites from harm (Deut 8:4; 29:5). That is why Moses said that Yhwh disciplined Israel, just as a man disciplines his son. A man (or a father) is aware of his son's vulnerability. He knows the limited resources his son possesses. As parent, the man thus seeks to improve his child's resources and knowledge by training him in the ways he should go. Yhwh did just that for Israel. As Vogel asserts, "God (the eagle) selects the weakest of His young (Israel in Egypt), delivers them safely to freedom (the exodus), and begins a period of training in the desert until, possessing the Torah, the young can 'fly' by themselves."[116]

The fourth theological truth of the fatherhood metaphor is that Yhwh is Israel's provider. He fed his people honey and olive oil and a variety of foodstuffs. He led them through the wilderness and brought them to the Promised Land, a "land flowing with milk and honey," a truth emphasized over and over in the book of Deuteronomy (6:3; 11:9; 26:9; 27:3; 31:20). As Brown declares, "It was Yahweh, not Baal, the agricultural deity of the Canaanite people, who *fed him with the fruit of the fields... and the finest grains of wheat* (13–14)."[117] Furthermore, he writes, "In the fissures of Canaan's rocks, the bees were there to provide Israel with nourishing honey; the olive trees would flourish in

---

115. Nathan MacDonald, *Deuteronomy and the Meaning of "Monotheism"* (Tübingen: Mohr Siebeck, 2003), 180.

116. Dan Vogel, "Ambiguities of the Eagle," *JBQ* 26, no. 2 (1998): 87.

117. Brown, *The Message of Deuteronomy*, 298.

unlikely places, even where other trees would find insufficient soil to root."[118] Yhwh provides for his people in unlikely circumstances because he is their father, and as such, he cares for them.

In summary, the "father" imagery serves to remind the Israelites that God is their Father, the one who elected them as his own possession. Yhwh creates the Israelites as his own family (vv. 7–9). He supports and loves them (v. 10). He knows when his people experience difficult times and is always ready to help them (vv. 11–14). Unfortunately, God's people (Israel) fail to show gratitude to him. They do not act like his children; rather, they act corruptly toward him (v. 5). They acknowledge heathen gods as their father, gods that recently appeared (v. 17). They completely ignore the God who begot them and live as disobedient and senseless children (vv. 18, 28). Since Yhwh is holy and pure, he cannot tolerate sins. He will act as an avenging warrior to judge his people (vv. 22–25). Yet, because of his love and his mercy toward his covenant children, Yhwh will limit their judgment, render vengeance on his enemies (vv. 39–42), and make atonement for his people (v. 43).

---

118. Brown, *The Message of Deuteronomy*, 298.

*Chapter Five*

# Metaphor: God Is an Avenging Warrior

The Song of Moses portrays God as a warrior in three ways: (1) as a warrior fighting against his people when they reject him (vv. 22–25), (2) as a warrior fighting his foes in favor of his chosen people (vv. 39–42), and (3) as an avenging warrior making atonement for his people (v. 43). In analyzing some warrior metaphors in the book of Psalms, Brettler correctly states, "In determining whether a particular context presupposes the metaphor of YHWH as warrior, it is not sufficient to look for epithets such as גִּבּוֹר, "warrior" or אִישׁ מִלְחָמָה, "man of war," since a metaphor may be presupposed without its central term appearing explicitly."[1] Brettler's statement regarding the divine warrior in the Psalms is also true for the Song of Moses which does not use warrior epithets to depict Yhwh taking the role of a warrior. Therefore, in reading through the Song, interpreters must look for terms and features associated with warfare to identify and analyze the metaphor "God is a warrior." Fortunately, Trimm provides a list of common features found in divine warrior texts—apart from martial epithets, such as "man of war" (Exod 15:3) and "hero" (Ps 24:8)—that makes such a study easier.[2] His list includes the trembling of the earth and hills, and Yhwh's entrance into his sanctuary,

---

1. Marc Brettler, "Images of YHWH the Warrior in Psalms," in *Semeia* 61 (1993): 138.

2. Charlie Trimm, *"YHWH Fights for Them!": The Divine Warrior in the Exodus Narrative* (Piscataway, NJ: Gorgias Press, 2014), 36–42.

where he is proclaimed as king (Exod 15:1–18; Deut 33:2–5; Pss 24; 68:7–10 [6–9]; Hab 3:3–7).[3] The list also includes terms such as "arrows" (Hab 3:11), "swords, bow, and other deadly weapons" (Ps 7:13–14[12–13]), the presence of a heavenly army accompanying Yhwh to battle (Deut 33:2; Zech 14:5; Isa 13:13:3), anthropomorphic descriptions of God's powerful hand, arm, and breath (Exod 15:6, 10, 12, 16), and Yhwh's incomparability among the gods (Exod 15:11; Deut 33:26; 2 Sam 22:32) which leads the universe to recognize his power (Deut 33:28–29; 2 Sam 22:50–51).[4] This list will help us to identify the divine warrior motif in the Song of Moses.

It is noteworthy that Yhwh is not a warrior merely eager to fight for no apparent reason. The text makes it clear that Yhwh is an avenging warrior, one who inflicts vengeance on his people when they violate his covenant (vv. 19–25), and one who fights against his foes who hate him (vv. 39–42) in order to make atonement for his people (v. 43). This aligns with the major theme of the Song, namely, Yhwh is faithful, just, righteous, and perfect (v. 4). There is no injustice in him (v. 4).

# Identification and Interpretation of the Metaphor "God is an Avenging Warrior"

Since the poet used motifs associated with the role of a warrior, the first step leading to a good understanding of the metaphor is to look at the meaning of the term to see how God can be pictured as a warrior. To quote Ryken again, "Metaphor and simile first demand that we take the time to let the literal situation sink in. Then we must make a transfer of meaning(s) to the topic or experience the poem is talking about."[5] This entails defining the term and surveying a few other biblical texts to see how it is used literally.

---

3. Trimm, *YHWH Fights for Them*, 36–37.
4. Ibid.
5. Leland Ryken, *How to Read the Bible as Literature* (Grand Rapids: Zondervan, 1984), 95.

## Literal Meaning of the Term "Warrior"

The term "warrior" refers to someone who is mighty, one whose strength surpasses ordinary strength.[6] It describes the one who knows how to use the various weapons of war such as swords, spears, javelins, bows, and arrows, in combat.[7] The Hebrew Bible contains references of people who were regarded as warriors. For instance, when Gideon was beating out wheat in the wine press to save it from the Midianites, the angel of Yhwh appeared to him and said, "Yhwh is with you, O valiant warrior" (Judg 6:11-12). Another example of a warrior would be the man named Goliath, the one who was chosen to represent the Philistines in battle against Israel. In this story recorded in 1 Samuel, the Bible explains that Goliath was well prepared for the battle. He had a bronze helmet on his head and was clothed with scale-armor weighing five thousand shekels of bronze (1 Sam 17:4-5). He also had bronze greaves on his legs and a bronze javelin slung between his shoulders (v. 6). According to Longman and Reid, "Goliath was everything an ancient warrior could be: large, powerful, experienced, and armed with the most advanced weapons."[8]

## Divine Warrior in the Hebrew Bible

The Hebrew Bible is replete with examples of God being a warrior. As Klingbeil states, "The presence in the biblical texts of descriptions of hostile activities, implements of warfare, semantic domains of warfare, etc., are indicative of the utilization of the metaphor of God as warrior."[9] Similarly, Fredriksson

---

6. See William D. Mounce, *Complete Expository Dictionary of Old & New Testament Words* (Grand Rapids: Zondervan, 2006), 775.

7. For more details on the use of these military terms, see Philip J. King and Lawrence E. Stager, *Life in Biblical Israel* (Louisville: Westminster John Knox Press, 2001), 224-27.

8. Tremper Longman III and Daniel G. Reid, *God is a Warrior*, Studies in Old Testament Biblical Theology (Grand Rapids: Zondervan, 1995), 38.

9. Martin Klingbeil, *Yahweh Fighting from Heaven: God as Warrior and as God of Heaven in the Hebrew Psalter and Ancient Near Eastern Iconography*, OBO 169 (Göttingen: Vandenhoeck & Ruprecht, 1999), 2-3.

# THE FIRST ROCK SONG:
## Contributions of Divine Metaphors to the Theology of the Song of Moses

declares, "Kriegsgott ist Jahwe, wenn er in kriegerische Konflikte eingreift."[10] These authors have correctly recognized Yhwh's frequent involvement in battle in the Hebrew Bible. Sometimes he fights for his people (Exod 15:1–18); at other times he fights against them when they violate his covenantal precepts (Deut 32:19–25). The divine warrior motif is so frequent in the Hebrew Bible that space does not permit a discussion of all its occurrences. However, one important divine warrior text will be noted since it is the first biblical text in which God is portrayed as such.

The first explicit statement of God acting as a warrior is found in Exod 15:3 where God is called אִישׁ מִלְחָמָה a "warrior." In fact, this poetic text is perhaps the earliest text describing God as a warrior in the Hebrew Bible. As Longman correctly asserts, "This poem represents the first explicit statement of the warlike nature of God."[11] In this poem, Moses and the Israelites praise Yhwh for his actions against the Egyptians. This poem occurs at the point in the history of Israel when Yhwh followed plagues (signs and wonders) sent against Pharaoh and the Egyptians for not wanting to release the Israelites (Exod 7–12). After the tenth plague by which God killed all the firstborn of the Egyptians but spared the Israelite firstborn, Pharaoh finally decided to let the Israelites go their way. Afterwards, Yhwh not only instituted his regulations for his chosen people concerning how they were to serve him but also led them through their wilderness wandering (Exod 12–14). The Israelites were thus delivered out of the hand of the Egyptians as they witnessed Yhwh killing the Egyptians and "saw the Egyptians dead on the seashore" (Exod 14:30, ESV). Therefore, the people of God could not help but praise Yhwh to celebrate his magnificent power (Exod 15). As the Israelites celebrated God's power and their deliverance from the Egyptian army, they envisioned Yhwh as אִישׁ מִלְחָמָה "a man of war," or simply "a warrior" (Exod 15:3). After this description, the Israelites described how Yhwh was a warrior on their behalf: He threw Pharaoh's chariots and his army into the sea (v. 4) and allowed the depths to cover them (v. 5). He stretched out his right hand which held the weapons, and the earth swallowed the enemy

---

10. Henning Fredriksson, *Jahwe Als Krieger: Studien Zum Alttestamentlichen Gottesbild* (Lund: C. W. K. Gleerup, 1945), 1. This quote is translated as follows: "Yahweh is a warrior God when he intervenes in armed conflicts."

11. Longman and Reid, *God is a Warrior*, 32.

(v. 12). His strong arm caused the enemy to be defeated and be motionless as a stone (v. 16). This narrative sequence resembles other ancient Near Eastern divine warrior texts, such as *Enuma Elish* and the Baal Cycle, where Marduk and Baal respectively prevailed over their enemies, erected houses for themselves, and ruled as kings.[12] Yhwh's victory over the Egyptians causes the Israelites to remember him as their king, since he alone redeemed them from slavery in Egypt. This divine warrior text serves to demonstrate God's role as warrior. As such, it paves the way for the analysis of the imagery "God is a warrior" in the song that Moses sings in Deuteronomy.

## "Warrior" as a Metaphor for God in the Song of Moses

The first instance in which God is portrayed as taking the role of a warrior is in vv. 22–25. This strophe is part of the third stanza (vv. 19–25). In this strophe, the righteous God says he will execute judgment on his people for their foolishness. The Israelites have rejected the rock who begot them; they have forgotten the God who birthed them (v. 18). Therefore, Yhwh responds to the provocation of his people and says he will judge them measure for measure, treating them just as they treated him (vv. 19–21). God will use other nations as the primary instrument by which he will carry out his judgment on Israel (v. 21). Thus, as Deanna Thompson states, "This God not only fights on behalf of Israel but also disciplines his own people."[13]

## Deut 32:22–25 God is an Avenging Warrior: Identification and Interpretation

A כִּי־אֵשׁ קָדְחָה בְאַפִּי
B וַתִּיקַד עַד־שְׁאוֹל תַּחְתִּית
A וַתֹּאכַל אֶרֶץ וִיבֻלָהּ
B וַתְּלַהֵט מוֹסְדֵי הָרִים׃

---

12. See Trimm, *YHWH Fights for Them*, 18–19.

13. Deanna A. Thompson, *Deuteronomy: A Theological Commentary on the Bible* (Louisville: Westminster John Knox Press, 2014), 227.

## THE FIRST ROCK SONG:
### Contributions of Divine Metaphors to the Theology of the Song of Moses

²²For fire is kindled by my anger,
And burns to Sheol below,
And eats the land and its produce,
And flames the foundations of mountains.

A אַסְפֶּה עָלֵימוֹ רָעוֹת
B חִצַּי אֲכַלֶּה־בָּם:

²³I will gather upon them disasters;
My arrows I will use up on them.

A מְזֵי רָעָב
B וּלְחֻמֵי רֶשֶׁף
C וְקֶטֶב מְרִירִי
A וְשֶׁן־בְּהֵמוֹת אֲשַׁלַּח־בָּם
B עִם־חֲמַת זֹחֲלֵי עָפָר:

²⁴Weakened through famine
And consumed by flame
And bitter plague;
And the tooth of beasts I will turn loose on them;
With the venom of crawlers in the dust.

A מִחוּץ תְּשַׁכֶּל־חֶרֶב
B וּמֵחֲדָרִים אֵימָה
A גַּם־בָּחוּר גַּם־בְּתוּלָה
B יוֹנֵק עִם־אִישׁ שֵׂיבָה:

²⁵From outdoors the sword will bereave;
And from indoors, terror!
Both young man and young woman,
Infant with the man of gray hair.

Structurally, this strophe contains various levels of parallelism. In v. 22, lines A and B contain a lexical parallelism with "is ignited" and "burns." They are also parallel grammatically with the subject-verb-prepositional phrase versus no subject-verb-prepositional phrase. Line B expands line A, explaining to what extent Yhwh is angry with his people.

Lines A and B in the second bicolon are parallel lexically: "eats" parallels "flames," and "land and its produce" parallels "foundations of mountains." Line B serves to expand line A, going from land to foundations of mountains.

## Metaphor: God Is an Avenging Warrior

There is a parallelism between line B in the first bicolon and line B in the second, whereas "burns" and "flames" correspond to "Sheol" and "foundations of mountains." Thus, the parallelism in this verse describes the power of Yhwh to punish people. In fact, this verse begins with the כִּי particle which explains the course of action that Yhwh will undertake to provoke his people. The word אֵשׁ "fire" represents God's anger, and the word אַף translated as "anger" can also mean "nose."[14] The term שְׁאוֹל "Sheol" stands for grave; it is the place of destruction, a place for the dead. The verb וַתִּלְהַט "flame" is a hyperbole showing the extent of God's destruction.

In v. 23, lines A and B are parallel lexically. The phrase "gather upon them" corresponds to "use up on them" and "disasters" corresponds to "arrows." The lines are also parallel grammatically with an inverted order: verb-preposition-object versus object-verb-preposition. Line B specifies "arrows" as the instruments in line A that will be used for the disasters. Turning to the imagery of a consuming fire (v. 22), Yhwh now describes his wrath with the term חִצַּי (arrows). That metaphor presents Yhwh as a divine warrior, and as such, he will use his חִצַּי to fight against his enemies (as in Ps 7:13).

In v. 24, lines A, B and C of the tricolon are parallel lexically. The verb "weakened" in line A goes with the verb "consumed" in line B. The noun "famine" in line A corresponds with the noun "flame" in line B and "bitter plague" in line C. Moreover, lines B and C intensify line A, adding descriptions regarding the distress that encompasses the people. Lines A and B of the bicolon are also parallel lexically. The construct phrase "tooth of beasts" corresponds to the construct phrase "venom of crawlers." Thus, unlike human warriors, Yhwh can use any natural elements—such as hail, thunder, lightning, fire—and any other supernatural elements like disease or plague as weapons to combat his foes.[15] In the Song, the poet lists at least five different weapons Yhwh will use to carry out his avenging judgment (famine, consuming flame, bitter plague, the tooth of beasts, and the venom of crawlers).

In v. 25, lines A and B are parallel lexically with "outdoors" corresponding to "indoors" and "sword" corresponding to "terror." Lines A and B of this

---

14. BDB, 60.

15. For more on the use of natural and supernatural weapons by Yahweh, see Trimm, *YHWH Fights for Them*, 47–66.

# THE FIRST ROCK SONG:
## Contributions of Divine Metaphors to the Theology of the Song of Moses

first bicolon contain a merism with מִחוּץ "outdoors" and חֲדָרִים "indoors." This merism encompasses every place where someone would go to hide himself. Therefore, line B serves to intensify line A.

Lines A and B of the second bicolon are parallel grammatically with each colon having a noun pair that contrasts either in sex or in age. Additionally, the word pairs בָּחוּר "young man" and בְּתוּלָה "young woman" stand for all young people, no matter the sex to which they belong. Then, the merism of יוֹנֵק "infant," and the correspondings אִישׁ שֵׂיבָה "man of gray hair or elders," stand for everyone. Line B expands line A to include everyone in the judgment of God. Therefore, the parallelism explains that no one will be spared in God's judgment.

The structure demonstrates that it is God who will gather his various arrows and his sword to punish his people. This language, usually used of human warriors, is here used of God. Since God has the selection restrictions of *deity, spirit,* and warrior has the selection restrictions of *human, physical being,* the language is deviant or metaphorical. God is thus the tenor and warrior (avenging warrior) is the vehicle.

As Yhwh sentences Israel for rejecting him (vv. 19–21), he explains how his judgment will be carried out. He begins by saying כִּי־אֵשׁ קָדְחָה בְאַפִּי "For fire is kindled by my anger." The כִּי particle explains the course of action Yhwh will undertake to provoke and judge his people. God's anger will ignite אֵשׁ "fire." The term אֵשׁ "fire" denotes the physical manifestation of burning.[16] In ancient times, fire was often used to cook food (Ex 12:8; Is 44:15–16), to give people light to see (Is 50:11), to refine metals (Is 1:25; Mal 3:2–3), and to burn refuse (Lev 8:17).[17] It also served as an instrument of warfare with which conquerors burned down cities of those who were overcome in battle (Josh 6:24; 8:8; Judg 1:8; 1 Kgs 9:16). Metaphorically, אֵשׁ "fire" is used as an instrument of divine

---

16. See Chad Brand, Charles Draper, and Archie England, *Holman Illustrated Bible Dictionary* (Nashville: Holman Bible Publishers, 2003), 575.

17. See Leland Ryken, James C. Wilhoit, and Tremper Longman III, eds., *Dictionary of Biblical Imagery: An Encyclopedic Exploration of the Images, Symbols, Motifs, Metaphors, Figures of Speech and Literary Patterns of the Bible* (Downers Grove: InterVarsity Press, 1998), 286.

punishment.[18] This metaphor represents God's anger.[19] The verb קָדְחָה means "to flare" or "to kindle."[20] The word אַף "nose" in the same line can also mean "anger."[21] The idea is that Yhwh's anger will burn just like fire flares up. In the second poetic line, Yhwh says וַתִּיקַד עַד־שְׁאוֹל תַּחְתִּית "and burns to Sheol below." The verb וַתִּיקַד was used in the past to imply that God's punishment is a done deal; it will surely come to pass.[22] The word שְׁאוֹל "Sheol" stands for grave and represents the lowest and deepest place imaginable; it is the underworld, the realm of the dead.[23] Thus, as Bratcher and Hatton state, "God's fire burns all the way through the surface of the earth to the very bottom of the world of the dead."[24] Therefore, nobody can escape Yhwh's judgment. In the second bicolon, Yhwh says that his divine wrath: וַתֹּאכַל אֶרֶץ וִיבֻלָהּ וַתְּלַהֵט מוֹסְדֵי הָרִים "eats land and its produce, and flames the foundations of mountains." The verb וַתֹּאכַל "to eat" can be translated as "to consume" or "to devour" as in Deut 4:24 where Yhwh is spoken of as a consuming fire. In this case, the verb carries the idea of judgment and destruction. In the second line, the verb וַתְּלַהֵט "flame" is a hyperbole showing the extent of the destruction. It can also be translated as "to devour."[25] God says he will devour מוֹסְדֵי הָרִים "the foundations of mountains." According to Walton, Matthews, and Chavalas, "In the ancient worldview the netherworld, the realm of the dead, was down beneath the earth where one found the foundations of the mountains, especially those mountains that were believed to support the dome of the heavens."[26] This helps to explain the meaning of this

---

18. In the ancient Near East, especially in Canaanite mythology, fire was frequently used to represent weapons of the divine warrior. See Thomas W. Mann, "Pillar of Cloud in the Reed Sea Narrative," *JBL* 90 (1971):15–30.

19. Jeffrey H. Tigay, *Deuteronomy* (Philadelphia: Jewish Publication Society, 1996), 308.

20. *HALOT*, 3:1067.

21. BDB, 60.

22. Tigay, *Deuteronomy*, 308.

23. *HALOT*, 4:1369.

24. Robert G. Bratcher and Howard A. Hatton, *A Handbook on Deuteronomy* (New York: United Bible Societies, 2000), 549.

25. *HALOT*, 4:521.

26. John Walton, Victor H. Matthews, and Mark W. Chavalas, *The IVP Bible Background Commentary: Old Testament* (Downers Grove: InterVarsity Press, 2012), 206.

# THE FIRST ROCK SONG:
## Contributions of Divine Metaphors to the Theology of the Song of Moses

bicolon: Yhwh will use his divine power to destroy everything. His wrath will consume the earth and all its produce and will destroy even the deepest roots of the netherworld and the mountains.

In vv. 23-24, Yhwh spells out the various tools he will use to carry out his judgment: famine, disease, war, wild beasts, and venomous snakes. Walton et al note that these tools were the most common ones used by the ancient Near Eastern gods to punish their human subjects.[27] Despite this similarity, the difference between Yhwh and the pagan gods is worth noting. Yhwh always identifies or outlines the reasons for his avenging wrath, and he often uses his prophets to warn his people so that they can repent before he sends his judgment (2 Chr 24:19). However, the pagan gods do not spell out the reasons of their judgment.[28] They are taken by their adherents to punish their subjects due only to anger, and for no apparent reason, leaving their adherents to invent a reason for gods that do not reason. This capriciousness by pagan gods is exemplified in the prayer of the Hittite king named Mursilis, where he prayed asking the gods to lift up a violent plague that erupted in Hatti and decimated its population for over two decades.[29] After outlining various reasons as possible causes of the plague, Mursilis says,

> See! I am praying to thee, Hattian Storm-god, my lord. So save my life! If indeed it is for those reasons which I have mentioned that people are dying, — as soon as I set them right, let those that are still able to give sacrificial loaves and libations die no longer! If, on the other hand, people are dying for some other reason, either let me see it in a dream, or let it be found out by an oracle, or let a prophet declare it, or let all the priests find out by incubation whatever I suggest to them. Hattian Storm-god, my lord, save my life! Let the gods, my lords, prove their divine power! Let someone see it in a dream! For whatever reason people

---

27., Walton, Matthews, and Chavalas, *The IVP Bible Background Commentary: Old Testament*, 206.

28. Ibid.

29. See Kenton L. Sparks, *Ancient Texts for the Study of the Hebrew Bible: A Guide to the Background Literature* (Peabody, MA: Hendrickson Publishers, 2005), 114.

are dying, let that be found out! ... Hattian Storm-god, my lord, save my life! Let this plague abate again in the Hatti land!³⁰

Contrary to the pagan gods who are taken to be capricious in their judgment, Yhwh is always perfect and just (Deut 32:4). He always deals with people according to their deeds. Therefore, he always makes sure to warn his people of judgment so that he might be justified when he judges (Ps 51:4).

In the first line of v. 23, Yhwh says אַסְפֶּה עָלֵימוֹ רָעוֹת "I will gather upon them disasters." The word רָעָה is often translated as "evil" or "wickedness" as in Gen 6 where Moses says Yhwh saw the רָעָה "wickedness" of man, that it was great on the earth and that man's desire only inclined toward evil (Gen 6:5). However, in the Song of Moses, the word is best translated as "calamity" or "misfortunes" brought by Yhwh upon his people for disobedience. In the second line, Yhwh states חִצַּי אֲכַלֶּה־בָּם "My arrows I will use up on them."³¹ Yhwh would use arrows to shoot at his people because they rejected him in favor of false and powerless gods (32:15–18). This is emphasized by the verb כלה which means "to use" or "to use up." God will employ every arrow to judge his people. These arrows are outlined as famine, consuming flame, bitter plague, tooth of beasts, and venom of crawlers (v. 24).

In the first bicolon, Yhwh declares מְזֵי רָעָב וּלְחֻמֵי רֶשֶׁף "Weakened through famine and consumed by flame." The term רָעָב "famine" refers to hunger. The ancient Near Eastern nations, which essentially lived on agricultural products or trade, were often victims of climatic changes that caused poor harvests leading to a lack of food (Gen 41:29–31; 2 Kgs 4:38).³² Because such conditions were unpredictable, the Israelites understood the necessity of trusting God to provide for them (Ps 33:18–19; 37:19). In such a case, absence of famine was a blessing from Yahweh (Ezek 34:29). In the Song of Moses, famine is thus one of the weapons the warrior God promises to use against his people if they disobey his covenantal laws (Deut 28:48). God's people will be מְזֵי weak-

---

30. *ANET*, 394–96. See also *COS*, 1:28.

31. According to King and Stager, "Arrows were tipped with points made of extremely hard material: flint, bone, bronze, or iron. Hundreds of arrowheads were recovered at Lachich; most were iron, only a few bronze." King and Stager, *Life in Biblical Israel*, 227.

32. See Ibid., 267.

# THE FIRST ROCK SONG:
## Contributions of Divine Metaphors to the Theology of the Song of Moses

ened through severe famine, and this would cause them to turn from their evil ways. The term רֶשֶׁף translated here as "flame" refers to the "ravage of the plague" or "pestilence."[33] It is followed by the phrase וְקֶטֶב מְרִירִי "bitter plague," a reference to epidemic or natural disasters.[34] The terms וְשֶׁן־בְּהֵמוֹת "tooth of beasts" and חֲמַת זֹחֲלֵי "venom of crawlers" refer to wild beasts such as lions and bears, and to venomous snakes God will send to kill his people. These terms were figured on the list of curses the divine warrior threatened to bring upon his people when they disobeyed him (Deut 28:15–68).[35]

In v. 25, God describes the scope of his judgment. In the first bicolon, he says, מִחוּץ תְּשַׁכֶּל־חֶרֶב וּמֵחֲדָרִים אֵימָה "From outdoors the sword will bereave; and from indoors, terror." The terms "outdoors" and "indoors" together is a merism implying that God's judgment will be everywhere: both in the streets and in people's houses. The instrument God will place in the hand of the enemy to judge his people is חֶרֶב "the sword."[36] According to Ryken, "The sword was the most important weapon of warfare in the ancient Near East and in the Greco-Roman world. Ranging from sixteen inches to three feet in length, with one or both sides sharpened, this implement was used for thrusting and slashing opponents in armed conflicts."[37] In the Song, the sword symbolizes divine punishment (cf. Ps 7:13). God's judgment will be so severe that חֶרֶב "the sword" will kill those who are in the streets (in the battlefield) and אֵימָה "terror" or "fright" will kill those inside their homes. In this case, אֵימָה "terror" is another adversary like חֶרֶב "the sword." Both will be used in God's judgment, which will not exclude anyone. It will include גַּם־בָּחוּר גַּם־בְּתוּלָה "both young man and young woman" and יוֹנֵק עִם־אִישׁ שֵׂיבָה "infant with the man of gray hair," two additional merisms which imply that nobody will be spared.

---

33. *HALOT*, 3:1297.

34. *HALOT*, 2:1091.

35. See Trimm, *YHWH Fights for Them*, 236–37.

36. For more information on the term "sword," see Brand, Draper, and England, *Holman Illustrated Bible Dictionary*, 1542.

37. Ryken, Wilhoit, and Longman, *Dictionary of Biblical Imagery*, 835.

*Metaphor: God Is an Avenging Warrior*

# Deut 32:39–42 God is an Avenging Warrior: Identification and Interpretation

The second instance in which God is portrayed as a warrior is found in vv. 39–42. Although Yhwh threatened to destroy his chosen people because of their disobedience, he decided to limit their punishment. He would show compassion and mercy on them so that his enemies might not misinterpret his actions (vv. 26–31). Then, he would avenge Israel by punishing the nations, lest they boast in their accomplishments (vv. 32–35). God will demonstrate that he alone is God and that there are no other gods besides him (vv. 39–42).

A רְאוּ עַתָּה
B כִּי אֲנִי אֲנִי הוּא
A וְאֵין אֱלֹהִים עִמָּדִי
B אֲנִי אָמִית וַאֲחַיֶּה
A מָחַצְתִּי וַאֲנִי אֶרְפָּא
B וְאֵין מִיָּדִי מַצִּיל׃

<sup>39</sup>See now,
That I, I am he!
And there is no god besides me!
I myself kill and bring to life,
I wound and I myself heal,
And there is no one who can rescue from my hand.

A כִּי־אֶשָּׂא אֶל־שָׁמַיִם יָדִי
B וְאָמַרְתִּי חַי אָנֹכִי לְעֹלָם׃

<sup>40</sup>For I raise my hand to heaven;
And say, "Alive I am forever!

A אִם־שַׁנּוֹתִי בְּרַק חַרְבִּי
B וְתֹאחֵז בְּמִשְׁפָּט יָדִי
A אָשִׁיב נָקָם לְצָרָי
B וְלִמְשַׂנְאַי אֲשַׁלֵּם׃

<sup>41</sup>If I sharpen my flashing sword,
And my hand seizes in justice;
I will return vengeance on my enemies,
And to those who hate me I will repay.

# THE FIRST ROCK SONG:
## Contributions of Divine Metaphors to the Theology of the Song of Moses

A אַשְׁכִּיר חִצַּי מִדָּם
B וְחַרְבִּי תֹּאכַל בָּשָׂר
A מִדַּם חָלָל וְשִׁבְיָה
B מֵרֹאשׁ פַּרְעוֹת אוֹיֵב׃

⁴²I will make my arrows drunk from blood,
And my sword will eat flesh;
From the blood of the slain and the captive,
From the long-haired heads of the enemy."

Structurally, this stanza contains various levels of parallelism. In v. 39, the first line introduces this stanza as the climax of the Song, directing the listeners to pay attention to the concluding statements about Yhwh. Line B provides specific details about what the listeners are called to understand in line A. Moreover, the last two bicola serve to reinforce the first bicolon, namely that Yhwh is unique. In this verse, the repetition of the first-person pronoun אֲנִי אָנִי in the second line is an intensification which emphasizes that Yhwh alone is God. The words "kill and bring to life" in line B of the second bicolon parallel the words "wound and heal" in line A of the third bicolon. The first-person pronoun is repeated in the second line of the second bicolon to emphasize that Yhwh alone is the creator of life and everything else. The second line of the third bicolon further indicates that Yhwh will carry out his judgment and mercy without the help of anyone.

In v. 40, lines A and B are parallel semantically. In this verse, the poet depicts Yhwh taking an oath. Thus, line A serves to give the oath gesture and line B states the oath formula. In v. 41, line B of the first bicolon parallels line A lexically: "sharpen" corresponds with "seizes," and "flashing sword" corresponds with "justice." Line B amplifies line A by stating the reason why Yahweh prepares his flashing sword is to execute judgment. In the second bicolon, line B parallels line A lexically: "return vengeance" corresponds with "repay" in the first line, and "enemies" goes with "those who hate me" in the second.

In v. 42, line B is parallel with line A on a lexical level: "arrows" in the first line corresponds with "sword" in the second. Moreover, "drunk from blood" in the first line corresponds with "eat flesh" in the second line. In the second bicolon, the terms "blood of the slain" and "captive" in the first line corresponds with "long-haired heads and the enemy" in the second.

The poetic structure shows that the language of the stanza is metaphorical. Yhwh is the one who would use the arrows and swords to combat his foes. As such, there is a metaphor involved. God is the tenor and warrior is the vehicle.

The poetic unit describes the greatness of God in contrast to the impotence of the pagan deities who cannot save Israel from God's justice. In v. 39, Yhwh invites people to pay careful attention to his speech when he says רְאוּ עַתָּה "See now" followed by the statement כִּי אֲנִי אֲנִי הוּא "that I, I am he!" The clause רְאוּ עַתָּה "see now" is transitional as it shifts the focus from the pagan and powerless gods to the true God (Yhwh) who is all powerful. It also serves to direct the attention of the listeners to pay attention to the concluding statements about Yhwh. In the phrase אֲנִי אֲנִי הוּא, Yhwh utilizes the repetition of the first-person personal pronoun אֲנִי to focus on his uniqueness and singularity. As Lundbom explains, these duplicated personal pronouns serve to provide "emphasis and betray divine passion."[38] This emphatic pronoun is further highlighted by the statement וְאֵין אֱלֹהִים עִמָּדִי "there is no god besides me." The ancient Near Eastern world was polytheistic, that is, they believed in the worship of many gods. The idea behind this polytheistic view was that no one god possessed absolute power and wisdom; no one god possessed all knowledge.[39] Therefore, these gods were seen more like superhumans than sovereign deities, and the pagan people needed to serve more than one god in order for their needs to be met.[40] It was amid this pagan, polytheistic context that the true God (Yhwh) states וְאֵין אֱלֹהִים עִמָּדִי "there is no god besides me." This statement is to cause people to acknowledge Yhwh as the only true God because the other gods were merely idols who had no power (Deut 32:21).

Yhwh's incomparability is further explained by four prominent action verbs using a literary device called "antithesis."[41] Yhwh declares אֲנִי אָמִית וַאֲחַיֶּה "I myself kill and bring to life." The first-person pronoun is added for emphasis. The idea conveyed by this pronoun is that only Yhwh is omnipotent, not any

---

38. Jack R. Lundbom, *Deuteronomy: A Commentary* (Grand Rapids: Eerdmans, 2013), 899.

39. Mark F. Rooker, *The Ten Commandments: Ethics for the Twenty-First Century* (Nashville: B&H Publishing Group, 2010), 24.

40. Ibid.

41. See David L. Petersen and Kent Harold Richards, *Interpreting Hebrew Poetry* (Minneapolis: Fortress Press, 1992), 79.

## THE FIRST ROCK SONG:
### Contributions of Divine Metaphors to the Theology of the Song of Moses

other god. Yhwh declares that he is the one who kills. That is, God may choose to inflict death as a penalty for disobedience. Conversely, God says וַאֲחַיֶּה "I bring to life." The verb חָיָה "to live" means "to restore life" or "to refresh."[42] In this case, God has the power to kill people and restore them to life because he is the one who creates life (Gen 1:26). Yhwh also says, מָחַצְתִּי וַאֲנִי אֶרְפָּא "I wound and I myself heal." To wound means to "smite through" or "to shatter" and is commonly used for someone defeating his foes.[43] The verb רָפָא "to heal" is commonly used by a medical doctor or a physician treating patients' diseases.[44] Thus, Yhwh says he can wound people and then heal them (Jer 30:17). These four verbs describe Yhwh's activity as both the giver and the sustainer of life. Yhwh reminds his people of his incomparability. As Petersen and Richards correctly state, "A human can slay, but only a deity can bring to life. Moreover, if one human kills another, one does not expect the slayer even to attempt to heal, much less to revivify the corpse. Such bizarre things are possible only with Yhwh."[45] Therefore, Yhwh summarizes this thought by saying וְאֵין מִיָּדִי מַצִּיל "And there is no one who can rescue from my hand." The term יָד literally refers to the body part located at the end of the arm (Gen 3:22). It allows people to grasp certain objects (Ezek 39:9), to perform certain tasks (Judg 5:26), and to hold tools and weapons (Num 35:18). However, in the Song, the word "hand" is used metaphorically to evoke the image of power and strength.[46] The verb נָצַל "to rescue" means "to snatch away" or "to take away."[47] That is, when Yhwh decides to take a certain course of action such as punishing people, no god can dare stop him.[48]

In v. 40, the כִּי particle serves to introduce further details about the power of Yhwh. The verb נָשָׂא means "to lift" or "to carry" or "to raise."[49] The word יָד "hand" is a synecdoche used for God's power. The phrase כִּי־אֶשָּׂא אֶל־שָׁמַיִם יָדִי "for I raise my hand to heaven" is a picture of someone who swears an oath.[50]

---

42. GKC, 274.
43. BDB, 563.
44. BDB, 950–51.
45. Petersen and Richards, *Interpreting Hebrew Poetry*, 79.
46. Ryken, Wilhoit, and Longman, *Dictionary of Biblical Imagery*, 360–61.
47. BDB, 664.
48. See Tigay, *Deuteronomy*, 313.
49. BDB, 669.
50. In כִּי־אֶשָּׂא אֶל־שָׁמַיִם יָדִי וְאָמַרְתִּי "for I raise my hand to heaven and I say," the poet

## Metaphor: God Is an Avenging Warrior

It was a common practice in ancient times to lift the hand up when taking an oath to demonstrate one's intention to keep the prescribed obligations. This oath taking usually involved calling on the name of a god to attest to the oath transactions. For example, in an Egyptian prayer, a man says,

> I am a man who swore falsely by Ptah, lord of Maat,
> And he made me see darkness by day.
> I will declare his might to the fool and the wise,
> To the small and great:
> Beware of Ptah, Lord of Maat!
> Behold, he does not overlook anyone's deed!
> Refrain from uttering Ptah's name falsely.
> Lo, he who utters it falsely, lo he falls![51]

Since the ancient people believed that a god would punish those who violated the agreement, they were forced to tell the truth.[52] That is why, instead of being punished by a god for not abiding by the agreement stipulations, some would refrain from taking oaths even when they had to pay a fine. Amid this ancient Near Eastern belief and practice, the true God declares that he will raise his hand in heaven swearing that his intentions are true. The raising of hands thus serves as an authentic element for the oath formula חַי אָנֹכִי לְעֹלָם "As I live forever!" Yhwh swears by his own existence that he is the warrior who will defeat his enemy.

In v. 41, Yhwh provides details about how his judgment on the enemy will be carried out. Biddle is of the opinion that the enemy in view may be either Israel's enemies or Israel itself.[53] However, it is best to see the reference as

---

juxtaposes "the instantaneous perfective with the incipient-progressive non-perfective." Bruce K. Waltke and Michael Patrick O'Connor, *An Introduction to Biblical Hebrew Syntax* (Winona Lake, IN: Eisenbrauns, 1990), 500.

51. Miriam Lichtheim, *Ancient Egyptian Literature*, 3 vols. (Berkeley: University of California Press, 1973–80), 2:110.

52. Raymond Westbrook, ed., *A History of Ancient Near Eastern Law*, 2 vols. (Leiden; Boston: Brill, 2003), 1:12–13, 24, 34, 84; 2:831.

53. Mark Biddle, *Deuteronomy*, SHBC (Macon, GA: Smyth & Helwys, 2003), 480–81.

# THE FIRST ROCK SONG:
## Contributions of Divine Metaphors to the Theology of the Song of Moses

Israel's enemies since Yhwh has already stated that he will limit Israel's judgment to make sure the enemies do not misjudge God's actions (vv. 26–27). In the ancient Near Eastern world, it was believed that divine warriors fought for and rescued their vassals when they faced danger. Tiglath-pileser I, for example, fought against the Hattians after they attacked šubartu, an Assyrian vassal.[54] Here Yhwh will fight against his foes because they misunderstand his judgment on Israel.

Therefore, Yhwh begins by saying אִם־שַׁנּוֹתִי בְּרַק חַרְבִּי "If I sharpen my flashing sword." The אִם particle which follows the oath formula serves to introduce the content of the formula. Lundbom rightly observes the non-conditional function of the particle when he states, "The statement is not conditional."[55] Other scholars have made the same observation, which led them to translate the "if" by "when."[56] The verb שָׁנַן means "to whet" or "to sharpen."[57] It is used metaphorically to explain how Yhwh, as a divine warrior, prepares himself for battle; בְּרַק "flashing" denotes the power of the sword. Here again (as in vv. 22–25), the word "sword" is used metaphorically for God's judgment.[58] This idea is further exemplified in the second poetic line which states וְתֹאחֵז בְּמִשְׁפָּט יָדִי "and my hand seizes in justice." The verb אָחַז means "to grasp" or "to take hold of something."[59] The term יָד "hand"—the body part located at the end of the arm—is used anthropomorphically for Yhwh to describe God's action in taking the sword to judge his foes. As Thompson rightly declares, "Yahweh is pictured as a warrior arming himself for battle (Ex. 15:3; Is. 42:13; 59:17). He seizes *judgment* as though it were a weapon, in order to bring judgment on His adversaries."[60] In the second bicolon, the adversaries are described as Yhwh's adversaries, that is, those who hate him. The first line reads אָשִׁיב נָקָם לְצָרָי "I will return vengeance on my enemies." The verb שׁוּב in the Hiphil

---

54. RIMA 2:17.

55. Lundbom, *Deuteronomy*, 901.

56. See Tigay, *Deuteronomy*, 313; Bratcher and Hatton, *A Handbook on Deuteronomy*, 562.

57. BDB, 1041.

58. Ryken, Wilhoit, and Longman, *Dictionary of Biblical Imagery*, 835.

59. BDB, 28.

60. J. A. Thompson, *Deuteronomy: An Introduction and Commentary* (Downers Grove: InterVarsity Press, 1974), 303.

stem has the idea of bringing something back or restoring something in the sense of paying for a recompense.⁶¹ In the Song, it is used to demonstrate how Yhwh will take reprisals against his enemies.⁶² He will punish the adversaries according to what they deserve. The second line of this second bicolon further clarifies the meaning of the word "adversaries" in the first line by stating that God's adversaries are specifically those who שֹׂנֵא "hate" him (Deut 7:10). Thus, he says וְלִמְשַׂנְאַי אֲשַׁלֵּם "And to those who hate me I will repay." That is, Yhwh will punish his foes, and their punishment will be well merited because they hate him.

In v. 42, Yhwh describes the devastating effects of his judgment. He says אַשְׁכִּיר חִצַּי מִדָּם "I will make my arrows drunk from blood." The term דָּם "blood" denotes the red liquid circulating through the body of humans and other vertebrate animals.⁶³ In the second line of the first bicolon, the poet says וְחַרְבִּי תֹּאכַל בָּשָׂר "and my sword will eat flesh." The hendiadys created by the word pair מִדָּם "blood" and בָּשָׂר "flesh" represents the human body. Thus, Yhwh's judgment will be devastating because his arrows will bring the enemy down to a bloody defeat.⁶⁴ As Merrill states, "The Lord spoke of intoxicating his arrows with the blood of his enemies and eating up (*ʾākal*) their flesh with the sword."⁶⁵

In the second bicolon, the imagery of bloodshed continues. Yhwh says his judgment will be so severe that even the וְשִׁבְיָה "captives" will be slain. Furthermore, he states מֵרֹאשׁ פַּרְעוֹת אוֹיֵב "from the long-haired heads of the enemy." Scholars disagree on the correct lexical meaning of the word פַּרְעוֹת. Some translate it as "long-haired heads of the enemy" and take it in a literal sense to mean that dedicated warriors would not cut their hair during battle.⁶⁶ Others think the word might refer to the strength of a warrior. Lundbom states, "Long, loosely-hanging hair went with the Nazirite vow (Num 6:5; 1 Sam 1:11) and may also have been a mark of extraordinary strength and fight-

---

61. BDB, 999.

62. *HALOT*, 4:1432.

63. See *BEB*, 366.

64. Tigay, *Deuteronomy*, 313.

65. Eugene H. Merrill, *Deuteronomy*, NAC 4 (Nashville: Broadman & Holman Publishers, 1994), 424–25.

66. Bratcher and Hatton, *A Handbook on Deuteronomy*, 563.

# THE FIRST ROCK SONG:
## Contributions of Divine Metaphors to the Theology of the Song of Moses

ing ability (Judg 5:2) or both, as in the case of Samson (Judg 13:5; 16:17)".[67] Still other scholars express mixed feelings and are ready to go either way. As Thompson declares, "The long-haired heads of the enemy may be a poetic expression either for the great strength of the enemy displayed by long hair (cf. Samson), or for the fact that they were consecrated to battle. However, the term translated long-haired means either 'hair' or 'leader,' and the phrase may mean 'from the head of the leaders of the enemy.'"[68] While one cannot be dogmatic, it seems reasonable to take the phrase in a figurative sense considering the warfare context in which it occurs. In other words, the phrase explains that Yhwh will defeat even those enemies who have extraordinary strength. They will bow down before Yahweh. Thus, as Merrill states, "The thrust of the whole is complete devastation of all God's enemies from the lowliest to the most exalted."[69]

## Deut 32:43 God is an Avenging Warrior: Identification and Interpretation

A הַרְנִינוּ גוֹיִם עַמּוֹ
B כִּי דַם־עֲבָדָיו יִקּוֹם
A וְנָקָם יָשִׁיב לְצָרָיו
B וְכִפֶּר אַדְמָתוֹ עַמּוֹ׃

[43] Rejoice, O nations, with his people!
For the blood of his servants, he will avenge;
And vengeance he will return on his enemies,
And he will atone for his land and people.

In this verse, line A parallels line B in the first bicolon. Line B expands line A by stating the reason all nations are invited to join the Israelites in honoring God for avenging the blood of his servants (Israel). The imperative form הַרְנִינוּ of the verb רָנַן "rejoice" resembles the first word of the poem הַאֲזִינוּ both morphologically and phonologically. The idea conveyed here is that when people listen attentively to the message of God (Deut 32:1), they will be able to rejoice (Deut 32:43). The כִּי particle is a causal conjunction that introduces

---

67. Lundbom, *Deuteronomy*, 902. See also Tigay, *Deuteronomy*, 313.
68. Thompson, Deuteronomy: An Introduction and Commentary, 330.
69. Merrill, *Deuteronomy*, 424–25.

the reason to rejoice, namely that God will direct his vengeance toward those who hate him but will show compassion on his people. He will cleanse, reconcile, and forgive the sins and guilt of his people and restore them to fellowship with him. Line B in the second bicolon serves to complete the thoughts of line A. This verse forms an inclusio established by the word עַמּוֹ in the first and last lines. This inclusio serves to unite the final two bicola of the poem together.[70] It also presents the reader with a parallelism of opposites. As Vogel observes, "*Vengeance* become a cleans[ing] of the land; His *foes* will be exchanged for His *people* whose land it is."[71] The message is clear: the poet invites the nations to congratulate Israel because Israel's God (Yhwh) will return vengeance on his adversaries and restore his chosen people.

In this stanza (v. 43), the narrator comments on Yhwh's speech (vv. 39–42) as he invites the nations to join in the celebration of God's gracious acts on Israel's behalf.[72] He begins with an imperative: הַרְנִינוּ גוֹיִם עַמּוֹ "Rejoice, O nations, with his people!" The verb רָנַן means "to bring to exultation" or "to cause to exult."[73] The Gentile nations are invited to congratulate Israel on its deliverance and full restoration.[74] According to Driver, "Such an invitation, addressed to the nations, involves implicitly the prophetic truth that God's dealings with Israel have, indirectly, an interest and importance for the world at large."[75] Therefore, by inviting all nations to rejoice, the poet anticipates a day when all people groups will acknowledge the God of Israel as the only righteous judge. Merrill puts it this way, "By offering their ringing cry (thus *rānan*; 'rejoice') of endorsement, all peoples would finally realize that the judge of all the earth would do right."[76]

---

70. See Petersen and Richards, *Interpreting Hebrew Poetry*, 80.

71. Dan Vogel, "Moses as Poet: Ha'azinu as Poem," *JBQ* 31, no. 4 (2003): 7.

72. The textual critical problems of this verse are beyond the scope of this project. Like most English translations, this dissertation follows the MT in presenting two bicola for the Song. For more information about the verse's textual issues, see Daniel I. Block, *How I Love Your Torah, O LORD!* (Eugene, OR: Wipf and Stock Publishers, 2011), 185–88; Lundbom, *Deuteronomy*, 902–5; Tigay, *Deuteronomy*, 516–18.

73. HALOT, 4:1248.

74. See Tigay, *Deuteronomy*, 314.

75. S. R. Driver, *A Critical and Exegetical Commentary on Deuteronomy* (New York: Charles Scribner's Sons, 1895), 380.

76. Merrill, *Deuteronomy*, 425. (Of many biblical occurrences, Rev 5:9; 7:9

# THE FIRST ROCK SONG:
## Contributions of Divine Metaphors to the Theology of the Song of Moses

In the second poetic line of the first bicolon, Moses provides the rationale for the celebration: כִּי דַם־עֲבָדָיו יִקּוֹם "For the blood of his servants he will avenge" (cf. Rev 6:10; 16:4–7). The term "blood," which denotes the red liquid circulating in the body of human beings and other vertebrate animals, is used figuratively in the Song to refer to violent death.[77] The verb נָקַם means to avenge someone, to take revenge.[78] The concept of blood revenge reflects an ancient Near Eastern practice by which a close relative was responsible to punish a criminal in a way that would fit the crime.[79] However, restrictions were placed on this practice in ancient Israel.[80] An avenger of blood was required to act only in cases of premeditated murder but not of accidental killing.[81] That is why Moses commanded the Israelites to set aside cities of refuge to provide asylum for the man who committed manslaughter accidentally (Deut 4:-41:43; 19:1–13). The purpose was so that innocent blood might not be shed in the land which Yhwh was going to give Israel as inheritance. In the Song, however, the avenger of blood is Yhwh: דַם־עֲבָדָיו יִקּוֹם "He will avenge the blood of his servants." The phrase עֲבָדָיו "his servants" refers to Israel.[82] All those who slew the Israelites will suffer destruction at the hands of God. The second bicolon makes clear that those who slew Israel are not God's servants but rather לְצָרָיו "his enemies." Therefore, God will defeat them to avenge the blood of his servants. Not only will Yhwh avenge the blood of Israel, he will also וְכִפֶּר אַדְמָתוֹ עַמּוֹ "atone for his land and people." The piel כִּפֶּר means "to cover over" or "to pacify."[83] It is taken up from the concept of the Old Testament sacrificial worship in which the Israelites performed certain rituals to receive God's forgiveness (Lev 16:11–22). In the Song, God is the one who performs the rituals. As Thompson rightly says, "God is here pictured as clearing away and covering over the guilt of his people and his land. He not only forgives his people but covers over their offence."[84] The term אֲדָמָה "ground" or

most agree with this point.)

77. See *BEB*, 366.
78. *HALOT*, 3:721.
79. Ryken, Wilhoit, and Longman, *Dictionary of Biblical Imagery*, 64.
80. Ibid..
81. See *BEB*, 235.
82. See Merrill, *Deuteronomy*, 425.
83. BDB, 497.
84. Thompson, *Deuteronomy: An Introduction and Commentary*, 331.

"land" refers to the Promised Land.⁸⁵ It is a technical term used in the book of Deuteronomy for the land of promise.⁸⁶ God's atoning work is needed because the shedding of the blood pollutes the land. As Hall rightly says, "If blood had been shed on the land, then atonement was required by the one who shed the blood in order to cleanse the land (Num 35:33).⁸⁷ Thus, the poet says that Yhwh will make atonement for his people — a cleansing that will remove all impurity and guilt in Israel.

# Function of the Metaphor "God is an Avenging Warrior"

Arthurs makes the point, "Through metaphor, the communicator hopes to convey a rich concept, and yet he or she carries that concept through the back door of the receiver's mind."⁸⁸ Arthurs further notes that the rhetorical significance of indirect communication is subtle but profound. It prompts the sender and receiver to collaborate, producing the meaning the author intends.⁸⁹ If, as Arthurs observes, the poet carries the metaphorical concept in the back door of the receiver's mind, the task of the exegete is to bring that concept to the front so that readers or receivers may understand the poet's message. Therefore, this section will survey the function of the metaphor "God is a Warrior" to understand what the poet wanted to convey to his audience.

## Deut 32:22–25

The use of the divine warrior metaphor in this strophe serves to instill the proper fear of Yhwh as one who would avenge wrong against himself and his

---

85. *HALOT*, 1:15.

86. This meaning is also found in Deut 7:13; 11:17; 12:19; 21:1, 23; 26:2, 10; 28:4, 11, 18, 21, 33, 51, 63; 29:27; 30:9; and 31:20.

87. Hall, *Deuteronomy*, 481.

88. Jeffreys D. Arthurs, *Preaching with Variety: How to Re-create the Dynamics of Biblical Genres* (Grand Rapids: Kregel, 2007), 47.

89. Ibid.

## THE FIRST ROCK SONG:
### Contributions of Divine Metaphors to the Theology of the Song of Moses

people. The poet uses various terms to warn the Israelites about God's judgment and to urge them to display covenantal obedience. One of these terms is אֵשׁ "fire" which explains God's destructive power (Deut 4:24). In this Song, fire is used to emphasize God's judging power to eliminate unrighteousness and cleanse it from the earth (v. 22). Thus, the poet utilizes this imagery to remind the listeners of God's severity. Moreover, the term אֵשׁ "fire" used in conjunction with the divine warrior would serve to remind the Israelites of their fearful experience when Yhwh was about to deliver the Ten Commandments to them (Exod 20). At Mount Sinai, Yhwh asked Moses to gather the people to him so that they could hear his words to learn to fear him (Deut 4:10). As the Israelites assembled to hear the divine truths, they became afraid when they heard God's voice from the midst of the darkness, while the mountain was burning with אֵשׁ "fire" (Deut 5:22-23); the people stood at a distance while all the heads of their tribes and their elders came near to Moses urging him to serve as covenant mediator between God and His people (Deut 5:24-27). Thus, just as Yhwh's manifestation at Mount Sinai used fire to instill the proper fear of God in the Israelites, the divine warrior metaphor uses fire to call them to covenantal obedience.

The warrior metaphor also uses three other terms to call the Israelites to covenantal obedience. Each of these terms is associated with a divine benefit which serves to teach the Israelites about what they will miss when they disobey and reject their covenant God. The first term is רָעָב "famine," a shortage of food which Israel will experience as a divine punishment. The Israelites will no longer have foods in abundance because Yhwh, the divine warrior, will send a severe famine which will destroy all agricultural products. Thus, Israel's disobedience will cause God to withdraw his provision of food (vv. 10-14) and to replace it by famine (v. 24). The second term associated with a divine benefit is קֶטֶב "plague" or "pestilence" (v. 24). The God who led the Israelites through the desert land, encircled them, and guarded them like the pupil of his eye (v. 10) will now send plagues to punish them (v. 23-24). Thus, Israel's disobedience will cause God to withdraw his protection from his people. The third term is *sword* which symbolizes war (v. 25). Rather than fighting for his people as he has done before (Exod 15:1-21), he will now deliver them into the hand of the enemy in warfare (v. 25). Israel's disobedience will cause

God to withdraw his peace. Yhwh will use all these circumstances to restore his children to fellowship with him because, as a father, he cares for all his children (v. 6).

## Deut 32:39–42

The function of the divine warrior metaphor in this stanza is fourfold. First, it functions as the poem's climax to focus the attention of the audience on Yhwh. This is indicated by the emphatic expression רְאוּ עַתָּה כִּי אֲנִי אֲנִי הוּא "See now, that I, I am he." The emphatic pronoun is used twice to explain who God is. According to Brown, "The choice of the 'I am' title for God is sensitive and deliberate. The name recalls the burning bush incident and the saving event of the exodus. It reminds the Israelites of the Lord's mercy to sinful individuals as well as enslaved communities."[90]

Second, the divine warrior serves to display God's absolute power and sovereignty. This is highlighted by the emphatic declaration, וְאֵין אֱלֹהִים עִמָּדִי "There is no god besides me." The statement וְאֵין אֱלֹהִים עִמָּדִי reminds the Israelites of the covenant affirmation in the Decalogue. This statement is similar to the reading of the first commandment Yhwh reiterated to them through Moses in Deuteronomy, saying, "You shall have no other gods before me" (Deut 5:7). As Block writes, "Yahweh alone controls the events of history. He is sui generis; no one shares status or rank with him."[91] Thus, the poet uses the divine warrior metaphor to encourage the Israelites to be loyal to God as they recognize his uniqueness.

Third, the statement אֲנִי אָמִית וַאֲחַיֶּה מָחַצְתִּי וַאֲנִי אֶרְפָּא "I myself kill and bring life; I wound and I myself heal" invites the audience to manifest a greater appreciation for God's absolute power. Yhwh alone has supreme authority over life and death. If the Israelites have suffered, it is not because their enemies are powerful. Rather, it is the work of Yhwh who has the power to wound and to heal. Therefore, in due time, Yhwh will heal his people. When God decides to

---

90. Raymond Brown, *The Message of Deuteronomy: Not by Bread Alone* (Downers Grove: InterVarsity Press, 1993), 305.

91. Daniel I. Block, *Deuteronomy*, The NIV Application Commentary (Grand Rapids: Zondervan, 2012), 765.

heal his covenant people, nobody will be able to prevent it (Deut 32:39; cf. Hos 6:1–2; Job 5:18).

Fourth, Yhwh's oath in which he lifts his hand to heaven and declares חַי אָנֹכִי לְעֹלָם "As I live forever" invites the Israelites to trust in God's power. It guarantees that God will overcome the adversaries and restore his people.[92] This is reinforced by the terms "flashing," "sword," "arrows," and "blood" (vv. 41–42). The warrior metaphor also invites the Israelites to wait patiently on Yhwh as he deals with the enemies and restores peace within the Israelite community. As Block states, "The sword he [Yahweh] had placed in the hands of Israel's enemies (v. 25) he will now wield against them to restore ethical balance."[93]

## Deut 32:43

The function of this stanza is twofold. First, it serves to teach the Israelites about God's mercy. Although Yhwh will punish the Israelites, he will have mercy on them because they are his people and servants. This was meant to provide hope for Israel. Second, by telling Israel that Yhwh will forgive their sins and restore them, the poet reminds the people of God's relationship with them (Exod 19–20). Such a reminder serves to motivate Israel to covenant faithfulness as they look forward to a time when their covenant partner, Yhwh, will make atonement for them and restore them to fellowship with him.

# Theological Contributions of the Metaphor "God Is an Avenging Warrior"

The first theological point to be derived from the divine warrior metaphor is that God is wrathful (vv. 22–25): Yhwh judges the sins of his people. As a just and blameless God, Yhwh cannot tolerate sin (v. 4). That is why he always warns his people of his judgment.

The second theological truth of this divine warrior metaphor is that God is personal. In v. 39, Yhwh says אֲנִי אֲנִי הוּא "I, I am he." This statement demon-

---

92. Brown, *The Message of Deuteronomy*, 305; Block, *Deuteronomy*, 766.
93. Block, *Deuteronomy*, 766.

strates that Yhwh is personal. Speaking about this attribute of God, Grudem declares, "He [God] interacts with us as a person, and we can relate to him as persons. We can pray to him, worship him, obey him, and love him, and he can speak to us, rejoice in us, and love us."[94]

Not only is God personal, but also his person is to be worshiped monotheistically.[95] In v. 39, God says וְאֵין אֱלֹהִים עִמָּדִי "And there is no god besides me." According to House, "This declaration separates the Lord from so-called gods who have no power to save their worshipers."[96] This uniqueness and exclusivity of God was already emphasized in the book of Deuteronomy where Moses told the Israelites that Yhwh their God is one (Deut 6:4). Goldingay writes, "The First Testament makes exclusive claims for Yhwh and for Israelite faith. Only Yhwh has real power; the Babylonians' belief about Marduk are fundamentally false. There is no hope for people who insist on continuing to adhere to this religion rather than accept Yhwh's claims."[97]

The fourth theological point that can be drawn from the divine warrior metaphor is that Yhwh is sovereign. This is reflected in God's own statement in the Song where he says אֲנִי אָמִית וַאֲחַיֶּה מָחַצְתִּי וַאֲנִי אֶרְפָּא "I myself kill and bring to life; I wound and I myself heal" (v. 39). This is in stark contrast to the pagan gods who operate at the mercy of nature. For instance, in the Epic of Gilgamesh, one section reads,

> The gods were frightened by the deluge,
> And, shrinking back, they ascended to the heaven of Anu,
> The gods cowered like dogs

---

94. Wayne Grudem, *Systematic Theology: An Introduction to Biblical Doctrine* (Grand Rapids: Zondervan, 2000), 167.

95. Oswalt says, "The single most obvious difference between the thought of the Old Testament and that of Israel's neighbors is monotheism. The Old Testament vehemently and continuously insists that Yahweh is one and that no other being is in the same category with him." John N. Oswalt, *The Bible among the Myths: Unique Revelation or Just Ancient Literature?* (Grand Rapids: Zondervan, 2009), 64.

96. Paul R. House, *Old Testament Theology* (Downers Grove: InterVarsity Press, 1998), 97.

97. John Goldingay, *Israel's Faith*, vol. 2 of *Old Testament Theology* (Downers Grove, IL: InterVarsity Press, 2006), 30.

## THE FIRST ROCK SONG:
### Contributions of Divine Metaphors to the Theology of the Song of Moses

> Crouched against the outer wall...
> The gods, all humbled, sit and weep.[98]

The fifth theological truth of this divine warrior metaphor is that God is a healer (v. 39). After redeeming the Israelites from the hand of Pharaoh in Egypt, Yhwh made a strong promise to them. He said, "If you will listen carefully to the voice of Yhwh your God, and do what is right in his sight, and give heed to his commandment and keep all his statutes, I will not bring upon you any of the diseases that I brought upon the Egyptians; for I am Yhwh, your healer" (Exod 15:26). This conditional statement presents God as a medical doctor who has the power to heal people. As Brueggemann notes, "Although not a major image for Yahweh, the doctor image occurs in Israel's speech at pivotal places, witnessing to Yahweh's capacity to restore, rehabilitate, and repair all that has been damaged or hurt."[99] Furthermore, he writes, "The claim that Yahweh has a healing capacity, however, is not limited to restoration of what Yahweh has damaged. Yahweh's healing capacity pertains to whatever damage has been done, by whatever agent."[100]

The sixth theological point of this warrior metaphor is that God is all-powerful. This is emphasized by God's own statement when he says אֲנִי אָמִית וַאֲחַיֶּה מָחַצְתִּי וַאֲנִי אֶרְפָּא "I myself kill and bring to life; I wound and I myself heal" (v. 39). Yhwh is the one who controls death and life. He will render vengeance on all his adversaries and will demonstrate the total weakness of their gods (vv. 40–42). As Hall boldly declares, "God's vindication also demonstrated the absoluteness of his power and authority. No god could stand up to him. Beside him there was no other (4:35, 39, 5:7; 7:9).... From the practical level of everyday life to national fortunes he is the only active and effective God because he is the only One."[101]

The seventh theological truth of this warrior imagery is that God is a righteous redeemer (v. 43). God redeemed Israel from slavery in Egypt and led the

---

98. *ANET*, 94.

99. Brueggemann, *Theology of the Old Testament*, 252.

100. Ibid.

101. Gary H. Hall, *Deuteronomy*, The College Press NIV Commentary (Joplin, MO: College Press, 2000), 480.

nation through the wilderness wandering (Deut 7:8; 9:26). He chose Israel out of all the nations of the earth and established a special covenant relationship with the nation (Exod 19:4-6; Deut 32:9). Despite of all God's goodness and benefactions to Israel, they reject him in favor of pagan gods (v. 18). For this reason, God will use foreign nations to carry out his plan of judgment on his chosen people (vv. 20-25). However, God will also limit Israel's judgment to render vengeance on his enemies and make atonement for Israel in the future (v. 43).

In sum, through the avenging divine warrior motif, the poet has spelled out several important truths about God to encourage the Israelites to live in perfect obedience to God. The poet tells Israel that God is wrathful, sovereign, personal, and unique. He is the one who kills and brings to life. He is a righteous redeemer. This message was given to the Israelites to teach them about God's sovereignty over the world he created. Such a powerful message was meant to go beyond Israel, as the last verse makes clear. One day all nations and people groups will acknowledge Yhwh as the only sovereign God as he deals with each person according to his/her deeds. This message also offered hope to Israel, reminding them of God's faithfulness to his promises and his wonderful grace and mercy to those with whom he has a covenant relationship.

*Chapter Six*

# Conclusion and Recommendations for Further Study

The purpose of this dissertation has been to undertake a biblical theological examination of three divine metaphors in the Song of Moses: God is a rock, God is a father, and God is a warrior. These metaphors have shed light on several truths. Thus, it is important to summarize the findings of this research and to propose some avenues for further study in the Song.

## Conclusion

This investigation of the divine metaphors in the Song of Moses has given rise to multiple observations. First, it demonstrates that it is possible to discern the intention of the original author even in metaphoric utterance by carefully looking at the biblical text. Such a careful look demands usage of a good method such as a text-based approach to study the metaphors.

To demonstrate the intention of the original author in the Song, this project surveyed various theoretical perspectives on metaphor, notably the works of Aristotle, I. A. Richards, Max Black, Lakoff and Johnson, and Janet Soskice, before providing its own definition. Next, it used Kittay's method to distinguish the metaphor from other tropes such as metonymy, hyperbole, and synecdoche. Kittay's model involves looking at the literal meaning of the vehicle to see if there is some level of incongruity. If there is an incongruity and the speaker is competent, then a metaphor is in view. Finally, to study the

## THE FIRST ROCK SONG:
### Contributions of Divine Metaphors to the Theology of the Song of Moses

metaphor, this dissertation followed a text-based approach, meaning that the poem is analyzed as part of its surrounding context. This project then looked at the rhetorical function of the metaphors to see how the original author intended to persuade his audience. Finally, the project drew theological conclusions regarding the use of each divine metaphor.

This study has shown that each metaphor portrays Yhwh in a unique way. Beginning with the metaphor "God is a rock," the poet invites his audience to ascribe greatness to Yhwh because he is perfect in all his ways (Deut 32:4a). He possesses all exceptional qualities and is unimpaired. He is a just God, one who executes justice with equity (v. 4b). He is faithful in all his dealings with humanity (v. 4c), and he is righteous and upright (v. 4d). God's deeds always show his integrity. The rock metaphor also demonstrates that Yhwh is a generous provider. He provides abundantly for his people (v. 15a). Israel's rock is the sole creator (v. 15c, 18). He is the savior who rescued Israel from slavery in Egypt (v. 15d) and is the ultimate judge of his people (v. 30). He is unique; he is the only God who provides full security and protection for his people (v. 37).

The fatherhood metaphor depicts God as the universal father who created heavens and earth without any outside help (vv. 6–9). As a father, Yhwh cares about his own family; he loves and sustains his people (vv. 6–10). He is their protector and trainer. He protects them just like an eagle spread out his wings (vv. 11–13). Yhwh provides abundantly for his people because he is one who cares (v. 14).

Lastly, the divine warrior metaphor portrays God in various ways. He is wrathful. Because of his holiness, he must judge sin (vv. 22–25). God is also personal (v. 39). His people can fellowship with him in prayer and in worship. God is unique. He is to be worshiped monotheistically. He alone, by his sovereignty, creates and sustains everything. Yhwh is also a healer, the one who kills and restores to life. As the sole cause of everything that happens in his world, Yhwh can heal people and restore them back to good health (v. 39). Yhwh is the righteous redeemer who avenges the blood of his servants to make atonement for them (v. 43).

These divine metaphors in the Song of Moses work together to teach the Israelites about the qualities of Yhwh and the kind of behavior they are to have toward him. The whole idea of the Song is that, as an immovable rock, Yhwh will not change. He will remain faithful and perfect in all his ways. Because Yhwh is a faithful and generous father, he will always provide for his children. Finally, as a warrior, Yhwh will lead Israel's army to fight for them against their foes. God will ultimately avenge his enemies, forgive Israel, and restore them to fellowship with him.

While the poet uses the divine metaphors to teach the Israelites about the qualities of Yhwh, he presents an honest assessment of Israel's condition. First, the metaphors have repeatedly shown that, whereas Yhwh is faithful, just, and perfect, the Israelites are faithless and rebellious (vv. 4–5). They refuse to give undivided allegiance to their father, the one who created them and provided for them in abundance (vv. 6–14). The Israelites are ungrateful and disloyal (v. 15). Instead of obeying God's covenantal precepts, the Israelites abandon God and turn to idolatry, thus ascribing to heathen gods distinct qualities that belong exclusively to Yhwh (vv. 15–18). In living the idolatrous life, the Israelites dishonor God's person, ignore his word and provisions, and provoke him to wrath and jealousy (vv. 19–22). They live as disobedient and loveless children who forget all they owe to their father, Yhwh (vv. 19–21). They are also a senseless nation with no wisdom or discernment in them (v. 28). They have made the wrong choice by forgetting their sole father to turn to worthless and demonic gods (vv. 28–33). Second, the divine metaphors demonstrate that the Israelites are unable to restore themselves. Although they turn to pagan gods for help, they are still desperate without Yhwh because the other gods are insignificant (vv. 21, 37, and 38). Therefore, the Israelites will be severely judged by God. But God's judgment will not be the final word. The Israelites will obtain the mercy of God who will bring reconciliation and hope to them when he atones for the land and the people.

# Recommendations for Further Study

Although this dissertation has examined the rhetorical effects and theological contributions of the divine metaphors of the Song of Moses, much remains to be done. Three primary recommendations stem from this research. First, it would be profitable to employ the methodology used in this project to study the similes of the Song. Since similes are used throughout the poem (vv. 2, 10, 11, 31), this approach would help to uncover their rhetorical effects and their contribution to the theology of the poem.

Second, it would be beneficial to do an in-depth study of the four rhetorical questions of the Song (vv. 6, 30, 34, 37). Since rhetorical questions often occur in strategic collocations to begin a discourse unit, continue the unit, or end the unit, it would be essential to see their rhetorical function and theological contributions in the Song.

Third, since the Song of Moses was to serve as didactic material to motivate Israel's future behavior and to witness for God against his faithless people when they disobey him, an important task would be to study the allusions and quotations of the Song in later revelations in the history of Israel. Doing so would help to see how much later prophets relied on the Song in their teaching. It would also be useful to employ the linguistic approach utilized in this research to study the divine metaphor "rock" in the other books of the Hebrew Bible, especially in the book of Psalms and in Isaiah where the term is frequently used.

# Bibliography

Aaron, David. *Biblical Ambiguities: Metaphor, Semantics, and Divine Imagery*. Brill Reference Library of Ancient Judaism 4. Leiden: Brill Academic Publishers, 2001.

Abel, Félix-Marie. *Géographie de la Palestine*. Vol. 1. Paris: Gabalda, 1933.

Adler, Elaine June. "The Background for the Metaphor of Covenant as Marriage in the Hebrew Bible." PhD diss., University of California, Berkeley, 1989.

Aharoni, Yohanan. *The Land of the Bible: A Historical Geography*. Revised and Enlarged Edition. Translated by Anson Rainey. Philadelphia: Westminster, 1979.

Albright, William F. *Yahweh and the Gods of Canaan: A Historical Analysis of Two Contrasting Faiths*. Winona Lake, IN: Eisenbrauns, 1994.

Alday, Carrillo S. *El Cántico de Moisés (Dt 32)*. Madrid: Instituto Francisco Suarez, 1970.

Alexander, T. Desmond. *From Paradise to the Promised Land: An Introduction to the Pentateuch*. 3rd ed. Grand Rapids: Baker Academic, 2012.

Allen, David. "'Paul Donning Mosaic Garb?' The Use of Deuteronomy 32 in Philippians 2:12–18." *European Journal of Theology* 26, no. 2 (October 2017): 135–43.

# THE FIRST ROCK SONG:
## Contributions of Divine Metaphors to the Theology of the Song of Moses

Alt, A., O. Eissfeldt, P. Kahle, Rudodlf Kittel, and Karl Elliger, eds. *Biblia Hebraica Stuttgartensia*. Editio quarta emendata. Stuttgart: Deutsche Bibelgesellsschaft, 1990.

Alter, Robert. *The Art of Biblical Narrative*. New York: Basic Books, 1981.

———. *The Art of Biblical Poetry*. Rev. and updated ed. New York: Basic Books, 2011.

———. *The Five Books of Moses: A Translation with Commentary*. New York: W. W. Norton, 2004.

Anderson, Jeff S. "The Social Function of Curses in the Hebrew Bible." *Zeitschrift für die Alttestamentliche Wissenschaft* 110 (1998): 223–37.

Archer, Gleason L. *A Survey of Old Testament Introduction*. Rev. and expanded ed. Chicago: Moody Press, 1994.

Aristotle. *Poetics*. Vol. 23 in *Aristotle in 23 Volumes*. Translated by W. H. Fyfe. Medford, MA: Harvard University Press, 1932.

Arminion, Blaise. *Sur la lyre à dix cordes: À l'écoute des psaumes au rythme des Exercises de Saint Ignace*. Montréal: Bellarmin, 1990.

Arnold, Bill, and John H. Choi. *A Guide to Biblical Hebrew Syntax*. Cambridge: Cambridge University, 2003.

Arthurs, Jeffrey D. *Preaching with Variety: How to Re-create the Dynamics of Biblical Genres*. Grand Rapids: Kregel Publications, 2007.

Askénazi, Léon. *La Parole et l'Écrit*. Vol. 1. Paris: Albin Michel, 1999.

Audirsch, Jeffrey G. *The Legislative Themes of Centralization: From Mandate to Demise*. Eugene, OR: Pickwick, 2014.

Avalos, Hector. *Fighting Words: The Origins of Religious Violence*. Amherst: Prometheus, 2005.

Baker, David W. *Nahum, Habakkuk and Zephaniah: An Introduction and Commentary*. Tyndale Old Testament Commentaries 27. Downers Grove: InterVarsity Press, 1988.

Ballard, Harold, Jr. *The Divine Warrior Motif in the Psalms*. BIBAL Dissertation Series 6. Richland Hills, TX: BIBAL, 1999.

Barker, Kenneth L., and D. Waylon Bailey. *Micah, Nahum, Habakkuk, Zephaniah*. New American Commentary 20. Nashville: Broadman & Holman Publishers, 1999.

Barr, James. *The Semantics of Biblical Language*. London: Oxford University Press, 1961.

Barré, Michael L. "'My Strength and My Song' in Exodus 15:2." *Catholic Biblical Quarterly* 54 (1992):623–37.

Basson, Alec. *Divine Metaphors in Selected Hebrew Psalms of Lamentation*. Tübingen: Mohr Siebeck, 2006.

———. "'You Are My Rock and Fortress.' Refuge Metaphors in Psalm 31. A Perspective from Cognitive Metaphor Theory." *Acta Theologica* 25, no. 2 (2005): 1–17.

Bensussan, Gérard. *Qu'est-ce La Philosophie Juive?* Paris: Desclée de Brouwer, 2003.

Bergen, Robert D. *1, 2 Samuel*. The New American Commentary 7. Nashville: Broadman & Holman Publishers, 1996.

Bergey, Ronald. "Le Cantique de Moïse — Son Reflet dans le Prisme du Canon des Ecritures." *La Revue réformée* 223, no. 3 (2003).

Berlin, Adele. *The Dynamics of Biblical Parallelism*. Rev. and expanded ed. Grand Rapids: Eerdmans, 2008.

———. "On the Meaning of *rb*." *Journal of Biblical Literature* 100 (1981):90–103.

———. *Poetics and Interpretation of Biblical Narrative*. Winona Lake: Eisenbrauns, 1994.

———. "The Role of Metaphor." Pages 25–36 in *Congress Volume: Cambridge 1995*. Edited by J. A. Emerton. Leiden: Brill, 1997.

Biddle, Mark E. *Deuteronomy*. Smyth & Helwys Bible Commentary. Macon, GA: Smyth & Helwys, 2003.

Black, Max. "Metaphor." *Proceedings of the Aristotelian Society*, New Series, 55 (1954): 273–94.

———. *Models and Metaphors: Studies in Language and Philosophy*. Ithaca: Cornell University Press, 1962.

Block, Daniel I. *Deuteronomy*. The NIV Application Commentary. Grand Rapids: Zondervan, 2012.

———. *The Gospel According to Moses: Theological and Ethical Reflections on the Book of Deuteronomy*. Eugene, OR: Cascade Books, 2012.

———. *How I Love Your Torah, O LORD!* Eugene, OR: Wipf and Stock Publishers, 2011.

———. *Judges, Ruth*. New American Commentary 6. Nashville: Broadman & Holman Publishers, 1999.

———. "Recovering the Voice of Moses: The Genesis of Deuteronomy." *Journal of the Evangelical Theological Society* 44, no. 3 (September 2001): 385–408.

Block, Daniel I., and Richard L. Schultz. *Sepher Torath Mosheh: Studies in the Composition and Interpretation of Deuteronomy*. Peabody, MA: Hendrickson Publishers, 2017.

Boadt, Lawrence. "Reflections on the Study of Hebrew Poetry Today." *Concordia Journal* (1998): 156–63.

Bobbs, Allsopp F. W. *On Biblical Poetry*. New York: Oxford University Press, 2015.

Bogaert, P-M. "Les trois rédactions conservées et la forme originale de l'envoi du Cantique de Moïse (Dt 32, 43)." Pages 329–40 in *Das Deuteronomium, Entstehung, Gestalt und Botschaft*. Edited by N. Lohfink. Bibliotheca Ephemeridum Theologicarum Lovaniensium 68. Leuven: University Press, 1985.

Booth, Wayne C. *The Rhetoric of RHETORIC: The Quest for Effective Communication*. Malden, MA: Blackwell Publishing, 2004.

Boston, James A. "The Wisdom Influence upon the Song of Moses." *Journal of Biblical Literature* 87, no. 2 (1968): 198–202.

Botterweck, Johannes G., Helmer Ringgren, and Heinz-Jozef Fabry, eds. *Theological Dictionary of the Old Testament*. Translated by Douglas W. Stott. Grand Rapids: Wm. B. Eerdmans, 2003.

Bourguet, Daniel. *Des Métaphores de Jérémie*. Paris: Librairie Lecoffre, 1987.

Brand, Chad, Charles Draper, and Archie England. *Holman Illustrated Bible Dictionary*. Nashville: Holman Bible Publishers, 2003.

Bratcher, Robert G., and Howard A. Hatton. *A Handbook on Deuteronomy*. New York: United Bible Societies, 2000.

Braulik, Georg. *Deuteronomium*. Vol. 2 (16, 18–34, 12). Neue Echter Bibel 28. Würzburg: Echter, 1992.

Brettler, Marc Zvi. *God Is King: Understanding an Israelite Metaphor*. Journal for the Study of the Old Testament Supplement Series 76. Sheffield, UK: JSOT Press, 1989.

———. "Images of YHWH the Warrior in Psalms." *Semeia* 61 (1993): 135–65.

———. "Incompatible Metaphors for YHWH in Isaiah 40–66." *Journal for the Study of the Old Testament* 78 (1998): 97–120.

## THE FIRST ROCK SONG:
### Contributions of Divine Metaphors to the Theology of the Song of Moses

Britt, Brian M. "Deuteronomy 31–32 as a Textual Memorial." *Biblical Interpretation* 8, no. 4 (2000): 358–74. http://dx.doi.org/10.1163/156851500750118962.

———. "Rewriting Moses: The Narrative Eclipse of the Text." *Journal for the Study of the Old Testament* 402 (2004): 150.

Brown, F., S. Driver, and C. Briggs. *The Brown-Driver-Briggs Hebrew and English Lexicon*. Peabody, MA: Hendrickson Publishers, 2003.

Brown, Raymond. *The Message of Deuteronomy: Not by Bread Alone*. Leicester, UK: InterVarsity Press, 1993.

Brown, William P. "The Didactic Power of Metaphor in the Aphoristic Sayings of Proverbs." *JSOT* 29 (2004): 133–54.

———. *Seeing the Psalms: A Theology of Metaphor*. Louisville: John Knox Press, 2002.

Brueggemann, Walter. *Deuteronomy*. Abingdon Old Testament Commentaries. Nashville: Abingdon Press, 2001.

———. *Theology of the Old Testament: Testimony, Dispute, Advocacy*. Minneapolis: Fortress Press, 1997.

Buis, Pierre, and Jacques Leclercq. *Le Deutéronome*. Paris: Librairie Lecoffre, 1963.

Bullinger, Ethelbert William. *Figures of Speech Used in the Bible, Explained and Illustrated*. Grand Rapids: Baker Book House, 1968.

Butts, Aaron M. "Reduplicated Nominal Patterns in Semitic." *Journal of the American Oriental Society* 131 (2011): 83–108.

Caird, G. B. *The Language and Imagery of the Bible*. London: Duckworth, 1980.

Cairns, Ian. *Word and Presence: A Commentary on the Book of Deuteronomy.* International Theological Commentary. Grand Rapids: Wm. B. Eerdmans, 1992.

Cassuto, Umberto. *Bible.* Translated by Israel Abrahams. Vol. 1 in *Biblical and Oriental Studies.* Jerusalem: Magnes Press, 1973.

Causse, Antonin. *Les Plus Vieux Chants de la Bible.* Etudes d'Histoire et de Philosophie Religieuse 14. Paris: Alcan, 1926.

Charbonnel, Nanine. *Les Aventures de la Métaphore.* Strasbourg: Presses Universitaires de Strasbourg, 1991.

Chau, Kevin D. "A Poetics for Metaphor in Biblical Hebrew Poetry." PhD diss., University of Wisconsin at Madison, 2011.

Childs, Brevard S. *The Book of Exodus: A Critical, Theological Commentary.* Louisville: Westminster John Knox Press, 2004.

Chisholm, Robert B., Jr. "Divine Hardening in the Old Testament." *Bibliotheca Sacra* 153 (1996): 410–34.

———. "Does God Deceive?" *Bibliotheca Sacra* 155 (1998): 11–28.

———. *From Exegesis to Exposition: A Practical Guide to Using Biblical Hebrew.* Grand Rapids: Baker Book, 1998.

Chong, Joong Ho. *The Song of Moses (Deuteronomy 32:1–43) and the Hoshea-Pekah Conflict.* Ann Arbor: University Microfilms International, 1990.

Christensen, Duane L., ed. *Deuteronomy 21:10–34:12.* Word Biblical Commentary 6B. Nashville: Thomas Nelson, 2002.

———. *A Song of Power and the Power of Song: Essays on the Book of Deuteronomy.* Sources for Biblical and Theological Study 3. Winona Lake, IN: Eisenbrauns, 1993.

Claassens, Juliana M. *The God Who Provides: Biblical Images of Divine Nourishment.* Nashville: Abingdon Press, 2014.

Clifford, Richard J. *The Cosmic Mountain in Canaan and the Old Testament.* Harvard Semitic Monographs 4. Cambridge: Harvard University Press, 1972.

Clines, David J. A. *The Dictionary of Classical Hebrew.* Vol. 8. Sheffield, UK: Sheffield Phoenix Press, 2011.

———. "The Parallelism of Greater Precision." Pages 77–100 in *Directions in Hebrew Poetry.* Edited by Elaine R. Follis. Journal for the Study of the Old Testament Supplement Series 40. Sheffield, UK: Sheffield Academic, 1987.

Cocagnac, Maurice. *Les Symboles Bibliques. Lexique Théologique.* Paris: Cerf, 1993.

Cohen, Mordechai Z. *Three Approaches to Biblical Metaphor.* Netherlands: Koninklijke, 2003.

Cohen, Ted. "Notes on Metaphor." *Journal of Aesthetics and Art Criticism* 34, no. 3 (1976): 249–59.

Cole, Dennis R. *Numbers.* New American Commentary 3b. Nashville: Broadman & Holman Publishers, 2000.

Cook, Stephen L. *Reading Deuteronomy: A Literary and Theological Commentary.* Macon, GA: Smyth & Helwys Publishing, 2015.

Cooper, John W. *Our Father in Heaven: Christian Faith and Inclusive Language for God.* Grand Rapids: Baker Books, 1999.

Craigie, Peter C. *The Book of Deuteronomy.* New International Commentary on the Old Testament 5. Grand Rapids: Eerdmans, 1976.

Creach, Jerome F. D. *Yahweh as Refuge and the Editing of the Hebrew Psalter.* Journal for the Study of the Old Testament 287. Sheffield, UK: Sheffield Academic Press, 1996.

Currid, John D. *Against the Gods: The Polemical Theology of the Old Testament.* Wheaton: Crossway, 2013.

———. *Ancient Egypt and the Old Testament.* Grand Rapids: Baker, 1997.

———. *A Study Commentary on Deuteronomy.* Darlington: Evangelical Press, 2006.

Davila, James R. *Liturgical Works.* Grand Rapids: Wm. B. Eerdmans, 2000.

Day, John. *Yahweh and the Gods and Goddesses of Canaan.* Journal for the Study of the Old Testament: Supplement Series 265. Sheffield, UK: Sheffield Academic Press, 2000.

Deignan, Alice. *Metaphor and Corpus Linguistics.* Amsterdam: John Benjamins, 2005.

De Regt, L. J., J. de Waard, and J. P. Fokkelman. *Literary Structure and Rhetorical Strategies in the Hebrew Bible.* Assen, Netherlands: Van Gorcum & Comp., 1996.

De Roche, M. "Yahweh's *Rîb* against Israel: A Reassessment of the So-Called 'Prophetic Lawsuit' in the Preexilic Prophets." *Journal of Biblical Literature* 102 (1983):563–74.

DesCamp, Mary Therese. *Metaphor and Ideology: "Liber Antiquitatum Biblicarum" and Literary Methods through a Cognitive Lens.* Biblical Interpretation Series 87. Leiden: Brill, 2007.

Dillard, Raymond B., and Tremper Longman III. *An Introduction to the Old Testament.* Grand Rapids: Zondervan, 1994.

Dille, Sarah J. *Mixing Metaphors: God as Mother and Father in Deutero-Isaiah.* London: T&T Clark, 2004.

Donoghue, Denis. *Metaphor*. Cambridge, MA: Harvard University Press, 2014.

Doyle, Brian. *The Apocalypse of Isaiah Metaphorically Speaking: A Study of the Use, Function, and Significance of Metaphors in Isaiah 24-27*. Leuven: Peeters Publishers, 2000.

Driver, S. R. *A Critical and Exegetical Commentary on Deuteronomy*. New York: Charles Scribner's Sons, 1895.

Dürrenmatt, Jacques. *La Métaphore*. Paris: Honoré Champion, 2002.

Dyer, Charles H. "The Date of the Exodus Reexamined." *Bibliotheca Sacra* 140 (1983): 225-42.

Easton, M. G. *Easton's Bible Dictionary*. New York: Harper & Brothers, 1893.

Ellman, Barat. *Memory and Covenant: The Role of Israel's and God's Memory in Sustaining the Deuteronomic and Priestly Covenants*. Minneapolis: Fortress Press, 2013.

Elwell, Walter A., ed. *Baker Encyclopedia of the Bible*. 2 vols. Grand Rapids: Baker Book House, 1988.

———. *Evangelical Dictionary of Biblical Theology*. Grand Rapids: Baker Books, 1996.

Erickson, Millard J. *Christian Theology*. 2nd ed. Grand Rapids: Baker Books, 1998.

Fee, Gordon D., and Mark L. Strauss. *How to Choose a Translation for All Its Worth: A Guide to Understanding and Using Bible Versions*. Grand Rapids: Zondervan, 2007.

Fildes, Valerie A. *Breasts, Bottles and Babies: A History of Infant Feeding*. Edinburgh: Edinburgh University Press, 1986.

Finkelstein, I. *The Archaeology of the Israelite Settlement*. Jerusalem: Israel Exploration Society, 1988.

Fisch, Harold. *Poetry with a Purpose: Biblical Poetics and Interpretation*. Bloomington: Indiana University Press, 1988.

Fishbane, Michael. *Biblical Interpretation in Ancient Israel*. Oxford: Clarendon, 1985.

Fogelin, Robert J. *Figuratively Speaking*. New Haven: Yale University Press, 1988.

Fokkelman, J. P. *85 Psalms and Job 4-14*. Vol. 2 in *Major Poems of the Hebrew Bible at the Interface of Prosody and Structural Analysis*. Studia Semitica Neederlandica. The Netherlands: Van Gorcum & Company, 2000.

———. *Ex. 15, Deut. 32, and Job 3*. Vol. 1 in *Major Poems of the Hebrew Bible at the Interface of Prosody and Structural Analysis*. Studia Semitica Neederlandica. The Netherlands: Van Gorcum & Company, 2000.

———. *Reading Biblical Poetry: An Introductory Guide*. Louisville: Westminster John Knox Press, 2001.

Foreman, Benjamin. *Animal Metaphors and the People of Israel in the Book of Jeremiah*. Göttingen: Vandenhoeck & Ruprecht, 2011.

Fredriksson, Henning. *Jahwe Als Krieger: Studien Zum Alttestamentlichen Gottesbild*. Lund: C. W. K. Gleerup, 1945.

Freedman, David Noel. *The Anchor Bible Dictionary*. 6 vols. New York: Doubleday, 1992.

Fullerton, Kemper. "On Deuteronomy 32 26-34." *Zeitschrift für die Alttestamentliche Wissenschaft* 46 (1928): 138-55.

Futato, Mark D. *Interpreting the Psalms: An Exegetical Handbook*. Grand Rapids: Kregel, 2007.

Gan, Jonathan. *The Metaphor of Shepherd in the Hebrew Bible: A Historical-Literary Study*. Lanham: University Press of America, 2007.

Garrett, Duane A. *A Commentary on Exodus*. Grand Rapids: Kregel Publications, 2014.

Geller, Stephen A. "The Dynamics of Parallel Verse: A Poetic Analysis of Deut 32:6–12." *Harvard Theological Review* 75, no. 1 (1982): 35–56.

———. *Parallelism in Early Biblical Poetry*. Harvard Semitic Monographs 20. Missoula: Scholars Press, 1979.

———. "Theory and Method in the Study of Biblical Poetry." *Jewish Quarterly Review* 73 (1982): 65–77.

Gernsbacher, Morton Ann, Boaz Keysar, Rachel R. W. Robertson, and Necia K. Werner. "The Role of Suppression and Enhancement in Understanding Metaphors." *Journal of Memory and Language* 45 (2001): 433–50.

Gesenius, Wilhem. *Gesenius' Hebrew Grammar*. 2nd English ed. Edited by E. Kautzsch. Translated by A. E. Crowley. Oxford: Clarendon Press, 1910.

Gibbs, R. W. *The Cambridge Handbook of Metaphor and Thought*. Cambridge: Cambridge University Press, 2008.

———. *The Poetics of Mind: Figurative Thought, Language, and Understanding*. New York: Cambridge University Press, 1994.

———. "The Process of Understanding Literary Metaphor." *Journal of Literary Semantics* 19 (1990): 65–79.

———. *Researching Metaphor in Researching and Applying Metaphor*. Cambridge Applied Linguistics Series. Cambridge: Cambridge University Press, 1999.

Gile, Jason. "Ezekiel 16 and the Song of Moses: A Prophetic Transformation?" *Journal of Biblical Literature* 130, no. 1 (2011): 87–108.

Gillingham, S. E. *The Poems and Psalms of the Hebrew Bible*. New York: Oxford University Press, 1994.

Glucksberg, Sam. *Understanding Figurative Language: From Metaphors to Idioms*. Oxford: Oxford University Press, 2001.

Goldingay, John. *Israel's Faith*. Vol. 2 of *Old Testament Theology*. Downers Grove: InterVarsity Press, 2009.

———. *Israel's Gospel*. Vol. 1 of *Old Testament Theology*. Downers Grove: InterVarsity Press, 2009.

———. *Israel's Life*. Vol. 3 of *Old Testament Theology*. Downers Grove: InterVarsity Press, 2009.

Gordley, Matthew E. *Teaching through Song in Antiquity: Didactic Hymnody among Greeks, Romans, Jews, and Christians*. Tübingen: Mohr Siebeck, 2011.

Gordon, C. H. *Ugaritic Textbook: Grammar, Texts in Translation, Cuneiform Selections, Glossary, Indices*. Analecta Orientalia 38. Rome: Pontifical Biblical Institute, 1965.

Gray, Alison Ruth. *Psalm 18 in Words and Pictures: A Reading through Metaphor*. Biblical Interpretation 127. Leiden: Brill, 2004.

Green, Alberto R. W. *The Storm-God in the Ancient Near East*. Biblical and Judaic Studies 8. Winona Lake, IN: Eisenbrauns, 2003.

Green, Garrett. "The Gender of God and the Theology of Metaphor." In *Speaking the Christian God: The Holy Trinity and the Challenge of Feminism*. Edited by Alvin F. Kimmel. Grand Rapids, MI: Eerdmans, 1992.

———. *Imagining God: Theology and the Religious Imagination*. Grand Rapids: Eerdmans, 1998.

Grollenberg, Lucas H. *Atlas of the Bible*. London: Nelson, 1956.

Gruber, Mayer I. "Breast-feeding practices in biblical Israel and in Old Babylonian Mesopotamia." *The Journal of the Ancient Near Eastern Society* 19 (1989):61–83.

———. "The Motherhood of God in Second Isaiah." *Revue Biblique* 90 (1983): 351–59.

Grudem, Wayne. *Systematic Theology: An Introduction to Biblical Doctrine*. Grand Rapids: Zondervan, 1994.

Hall, Gary H. *Deuteronomy*. The College Press NIV Commentary. Joplin, MO: The College Press Publishing Company, 2000.

Hallo, William W., ed. *The Context of Scripture*. 3 vols. Leiden: Brill, 1997–2002.

Harris, Robert A. *Discerning Parallelism: A Study in Northern French Medieval Jewish Biblical Exegesis*. Providence, RI: Brown Judaic Studies, 2004.

Heiser, Michael S. "Deuteronomy 32:8 and the Sons of God." *Bibliotheca sacra* 158 (2001): 52–74.

Held, Moshe. "Rhetorical Questions in Ugaritic and Biblical Hebrew." *Eretz-Israel: Archaeological, Historical and Geographical Studies* 9 (1969): 71–79.

Hirsch, E. D., Jr. *Validity in Interpretation*. New Haven: Yale University Press, 1967.

Hoffmeir, James K. *Ancient Israel in Sinai: The Evidence for the Authenticity of the Wilderness Tradition*. New York: Oxford, 2005.

House, Paul R. *Old Testament Theology*. Downers Grove: InterVarsity Press, 1998.

Jackendoff, Ray, and David Aaron. Review of "More than Cool Reason: A Field Guide to Poetic Metaphor," by George Lakoff and Mark Turner. *Language* 67, no. 2 (1991): 320-38.

Jenni, Ernst, and Claus Westerman. *Theological Lexicon of the Old Testament*. Peabody, MA: Hendrickson Publishers, 1997.

Jindo, Job Y. *Biblical Metaphor Reconsidered: A Cognitive Approach to Poetic Prophecy in Jeremiah 1-24*. Harvard Semitic Monographs 64. Winona Lake, IN: Eisenbrauns, 2010.

Johnson, Mark. *The Body in the Mind: The Bodily Basis of Meaning, Imagination, and Reason*. Chicago: University of Chicago Press, 1987.

———. "Metaphor in the Philosophical Tradition." Pages 3-47 in *Philosophical Perspectives on Metaphor*. Edited by Mark Johnson. Minneapolis: University of Minnesota Press, 1981.

Joosten, Jan. "A Note on the Text of Deuteronomy xxxii 8." *Vetus Testamentum* 57, no. 4 (2007): 548-55.

Joüon, Paul. *A Grammar of Biblical Hebrew*. 2 vols. Translated by Takamitsu Muraoka. Rome: Editrice Pontificio Istituto Biblico, 2003.

Kaiser, Walter, Jr. "The Single Intent of Scripture." Pages 123-41 in *Evangelical Roots: A Tribute to Wilbur Smith*. Edited by K. S. Kantzer. Nashville: Thomas Nelson, 1978.

———. *Toward an Exegetical Theology: Biblical Exegesis for Preaching and Teaching*. Grand Rapids: Baker Books, 1981.

Kang, Sa-Moon. *Divine War in the Old Testament and in the Ancient Near East*. Beihefte zur Zeitschrift für die alttestamentliche Wissenschaft 177. Berlin: W. de Gruyter, 1989.

Keel, Othmar. *The Symbolism of the Biblical World: Ancient Near Eastern Iconography and the Book of Psalms*. Translated by Timothy J. Hallett. New York: Seabury, 1978.

Keil, Carl Friedrich, and Delitzsch Franz. *Biblical Commentary on the Old Testament*. Vol. 10. Edinburgh: T&T Clark, 1873.

Keiser, Thomas A. "The Song of Moses: A Basis for Isaiah's Prophecy." *Vetus Testamentum* 55, no. 4 (2005): 486–500.

King, Philip J., and Lawrence E. Stager. *Life in Biblical Israel*. Louisville: Westminster John Knox Press, 2001.

Kittay, Eva Feder. *Metaphor: Its Cognitive Force and Linguistic Structure*. Oxford: Clarendon Press, 1987.

Kittay, Eva F., and A. Lehrer. "Semantic Fields and the Structure of Metaphor." *Studies in Language* 5, no. 1 (1981): 31–63.

Kline, Meredith G. *Treaty of the Great King: The Covenant Structure of Deuteronomy*. Studies and Commentary. Grand Rapids: Eerdmans, 1963.

Klingbeil, Martin. *Yahweh Fighting from Heaven: God as Warrior and as God of Heaven in the Hebrew Psalter and Ancient Near Eastern Iconography*. Orbis biblicus et orientalis 169. Göttingen: Vandenhoeck & Ruprecht, 1999.

Knight, George A. *The Song of Moses: A Theological Quarry*. Grand Rapids: Wm. B. Eerdmans, 1995.

Knowles, Michael P. "'The Rock, His Work Is Perfect': Unusual Imagery for God in Deuteronomy 32." *Vetus Testamentum* 39, no. 3 (1989): 307–22.

Koehler, Ludwig Hugo, Walter Baumgartner, and J. J. Stamm. *The Hebrew and Aramaic Lexicon of the Old Testament*. 4 vols. New York: E. J. Brill, 1994–1999.

Kotzé, Zacharias. "A Cognitive Linguistic Methodology for the Study of Metaphor in the Hebrew Bible." *Journal of Northwest Semitic Languages* 31, no. 1 (2005): 107–17.

Kövecses, Zoltán. *Metaphor: A Practical Introduction*. 2nd ed. Oxford: Oxford University Press, 2010.

Kowalski, Vesta M. H. "Rock of Ages: A Theological Study of the Word 'צוּר' as a Metaphor for Israel's God." PhD diss., Jewish Theological Seminary, 1996.

Kramer, Samuel Noah. *History Begins at Sumer: Thirty-nine Firsts in Man's Recorded History*. Philadelphia: University of Philadelphia Press, 1981.

Kugel, James L. *The Bible as It Was*. Cambridge, MA: The Belknap Press of Harvard University Press, 1997.

———. *How to Read the Bible: A Guide to Scripture, Then and Now*. New York: Free, 2007.

———. *The Idea of Biblical Poetry: Parallelism and Its History*. Baltimore: Johns Hopkins University Press, 1981.

———. *Traditions of the Bible: A Guide to the Bible As It Was at the Start of the Common Era*. Cambridge, MA: Harvard University Press, 1998.

Labahn, Antje. "Metaphor and Intertextuality: 'Daughter of Zion' as a Test Case. Response to Kirsten Nielsen 'From Oracles to Canon' — and the Role of Metaphor." *Scandinavian Journal of the Old Testament* 17 (2003):49–67.

Labuschagne, Casper J. *Deuteronomium*. De prediking van het Oude Testament 3. Baarn: Callenbach, 1997.

———. "The Song of Moses: Its Framework and Structure." Pages 85–98 in *De Fructu Oris Sui: Essays in Honour of Adrianus van Selms*. Edited by I. H. Eybers et al. Leiden: E. J. Brill, 1971.

Lakoff, George, and Mark Johnson. *Metaphors We Live By*. 2nd ed. Chicago: University of Chicago Press, 2003.

Lakoff, George, and Mark Turner. *More than Cool Reason: A Field Guide to Poetic Metaphor*. Chicago: University of Chicago Press, 1989.

Lange, John Peter, Philip Schaff, and Wilhelm Julius Schröeder. *A Commentary on the Holy Scriptures: Deuteronomy*. Bellingham, WA: Logos Bible Software, 2008.

Lanham, Richard A. *A Handlist of Rhetorical Terms*. 2nd ed. Berkeley, CA: University of California Press, 1991.

Leezenberg, Michiel. *Contexts of Metaphor*. Current Research in the Semantics/Pragmatics Interface 7. Amsterdam: Elsevier, 2001.

Leuchter, Mark. "Why is the Song of Moses in the Book of Deuteronomy?" *Vetus Testamentum* 57, no. 3 (2007): 295–317.

Levine, Etan. "The Land of Milk and Honey." *Journal for the Study of the Old Testament* 87 (2000): 43 57.

Levinson, B. M. *Deuteronomy and the Hermeneutics of Legal Innovation*. New York: Oxford University Press, 1997.

Lichtheim, Miriam. *Ancient Egyptian Literature*. 3 vols. Berkeley: University of California Press, 1973–80.

Lim, Johnson T. K. "Toward a Final Form Approach to Biblical Interpretation." *Stulos Theological Journal* 7, no. 1&2 (1999): 1–11.

Lind, Millard C. *Yahweh Is a Warrior: The Theology of Warfare in Ancient Israel*. Christian Peace Shelf. Scottdale: Herald Press, 1980.

Lioy, Dan. "A Comparative Analysis of the Song of Moses and Paul's Speech to the Athenians." *Conspectus* 16 (2013): 1–45.

Littlemore, Jeannette. "The Effect of Cultural Background on Metaphor Interpretation." *Metaphor and Symbol* 18, no. 4 (2003): 273–88.

Loewenberg, Ina. "Identifying Metaphors." Pages 154–81 in *Philosophical Perspectives on Metaphor*. Edited by Mark Johnson. Minneapolis: University of Minnesota Press, 1981.

Long, Gary A. "Dead or Alive? Literality and God-Metaphors in the Hebrew Bible." *Journal of the American Academy of Religion* 62, no. 2 (2004): 509–38.

Longman, Tremper, III. *Psalms*. Tyndale Old Testament Commentaries 15–16. Downers Grove: InterVarsity Press, 2014.

Longman, Tremper, III, and Daniel G. Reid. *God is a Warrior*. Studies in Old Testament Biblical Theology. Grand Rapids: Zondervan, 1995.

Lundbom, Jack R. *Deuteronomy: A Commentary*. Grand Rapids: Eerdmans, 2013.

Lunn, Nicholas P. *Word-Order Variation in Biblical Hebrew Poetry: Differentiating Pragmatics and Poetics*. Paternoster Biblical Monographs. Georgia: Paternoster, 2006.

Macchi, Jean-Daniel. *Israël et ses Tribus Selon Genèse 49*. Orbis Biblicus et Orientalis 171. Göttingen: Vandenhoeck & Ruprecht, 1999.

Mac Cormac, Earl R. *A Cognitive Theory of Metaphor*. Cambridge, MA: MIT Press, 1985.

MacDonald, Nathan. *Deuteronomy and the Meaning of "Monotheism."* Tübingen: Mohr Siebeck, 2003.

Macky, Peter W. *The Centrality of Metaphors to Biblical Thought: A Method for Interpreting the Bible*. Lewiston: E. Mellen Press, 1990.

Mann, Thomas W. *Deuteronomy*. Louisville: Westminster John Knox Press, 1995.

———. "Pillar of Cloud in the Reed Sea Narrative." *Journal of Biblical Literature* 90 (1971):15–30.

Martin, Janet. "Metaphor amongst Tropes." *Religious Studies* 17 (1981): 55–66.

Masson, Robert. *Without Metaphor, No Saving God: Theology After Cognitive Linguistics*. Leuven: Peeters, 2014.

Mayes, A. D. H. *Deuteronomy*. Grand Rapids: Wm. B. Eerdmans, 1981.

McCarthy, Carmel. *Deuteronomy*. Biblia Hebraica Quinta 5. Stuttgart: Deutsche Bibelgesellschaft, 2007.

McConville, J. G. *Deuteronomy*. Apollos Old Testament Commentary 5. Downers Grove, IL: InterVarsity, 2002.

McFague, Sallie. *Metaphorical Theology: Models of God in Religious Language*. Philadelphia: Fortress, 1982.

———. *Models of God: Theology for an Ecological, Nuclear Age*. Philadelphia: Fortress, 1987.

McGinniss, Mark. *Contributions of Selected Rhetorical Devices to a Biblical Theology of the Song of Songs*. Eugene, OR: Wipf & Stock, 2011.

Mendenhall, George E. "Covenant Forms in Israelite Tradition." *The Biblical Archeologist* 17, no. 3 (1954): 50–76.

Merrill, Eugene H. *Deuteronomy*. New American Commentary 4. Nashville: Broadman & Holman Publishers, 1994.

Meynet, Royland. *Rhetorical Analysis: An Introduction to Biblical Rhetoric*. Rev. ed. Journal for the Study of the Old Testament Supplement Series 256. Sheffield, UK: Sheffield Academic Press, 1998.

Millar, Gary J. *Now Choose Life: Theology and Ethics in Deuteronomy*. Grand Rapids: Eerdmans, 1998.

Miller, Cynthia L. "A Linguistic Approach to Ellipsis in Biblical Poetry." *Bulletin for Biblical Research* 13, no. 2 (2003): 251–70.

———. "A Reconsideration of 'Double-duty' Prepositions in Biblical Poetry." *Journal of the Ancient Near Eastern Society* 31 (2008): 99–110.

———. "The Relation of Coordination to Verb Gapping in Biblical Poetry." *Journal for the Study of the Old Testament* 32, no. 1 (2007): 41–60.

———. *The Representation of Speech in Biblical Hebrew Narrative: A Linguistic Analysis*. Harvard Semitic Museum Monographs 55. Atlanta: Scholars Press, 1996.

Miller, George A. "Images and Models, Similes, and Metaphors." Pages 22829 in *Metaphor and Thought*. Edited by A. Ortony. Cambridge: Cambridge University Press, 1993.

Miller, Patrick D. *Deuteronomy*. Louisville: John Knox, 1990.

———. *The Divine Warrior in Early Israel*. Harvard Semitic Monographs 5. Cambridge: Harvard University Press, 1973.

Mills, Michael S. *Concise Handbook of Literary and Rhetorical Terms*. USA: Estep-Nichols Publishing, 2010.

Moor, Johannes C. de. *The Rise of Yahwism: The Roots of Israelite Monotheism*. Second Edition. Bibliotheca Ephemeridum Theologicarum Lovaniensium 91. Leuven: Leuven University Press, 1997.

Mounce, William D. *Complete Expository Dictionary of Old & New Testament Words*. Grand Rapids: Zondervan, 2006.

Muraoka, T., ed. *Semantics of Ancient Hebrew*. Leuven: Peeters Louvain, 1998.

Nelson, Richard D. *Deuteronomy: A Commentary*. Old Testament Library. Louisville: Westminster John Knox Press, 2004.

Neufeld, E. "Insects as Warfare Agents in the Ancient Near East." *Orientalia* 49 (1980): 30–57.

Niccacci, Alviero. *The Syntax of the Verb in Classical Hebrew Prose*, trans. W. G. E. Watson, Journal for the Study of the Old Testament Supplement Series 86. Sheffield, UK: JSOT Press, 1990.

Niditch, Susan. *War in the Hebrew Bible: A Study in the Ethics of Violence.* New York: Oxford University Press, 1993.

Niehoff, Maren R. *Jewish Exegesis and Homeric Scholarship in Alexandria.* Cambridge: Cambridge University Press, 2011.

Nielsen, Eduard. *Deuteronomium.* Handbuch zum Alten Testament. Tübingen: J. C. B. Mohr, 1995.

Nielsen, Kirsten. "'From Oracles to Canon' — and the Role of Metaphor." *Scandinavian Journal of the Old Testament* 17 (2003): 22–33.

———. *There Is Hope for a Tree: The Tree as Metaphor in Isaiah.* Translated by Christine Crowley and Frederick Crowley. Journal for the Study of the Old Testament Supplement Series 65. Sheffield, UK: Sheffield Academic, 1985.

Nilsen, Tina Dykesteen. *The Origins of Deuteronomy 32: Intertextuality, Memory, Identity.* New York: Peter Lang, 2018.

Nocquet, Dany. *Le livret noir de Baal. La polémique contre le dieu Baal dans la Bible hébraïque et l'"Ancien Israël.* Genève: Labor et Fides, 2004.

O'Connor, M. *Hebrew Verse Structure.* 2nd rev. ed. Winona Lake, IN: Eisenbrauns, 1997.

Oestreich, Bernhard. "Metaphors and Similes for Yahweh in Hosea 14:2–9 (1–8): A Study of Hoseanic Pictorial Language." PhD diss., Seventh-day Adventist Theological Seminary, 1997.

Ollenburger, Ben C. *Old Testament Theology: Flowering and Future.* Winona Lake, IN: Eisenbrauns, 2004.

Olofsson, Staffan. *God is My Rock: A Study of Translation Technique and Theological Exegesis in the Septuagint.* Stockholm: Almqvist & Wiksell, 1990.

Olson, Dennis T. *Deuteronomy and the Death of Moses: A Theological Reading.* Eugene, OR: Wipf & Stock Publishers, 1994.

———. "God for Us, God against Us: Singing the Pentateuch's Songs of Praise in Exodus 15 and Deuteronomy 32." *Theology Today* 70 (2013): 54–61.

Orton, David E. *Poetry in the Hebrew Bible.* Leiden: Brill, 2000.

Osborne, Grant R. *The Hermeneutical Spiral: A Comprehensive Introduction to Biblical Interpretation.* Downers Grove: InterVarsity Press, 2006.

Oswalt, John N. *The Bible among the Myths: Unique Revelation or Just Ancient Literature?* Grand Rapids: Zondervan, 2009.

Pate, C. Marvin, et al. *The Story of Israel: A Biblical Theology.* Downers Grove: InterVarsity Press, 2004.

Patrick, Dale, and Allen Scult. *Rhetoric and Biblical Interpretation.* Bible and Literature Series 26. Sheffield, UK: Almond Press, 1990.

Petersen, David L., and Kent Harold Richards. *Interpreting Hebrew Poetry.* Minneapolis: Fortress Press, 1992.

Pritchard, James B., ed. *Ancient Near Eastern Texts Relating to the Old Testament.* 3rd ed. with supplement. Princeton: Princeton University Press, 1969.

Putnam, Frederic Clark. *Hebrew Bible Insert: A Student's Guide to the Syntax of Biblical Hebrew.* Quakertown, PA: Stylus Publishing, 2002.

Richards, I. A. *The Philosophy of Rhetoric*. Oxford: Oxford University Press, 1936.

Ricoeur, Paul. *The Rule of Metaphor: Multi-disciplinary Studies of the Creation of Meaning in Language*. Translated by Robert Czerny, Kathleen McLaughlin, and John Costello. Toronto: University of Toronto Press, 1977.

Robertson, O. Palmer. *Understanding the Land of the Bible: A Biblical-Theological Guide*. Phillipsburg, NJ: P&R, 1996.

Rogers, Nancy Louise. "Poetic Revelation: The Relationship Between Parallelism and Metaphor in Biblical Hebrew Poetry." PhD diss., Cornell University, New York, 2010.

Rooker, Mark F. *The Ten Commandments: Ethics for the Twenty-First Century*. Nashville: B&H Publishing Group, 2000.

Rosner, Brian S. "Biblical Theology." Pages 3–11 in *New Dictionary of Biblical Theology*. Edited by T. Desmond Alexander and Brian S. Rosner. Downers Grove, IL: InterVarsity Press, 2000.

Ross, Allen P. *A Commentary on the Psalms*. 3 vols. Grand Rapids: Kregel Publications, 2011.

Rouillard, Hedweige. *La Péricope de Balaam (Nombres 22–24): La Prose et les "Oracles."* Etudes Bibliques 4. Paris: Gabalda, 1985.

Ryken, Leland. *How to Read the Bible as Literature*. Grand Rapids: Zondervan, 1984.

———. *Sweeter than Honey, Richer than Gold: A Guided Study of Biblical Poetry*. Bellingham, WA: Lexham Press, 2015.

Ryken, Leland, James C. Wilhoit, and Tremper Longman III, eds. *Dictionary of Biblical Imagery: An Encyclopedic Exploration of the Images, Symbols, Motifs, Metaphors, Figures of Speech and Literary Patterns of the Bible*. Downers Grove: InterVarsity Press, 1998.

Sanders, Paul. *The Provenance of Deuteronomy 32*. Leiden: Brill, 1996.

Schenker, Adrian. "Le monothéisme Israélite: un dieu qui transcende le monde et les dieux." *Biblica* 78 (1997): 436–48.

Schmitt, John J. "The Motherhood of God and Zion as Mother." *Revue Biblique* 92 (1985):557–69.

Schökel, Luis Alonso. *A Manual of Hebrew Poetics*. Subsidia Biblica 11. Rome: Pontifical Biblical Institute, 1988.

Seitz, Christopher R. "The Canonical Approach and Theological Interpretation." Pages 85–110 in *Canon and Biblical Interpretation*. Edited by Craig G. Bartholomew et al. Scripture and Hermeneutics Series 7. Grand Rapids: Zondervan, 2006.

Sherwood, Stephen K. *Leviticus, Numbers, Deuteronomy*. Berit Olam: Studies in Hebrew Narrative and Poetry. Collegeville, MN: The Liturgical Press, 2002.

Silva, Moisés. *Biblical Words and Their Meaning: An Introduction to Lexical Semantics*. Grand Rapids: Zondervan, 1994.

Skehan, Patrick William. "Structure of the Song of Moses in Deuteronomy (Deut 32:1–43)." *The Catholic Biblical Quarterly* 13, no. 2 (1951): 153–63.

Smith, Mark S. *The Early History of God: Yahweh and the Other Deities in Ancient Israel*. 2nd ed. Biblical Resource Series. Grand Rapids: Eerdmans, 2002.

Smith, Mark S., and Wayne T. Pitard. *The Ugaritc Baal Cycle: Introduction with Text, Translation and Commentary of KTU/CTA 1.3-1.4*. Supplements to Vetus Testamentum 114. Leiden: Brill, 2009.

Soskice, Janet Martin. *The Kindness of God: Metaphor, Gender, and Religious Language*. Oxford: Oxford University Press, 2008.

———. *Metaphor and Religious Language.* Oxford: Clarendon Press Oxford, 1985.

Sparks, Kenton L. *Ancient Texts for the Study of the Hebrew Bible: A Guide to the Background Literature.* Peabody, MA: Hendrickson Publishers, 2005.

Stallman, Robert C. "Divine Hospitality in the Pentateuch: A Metaphorical Perspective on God as Host." PhD diss., Westminster Theological Seminary, 1999.

Stern, Josef. *Metaphor in Context.* Cambridge, MA: The MIT Press, 2000.

Stevens, David E. "Does Deuteronomy 32:8 Refer to 'Sons of God' or 'Sons of Israel'?" *BSac* 154, no. 614 (1997): 131–41.

Stienstra, Nelly. *YHWH Is the Husband of His People: Analysis of a Biblical Metaphor with Special Reference to Translation.* Leuven: Peeters Publishers, 1993.

Stone, Keith A. *Singing Moses's Song. A Performance-Critical Analysis of Deuteronomy's Song of Moses.* Boston: Ilex Foundation, 2016.

Strawn, Brent A. "Keep/Observe/Do—Carefully—Today! The Rhetoric of Repetition in Deuteronomy." Pages 215–40 in *A God So Near: Essays on Old Testament Theology in Honor of Patrick D. Miller.* Winona Lake, IN: Eisenbrauns, 2003.

———. "The Old Testament and Participation in God (And/In Christ?): (Re-)Reading the Life of Moses with Some Help from Gregory of Nyssa." *Ex Auditu* 33 (2017): 25–52.

———. *What Is Stronger than a Lion? Leonine Image and Metaphor in the Hebrew Bible and the Ancient Near East.* Orbis Biblicus et Orientalis 212. Freiburg: Herder, 2005.

Swete, Henry Barclay. *The Old Testament in Greek: According to the Septuagint.* 4 vols. Cambridge, UK: Cambridge University Press, 1909.

Tasker, David R. *Ancient Near Eastern Literature and the Hebrew Scriptures About the Fatherhood of God*. Studies in Biblical Literature 69. New York: Peter Lang, 2004.

Thiessen, Matthew. "The Form and Function of the Song of Moses (Deuteronomy 32:1–43)." *Journal of Biblical Literature* 123, no. 3 (2004): 401–24.

Thompson, Deanna A. *Deuteronomy: A Theological Commentary on the Bible*. Louisville: John Knox Press, 2014.

Thompson, J. A. *The Ancient Near Eastern Treaties and the Old Testament*. London: Tyndale Press, 1964.

———. *Deuteronomy: An Introduction and Commentary*. Downers Grove: InterVarsity Press, 1974.

Tigay, Jeffrey H. *Deuteronomy*. Philadelphia: Jewish Publication Society, 1996.

Tov, Emmanuel. *Textual Criticism of the Hebrew Bible*. Minneapolis: Fortress Press, 1992.

———. *Textual Criticism of the Hebrew Bible*. 3rd ed., rev. and exp. Minneapolis: Fortress Press, 2012.

Trible, Phyllis. *Rhetorical Criticism: Context, Method, and the Book of Jonah*. Minneapolis: Fortress Press, 1994.

Trimm, Charlie. *"YHWH Fights for Them!": The Divine Warrior in the Exodus Narrative*. Piscataway, NJ: Gorgias Press, 2014.

Ullmann, Stephen. *Semantics: An Introduction to the Science of Meaning*. New York: Barnes & Noble, 1962.

Ulrich, Eugene, Frank Cross Moore, Sidnie White Crawford, Julie Ann Duncan, Patrick W. Skehan, Emmanuel Tov, and Tulio Trebolle Barrera. *Qumran Cave 4.IX: Deuteronomy, Joshua, Judges, Kings*.

Discoveries in the Judaean Desert XIV. Oxford: Clarendon Press, 1995.

van der Merwe, Christo H. J. "Lexical Meaning in Biblical Hebrew and Cognitive Semantics: A Case Study." *Biblica* 87 (2006): 85–95.

van der Merwe, Christo H. J., Jackie A Naudé, and Jan H. Kroeze. *A Biblical Hebrew Reference Grammar*. Biblical Languages: Hebrew 3. London: Sheffield Academic Press, 2006.

VanGemeren, W. A., ed. *New International Dictionary of Old Testament Theology and Exegesis*. 5 vols. Grand Rapids: Zondervan, 1997.

Van Hecke, Pierre. *Metaphor in the Hebrew Bible*. Leuven: University Press, 2005.

Van Hecke, Pierre, and Antje Labahn, eds. *Metaphor in the Psalms*. Bibliotheca Ephemeridum Theologicarum Lovaniensium 231. Leuven: Uitgeverij Peeters, 2010.

Vannoy, Robert J. *1–2 Samuel*. Cornerstone Biblical Commentary 4a. Carol Stream, IL: Tyndale House Publishers, 2009.

Van Pelt, Miles V. *Basics of Biblical Aramaic: Complete Grammar, Lexicon, and Annotated Text*. Grand Rapids: Zondervan, 2011.

van Wijk-Bos, Johanna. *Reimagining God: The Case for Scriptural Diversity*. Louisville: Westminster John Knox, 1995.

Vogel, Dan. "Ambiguities of the Eagle." *Jewish Bible Quarterly* 26, no. 2 (1998):85–92.

———. "Moses as Poet: Ha'azinu as Poem." *Jewish Bible Quarterly* 31, no. 4 (2003): 1–9.

von Rad, Gerhard. *Holy War in Ancient Israel*. Translated by Marva J. Dawn. Grand Rapids: Eerdmans, 1991.

———. *Old Testament Theology*. Translated by D. M. G. Stalker. Peabody: Prince, 2005.

Waltke, Bruce K., and Michael Patrick O'Connor. *An Introduction to Biblical Hebrew Syntax*. Winona Lake, IN: Eisenbrauns, 1990.

Walton, John H. *Ancient Near Eastern Thought and the Old Testament: Introducing the Conceptual World of the Hebrew Bible*. Grand Rapids: Baker, 2006.

Walton, John H., Victor H. Matthews, and Mark W. Chavalas. *The IVP Bible Background Commentary: Old Testament*. Downers Grove: InterVarsity Press, 2012.

Ward, Wayne E. "Towards a Biblical Theology." *Review and Expositor* 74, no. 3 (1977): 371–87.

Watson, Wilfred G. E. *Classical Hebrew Poetry: A Guide to Its Techniques*. London: T&T Clark International, 2005.

———. *Traditional Techniques in Classical Hebrew Verse*. Journal for the Study of the Old Testament Supplement Series 170. Sheffield, UK: Sheffield Academic, 1994.

Watts, James W. *Psalm and Story: Inset Hymns in Hebrew Narrative*. Sheffield, UK: JSOT Press, 1992.

———. "'This Song' Conspicuous Poetry in Hebrew Prose." Pages 345–58 in *Verse in Ancient Near Eastern Prose*. Alter Orient und Altes Testament 42. Edited by Johannes C. de Moor and Wilfred G. Watson. Neukirchen-Vluyn: Neukirchen Verlag, 1993.

Weiss, Andrea L. *Figurative Language in Biblical Prose Narrative: Metaphor in the Book of Samuel*. Supplements to Vetus Testamentum 107. Leiden: Brill, 2006.

———. "Figures of Speech: Biblical Hebrew." In *Encyclopedia of Hebrew Language and Linguistics*. Leiden: Brill, 2013.

———. "Motives Behind Biblical Mixed Metaphors." Pages 317–28 in *Making a Difference: Essays on the Bible and Judaism in Honor of Tamara Cohn Eskenazi*. Edited by David J. A. Clines, Kent Harold Richards, and Jacob L. Wright. Sheffield, UK: Sheffield Phoenix Press, 2012.

———. "A New Approach to Metaphor in Biblical Poetry." Pages 475–86 in *Mishneh Todah: Studies in Deuteronomy and Its Cultural Environment in Honor of Jeffrey H. Tigay*. Edited by Nili S. Fox, David A. Glatt-Gilad, and Michael J. Williams. Winona Lake, IN: Eisenbrauns, 2009.

Wenham, Gordon J. *Numbers: An Introduction and Commentary*. Tyndale Old Testament Commentaries. Vol. 4. England: InterVarsity Press, 1981.

Westbrook, Raymond., ed. *A History of Ancient Near Eastern Law*, 2 vols. Leiden; Boston: Brill, 2003.

Wevers, John William. *Notes on the Greek Text of Deuteronomy*. SBL Septuagint and Cognate Series 39. Edited by Bernard A. Taylor. Atlanta: Scholars Press, 1995.

White, Roger M. *The Structure of Metaphor: The Way the Language of Metaphor Works*. Cambridge: Blackwell Publishing, 1996.

Wigram, George V. *The Englishman's Hebrew Concordance of the Old Testament*. Peabody, MA: Hendrickson Publishers, 2013.

Wikander, Ola. "Ungrateful Grazers: A Parallel to Deut 32:15 from the Hurrian/Hittite Epic of Liberation." *Svensk Exegetisk Årsbok* 78 (2013): 137–46.

Woods, Edward J. *Deuteronomy*. Tyndale Old Testament Commentaries 5. Downers Grove: InterVarsity Press, 2011.

Work, Telford. *Deuteronomy*. Brazos Theological Commentary on the Bible. Grand Rapids: Eerdmans, 2009.

Wright, Christopher J. H. *Deuteronomy*. New International Biblical Commentary on the Old Testament. Peabody: Hendrickson, 1996.

Wright, G. Ernest. "The Lawsuit of God: A Form-Critical Study of Deuteronomy 32." Pages 26–67 in *Israel's Prophetic Heritage: Essays in Honor of James Muilenburg*. Edited by Bernhard W. Anderson and Walter Harrelson. New York: Harper & Brothers, 1962.

Wüste, Christiane. *Fels – Geier – Eltern: Untersuchungen zum Gottesbild des Moseliedes (Dtn 32)*. Göttingen: V&R Unipress GmbH, 2018.

Yob, I. M. "Religious Metaphor and Scientific Model: Grounds for Comparison." *Religious Studies* 28 (1992): 475–85.

Zevit, Ziony. *The Religions of Ancient Israel: A Synthesis of Parallactic Approaches*. London: Continuum, 2001.

Zogbo, Lynell, and Ernst R. Wendland. *Hebrew Poetry in the Bible: A Guide for Understanding and for Translating*. New York: United Bible Societies, 2000.

Zonglin, Changlin. *Cognitive Linguistics and Culture*. Qingdao, China: Ocean University of China Press, 2005.

www.ingramcontent.com/pod-product-compliance
Lightning Source LLC
Chambersburg PA
CBHW070722240426
43673CB00003B/116